NATIVE AMERICAN ISSUES

A Reference Handbook, Second Edition

Other Titles in ABC-CLIO's
CONTEMPORARY
WORLD ISSUES
Series

Books in the Contemporary World Issues series address vital issues in today's society such as genetic engineering, pollution, and biodiversity. Written by professional writers, scholars, and nonacademic experts, these books are authoritative, clearly written, up-to-date, and objective. They provide a good starting point for research by high school and college students, scholars, and general readers as well as by legislators, businesspeople, activists, and others.

Each book, carefully organized and easy to use, contains an overview of the subject, a detailed chronology, biographical sketches, facts and data and/or documents and other primary-source material, a directory of organizations and agencies, annotated lists of print and nonprint resources, and an index.

Readers of books in the Contemporary World Issues series will find the information they need in order to have a better understanding of the social, political, environmental, and economic issues facing the world today.

NATIVE AMERICAN ISSUES

A Reference Handbook,
Second Edition

William N. Thompson

CONTEMPORARY WORLD ISSUES

A B C ● C L I O

Santa Barbara, California
Denver, Colorado
Oxford, England

Library of Congress Cataloging-in-Publication Data
Thompson, William Norman.
    Native American issues : a reference handbook / William N. Thompson. — 2nd ed.
        p. cm. — (ABC-CLIO's contemporary world issues)
    Includes bibliographical references and index.
    ISBN 1-85109-741-4 (hardback : alk. paper) — ISBN 1-85109-746-5 (ebook)
    1. Indians of North America—Politics and government—Handbooks, manuals, etc.   2. Indians of North America—Civil rights—Handbooks, manuals, etc.   3. Indians of North America—Legal status, laws, etc.— Handbooks, manuals, etc.   I. Title.   II. Series: Contemporary world issues.

    E98.T77T56 2005
    973.04'97—dc22

                                    2005007570

07   06   05   10   9   8   7   6   5   4   3   2   1

This book is also available on the World Wide Web as an e-book. Visit http://www.abc-clio.com for details.

ABC-CLIO, Inc.
130 Cremona Drive, P.O. Box 1911
Santa Barbara, California 93116-1911

Production Team:
Acquisitions Editor   Mim Vasan
Production Editor   Laura Esterman
Editorial Assistant   Cisca Schreefel
Production Manager   Don Schmidt
Manufacturing Coordinator   George Smyser

To Evan
A Legacy of One Community for All

Contents

Acknowledgments

Many people have contributed to my efforts to put this volume together. In the first edition of *Native American Issues,* I sought to mention as many helpers as I could. I ask their pardon if I only give a collective thanks and instead refer the reader to that list of acknowledgments, and here I'll add only the names of those who have contributed to this second edition.

First, I thank Mim Vasan of ABC-CLIO, who, as my primary editor, has guided my work. I also wish to thank the University of Nevada–Las Vegas for granting a sabbatical leave to me while I was working on this edition. Others whom I wish to thank are people who have offered me new and renewed connections to the indigenous world of humanity, a humanity that is really a single community. Rather than being just persons who provided contacts with other worlds, they have most of all been people who have given me contacts with our one Universe. They have helped me understand that the world is not 500 nations or 5,000 nations but one universal nation with one people. I am thankful to Las Vegas resident Roy Kawaguchi, who introduced me to Japanese society and connected me with my Japanese hosts Reiko and Ichiro Tanioka of the Osaka University of Commerce, and his colleagues, especially H. E. Yang of Asiana Airlines and Kotaro Fujimoto of the Dentsu Corporation. I also appreciate new connections to South America, which were made possible through my host Jorge Rodriguez, his family, and many new friends from Lima, Peru. Dennis Piotrowski of Las Vegas has also introduced me to many leaders in the Native American community.

In this note of thanks I wish to interject a word of sadness: while putting together this edition, I lost a dear friend and colleague, Asher Friedberg of Jerusalem. Asher was a professor at the University of Haifa, and he wrote articles with me and our colleague Carl Lutrin of California Polytechnic University on world cultures and gambling phenomena. Asher and his wonderful wife Iris, together with their family, hosted my wife and me on a most memorable Middle Eastern cultural tour in 2001. I miss him deeply. Asher and Iris remain in our prayers always.

Thanks go to Michael Green of Southern Nevada Community College, History Department, and to Guy Rocha, the Nevada state archivist, for providing materials on Sarah Winnemucca. While many in the University of Nevada–Las Vegas community have been helpful, including our departmental staff and, of course, our librarians, a special note of thanks goes to John Murphey, my graduate assistant in the Department of Public Administration. For a semester John has helped me track down page numbers for references, and he has proofread these pages. Most of all, he processed the pages through WordPerfect and Word and transformed the pages into a product that my editor could work with toward final publication.

My family has been the greatest force in connecting me to our one world. My wife Kay has traveled with me to parts of five continents. But mostly I appreciate a love that has brought us three wonderful children, who not only have meant the world to us but have also literally brought the world to us. Daughter Laura has worked with projects such as the University of Pittsburgh's Semester at Sea and the University of Redlands' European Semester. Tim hosted us in Panama, where he served in the Peace Corps. There he met fellow Peace Corps member Carmenza Cespedes, and they were married in 2004. Carmenza's family migrated from Colombia to Queens, New York, and the wedding was a veritable mini-United Nations, just across the river from the real thing.

Since the first edition was written, our son Stephen has taken Siqin as his wife. She is from Inner Mongolia, where her mother and father have been lead dancers with the Mongolia Folk Dance Company. Their love has given us our greatest joy, a grandson: Evan Agarra Thompson. Siqin's parents selected his middle name "Agarra." It is a Mongolian word meaning "the Universe." So now, my heritage and my legacy extend to homelands that have given birth to all peoples everywhere, peoples of a single enduring Universe. I dedicate this volume to Evan, and the legacy of a single community of all peoples always at peace, always united.

1

Introduction

The second edition of *Native American Issues: A Reference Handbook* updates the earlier volume of this work published by ABC-CLIO in 1996. Although many original materials remain, much is new in terms of policy developments and discussion. The greatest change that Native America has experienced since the first edition has been a vast expansion in gambling enterprise on reservation lands. The participation of Natives in gambling operations has come to overwhelm other aspects of policy concerning Native Americans. Accordingly, this edition presents an extensive treatment of gambling operations.

Sovereignty and Zero-Sum Games

This volume abandons the organizational thesis found in the earlier work, at least in terminology. In the 1996 edition, the notion of "sovereignty" was presented as a guiding concept for understanding political issues ranging from land claims and fishing rights to gambling. Sovereignty was defined, and a brief history was given of the status of sovereignty among indigenous population groups in North America extending from the time before the European exploration of the continent through the colonial era to the period when new nations—particularly the United States and Canada—dominated Native life. Contemporary struggles with problem issues were presented in the context of a waning and then a restored idea of sovereignty.

The approach taken was not unique, for other volumes on Native American political controversies have dwelled on the

1

concept of sovereignty. However, having reexamined many treatments of issues within the context of sovereignty, I find myself perplexed. The more I grab to hold onto the meaning of the singular concept, the more elusive it seems to get. The word "sovereignty" carries extraordinarily vague meanings. Often meanings given to it are so vast that they can be inclusive of many different concepts, and often they are so complex that concrete understandings fade away quickly. At times the notion of sovereignty is considered to be an absolute—ergo, a condition of a political unit possessing "all" power, or a power "eternal," that can never be extinguished. At times it is used to suggest merely that a unit has a degree of power, any degree of power. All definitions have some merit, and many do represent a rallying cry for participants acting within political arenas. Yet common knowledge tells us that no absolute power has ever been exercised by any government vis-à-vis all other governments, whether they are inside or outside of the geographical territory of the government in question. At the same time, the smallest unit of the political system—for example, the individual—almost always exercises some power over affairs that might be called political. Certainly at the time of voting the citizen is "sovereign" in terms of political decision making. Moreover, there is little doubt that for some political units sovereignty has been permanently extinguished. An example would be the Roman Empire. In addition, formerly "sovereign" or independent units have yielded such independence by joining together with other more inclusive units. The "state" of Alsace, for example, is now joined to France, just as the state of South Carolina is part of the United States. Once there were as many as 500 Native tribes in North America. Many are gone, having neither population nor territory, while all tribes have seen changes in territorial boundaries. Similarly, the geographical boundaries of almost every existing state in the world have been changed at some time in history.

The idea of sovereignty is often confused with the idea of nation. While the trouble with the concept is not any fatal flaw in its use, in political debates, the trouble is a lack of precision. We do not have precise operational definitions that tell us exactly when it is, where it is, when it is not, and where it is not. Unfortunately, this writer does not have the philosophical understanding or deep abilities of logic to seek what can be considered a needed operationalization of the term so that it can have an explicitly precise use in this book's political analysis.

There is yet another difficulty in orienting this edition around the concept of sovereignty. The concept invites emotions that cloud reality. Battles fought with a goal of "sovereignty" are zero-sum battles in which there must be a winner and a loser—indeed, a winner for every loser. One side seeks its claim, and if it wins, the other side loses something of equal worth. Accordingly, the many historical accounts of Native American relationships with non-Natives tend to take sides. In the first edition, I, too, played this zero-sum game, as I chronicled many critical events, and I offered the general lament regarding the course of history. A listing of dated events (Chronology) is preserved and expanded in this volume, but following the Introduction, the textual focus shifts to contemporary issues.

The historical accounts of the struggles of Native American peoples as non-Natives began to occupy the continent are generally presented by authors who seek to be advocates of Native America, calling for "justice now" in order to replace "injustices" of the past. In rereading the first edition, I see that I fell into that position as well. It is easy to do—to abandon a neutral stance for a stance of advocacy on behalf of Native peoples. Maybe I can now say, "Okay. Been there, done that, time for an alternative approach." Those who want to read detailed histories about the wrongs done to Native Americans in the past will have no trouble finding volumes giving them what they want in any library or bookstore. I include annotations of such works in my updated bibliographic section.

Alfred Marshall and Daniel Elazar: A Notion of Realism

Here I set aside many moral arguments pervasive in the existing literature and instead concentrate on conditions in Native America today, examining contemporary policies that may represent positive responses to those conditions. In doing so, I endorse two philosophies of politics and economics. The first is the philosophy of political economy advanced by Englishman Alfred Marshall. Marshall is best known for his theory of marginality in economics: the last dollar we spent, he stated, has less value than the next dollar we will spend. In colloquial terms, Marshall might have expressed his ideas with the phrase, "No matter where you go, there you are." The entire global society is here; the entire global society is now. The central question in policy making is: What is the next step we should take? Marshall might have added the question, "And how will that next step affect society now?" (Bucholtz 1989, 147–149).

The second philosophy of politics and economics that I endorse is that proposed by Daniel Elazar. He postulated that several types of political cultures surrounded policy making. In some places, the culture of politics could be called individualistic, and in other places moralistic or traditionalistic.

The *individualistic* culture envisions a democratic order expressed through a marketplace of issues and policy positions. Government does not exist to create "a good society," but rather to respond to demands of citizens on economic and other issues. Mass political participation is not encouraged, for politics is an activity reserved for "professionals," not amateurs. Policy making is transactional, a bargaining process between self-interested groups and individuals. Politics is like horse trading (Elazar 1972, 86–89).

The *moralistic* culture emphasizes the commonwealth as the basis for democratic government. Politics is considered a lofty pursuit in humankind's search for the "good society," and there are somehow eternal truths that should guide us. Those who serve their people assume high moral obligations (Elazar 1972, 89–92).

The *traditionalistic* culture had its roots in British royalty. It persisted past the Revolutionary years within the United States in the Plantation South, where citizens sought economic opportunity through their agricultural system. The culture is based on an ambivalent attitude toward the marketplace coupled with an elitist conception of society. The culture accepts a largely hierarchical society and expects those at the top of the social order to take a special and dominant role in government. That role is defined as maintaining the existing social order (Elazar 1972, 92–94).

Although many cry out that we must always be guided by moral principles in our political debates, and others decry that the power interests always rule for their own good, the individualistic political culture model dominates the American scene. It provides a realistic orientation to politics. Native American interests participate in styles of politics reflecting the model. Issues considered here will be examined with a Marshallian present-day focus and in the context of the wider "clash of issues" found on the North American political scene.

The Quest for Strong Community: A Positive-Sum Game

The analysis here need not abandon the concept of what is "good" or what is "best" for society. While dropping my explicit use of the concept of sovereignty, I do seek to replace it with a set of factors that some may feel in their totality add up to the same thing. So be it. However, as I look at issues, I wish to do so in the context of a positive-sum game where players on both sides can be winners. I suggest that policy debates be examined in light of how policy decisions impact upon the notion of "community." The question asked over and over again will be: "Does this policy decision strengthen communities?" And "how does it do so, and to what extent does it do so?" These are positive-sum perspectives because everyone wins when communities within the society are stronger. One community is helped, not hurt, when a neighboring community is stronger. The direct attention can be given to the question of how Native American communities are helped, but it also goes to the question of how their non-Native neighboring communities are helped as well.

Defining Community

Forty-six years ago George Hillery analyzed ninety-four different definitions of the term *community.* He found sixteen commonly agreed upon definitions indicating that communities possessed geographical areas inhabited with people with common ties who had a sense of identification and engaged in social interaction as groups (Hillery 1959).

Communities are very important to human survival. A strong community has a physical infrastructure (e.g., houses, roads, water supplies) capable of serving the needs of its members. A community is the critical set of institutions that instill the psychological dispositions and value structures that sustain growth and personal satisfaction. Strong communities provide individuals with an "internalized rationale for altruistic, humane, and moral behavior." A powerful community binds people with a sense of identity and feelings of mutual security. There is a consensus with respect to norms and values so that all people know what to expect from others. A community is composed of individuals and institutions that interact with external communities. As linkages to other communities are strengthened, the community itself may be strengthened and gain a greater capacity to pursue common goals. On the other hand, linkages to outside communities may also cause a community to lose autonomy and a sense of common identification.

Recent literature also speaks to community. In Mark Roseland's book, *Toward Sustainable Communities* (1998), community is defined as "a group of people bound by geography and with a shared destiny." The word "shared" is in the past tense, and it connotes a togetherness that has existed over time. However, the word "destiny" looks toward the future. Roseland sees the sustainable community as having both strong natural capital and strong social capital. Natural capital refers to natural resources, protection of the environment, good housing stock, transportation resources, and opportunities for economic development. Social capital incorporates "shared knowledge, understandings, and patterns of interaction that a group of people bring to any productive activity." It looks to organizations and structures, information flows, social relationships, imagination, and notions of trust and interpersonal solidarity. It involves a sense of place and "civicness." Social capital is created "when individuals learn to trust one another so that they are able to make credible commitments and rely on generalized forms of reciprocity rather than on narrow sequences of specific quid pro quo relationships." Social capital does not wear out through use; yet, if it is unused, it may deteriorate. It takes time to nurture and develop (Roseland 1997, 8–9).

Tyler Norris Associates published *The Community Indicators Handbook* in 1997. They present lists of factors developed by organizations seeking "sustainability" in communities across North America. Recurring factors include:

1. The economy (business—vitality and investment, employment—job quality and job growth, income, prosperity—low poverty)
2. Health—alcohol, drug, tobacco use
3. Education—graduation rates, literacy, skills development

4. Government and civic engagement, participating
5. Livability—environmental health, safety, recreation, transportation, cultural events, child care, proper land-use policies
6. Housing
7. Neighborliness, respect for others, appreciation of the efforts of others past and present.

These factors are not presented in the literature as a formula that is available to "score" or rank communities. Rather, they exist as parts of measuring sticks for qualitatively judging community strength. The factors are incorporated by Native Americans themselves as well as by scholars who speak of social vitality in keeping the "circle whole." Canadian sociologist J. Rick Ponting asks parenthetically, "How is the circle made whole?" He answers by saying that wholeness comes with "keeping the (Native) culture and identity strong; developing trusted government at the local level and displaying good leadership and followership . . . (and) developing the human potential of members of the community." He adds a critical factor only hinted at above. The complete circle must keep "some boundaries between the community and outsiders" (Ponting 1994, 59).

By concentrating on attributes of community strength, we can establish a better understanding of positive development among tribal populations; it is related to public policies.

The Order of the Book

This first chapter introduces many of the issues currently facing Native American communities. Chapter 2 presents an overview of Native America through millennia from a time of basically autonomous tribal units to a contemporary era of special federally recognized units within a broader scheme of political organization. The chapter also presents a concise picture of Native American communities, their populations, and their socioeconomic attributes.

Chapters 3 and 4 treat major issues facing Native America today and examine how public policy regarding the issues impacts the strength of Native American communities. Chapter 3 offers an in-depth treatment of the subject of gambling, and Chapter 4 covers other issues. Most of these important but "secondary" issues are seen in aspects of how the gambling issue is evolving. We look at concerns about political jurisdiction and the Native American Bill of Rights; land claims, natural resources, and environmental protection, including water rights and hunting and fishing rights; health, education, housing, and welfare; religious practices, sacred sites, and burial practices; and stereotyping and discrimination. Chapter 4 also examines these issues in the context of Canadian tribal communities.

Chapter 5 presents a chronology of critical events, and Chapter 6 presents biographical sketches of important figures.

Chapter 7 offers an annotation of major legislation and court cases pertaining to Native Americans and their communities as well as tables of statistical data. Chapter 8 is a collection of thoughts and words regarding Native America. It also features a compendium of statements from the presidents of the United States. Chapter 9 presents a detailed listing of organizations.

Chapter 10 provides annotations for over 100 print and non-print sources, as well as descriptions of sixty feature films.

References

Bucholtz, Todd. *New Ideas from Dead Economists*. New York: Plume, 1989.

Elazar, Daniel. *American Federalism: A View from the States*. New York: Crowell, 1972.

Hillery, George. "A Critique of Selected Community Concepts." *Social Forces* 37, no. 3 (March 1959): 237–242.

Ponting, J. Rick. "The Paradox of On-Reserve Casino Gambling: Musings of a Nervous Sociologist." In Colin Campbell, ed. *Gambling in Canada: The Bottom Line*. Burnaby, B.C.: Simon Fraser University, 1994, pp. 57–68.

Roseland, Mark. *Toward Sustainable Communities: Resources for Citizens and Their Governments*. New Haven, CT: New Society Publ., 1998.

Tyler Norris Associates. *The Community Indicators Handbook*. San Francisco: Redefining Progress, 1997.

2

Native Communities in History and Native Peoples Today

Communities of indigenous Native peoples have lived in the Western Hemisphere for thousands of years. The ancestors of present-day North Americans arrived as many as 50,000 years ago. While most scholars agree that the first of these peoples came to the Americas across a land bridge between Asia and Alaska, the earliest evidence of significant cultural development is found in Central and South America. There agriculture-based empires with complex societies flourished. The early Native peoples of North America also exhibited agricultural and hunting and fishing societies, as well as formal ongoing political structures.

The first peoples of North America were organized into many diverse groups. There were over 500 languages spoken among 240 or more tribes. Some authors indicate there were 500 "nations" of Native peoples at the time of the first European contacts. The population at that time is estimated to have been two million (in the area of the present-day United States), although some scholars support much higher numbers. One indicates that as many as 15 million were on the continent (Stiffarm and Lane 1992, 33–55).

Before the arrival of Europeans, many of the Native peoples lived in communities with a common geographical space; a strong sense of identity with one another as a distinct population and extensive social interactions, based upon common interests as well as a common heritage and cultural practices; and a physical infrastructure with housing, water and food supplies, roads facilitating economic and trade activity, and a structure of defense against potential enemies. Whereas communities displayed autonomy, they also interacted with other communities.

The collective strength of the Native community has been severely tested over the past 500 years as a result of contacts with new groups migrating to North America. The first Europeans to cross the Atlantic Ocean and "find" new lands of the Western Hemisphere cannot be firmly identified. Celtic and Viking navigators may have come over a thousand years ago, landing in Newfoundland in eastern Canada and perhaps northern areas of New England. Although these venturers established rudimentary communities, their presence was not permanent. Such was not the case with the Spanish immigrations in the late fifteenth century.

The adventures of Columbus and his sailors were organized in part as a means of gaining permanence in communities in order to obtain economic advantages for transplanted Europeans. Soon Spanish explorations and migrations were followed by those from other countries, notably England, France, Denmark, Sweden, The Netherlands, and Portugal, with several of these establishing colonies. These migrating people also established the practice of importing slaves from African lands.

The various countries formed different patterns of relationships with the indigenous communities. The French migrations consisted initially of personal adventurers seeking wealth in fur trading. They interacted with Native communities on somewhat of an equal footing, and they found value in assimilating with the populations they encountered. The British who came to dominate the entirety of the European North American settlements did not find value in assimilation policies. A decided "we/they" posture guided their policies. Such a posture persisted after the United States was established. At times when notions of assimilation were made part of the relationships, the direction was one way, as Native peoples were expected to assimilate with the new Americans.

Because the French incursions into North America were designed with goals of trade rather than sustained migrations of peoples onto new lands, the French relationships with Native peoples were in many senses symbiotic and to a degree positive for both sides. This was less the case with the English and the later American contacts. Both British and Americans pursued goals of occupation and expanded settlements into lands surrounding and incorporating indigenous communities.

Government-to-government contacts developed into relationships between a dominant American national government and subordinate tribal governments. The relationships persisted on the basis of treaties until 1871 when the U.S. Congress decreed that treaty relationships would no longer be pursued. By that time the U.S. government had made 389 treaties with tribal governments.

The Articles of Confederation and the U.S. Constitution vested plenary powers over relationships with Native peoples in the hands of Congress. American state governments were guided in their relationships with tribes by the edicts of the national government. A critical first act of Congress declared that all transfers of Native lands to non-Native persons or authorities had to be made with the approval of the national government.

The Northwest Ordinance passed in 1787 by Congress provided that lands would not be taken from the Native peoples without their consent unless they were taken in a "just" war. During the English colonial era (prior to 1776 in the United States), tribes were moved by consent and otherwise onto reservations of land designated for their exclusive use. The removals were made with a recognition that symbiotic relationships between tribes and new settlers were not feasible.

President Thomas Jefferson had desired assimilation for the "betterment" of Native peoples; nonetheless, reservation policies persisted. In 1830, Congress passed the Indian Removal Act, which transferred Indian ownership of lands east of the Mississippi River to lands west of the river. Minimal compensation was given to tribes for the costs of moving their populations. Over 100,000 members of what were called the five civilized tribes (Cherokee, Choctaw, Chickasaw, Creek, and Seminoles) were moved involuntarily (Cohen 1982, 78–92).

When the Mexican War ended in 1848, the United States found that its newly won territories included 150,000 Natives. Attempts to impose political control over Native communities led to decades of war between the United States and indigenous western tribes. Eventually, tribes were subdued, and their peoples confined to reservation communities.

Under the Major Crimes Act of 1885, the jurisdiction over ten crimes was transferred directly to federal authorities. The federal government also took over many civil functions for the people, including the education of young people.

A major change in policy direction came with passage of the General Allotment (Dawes) Act of 1887. The act was the result of a recognition that the reservation policies had severely failed Native peoples. Helen Hunt Jackson's books, *A Century of Dishonor* and *Ramona*, graphically portrayed for a wide reading American public that most Native peoples were living under severe deprivations and abject poverty, being ill housed, ill fed, sick, and ailing. Her solution was the Jeffersonian dream: assimilation of indigenous people with their adoption of the social and cultural patterns of non-Natives (Jackson 1881, 1884).

The Dawes Act divided existing reservations into parcels of land that were granted to Native peoples as individual parcels with individual private ownership. Under the formula established, surplus lands were sold to non-Natives. The result of this attempt to "help" Native peoples was a disaster. The first result was that Natives lost great quantities of lands. Second, the individual land-owning Native populations were not given the "tools" to exploit the lands as individuals—tools such as agricultural equipment and specific education for land development. While it took several decades, the assimilation notion did result in a 1924 Act of Congress that decreed that Native peoples were citizens of the United States.

Another study influenced policy once again. The Meriam Report of 1928 was not a popular book, but rather a set of revelations from a government study of conditions of Native peoples. The conclusions were the same as those offered by Helen Hunt Jackson: the peoples were in dire conditions. However, the policy recommendations that came from the Meriam Report were different from those advocated by Jackson. As a result of the Meriam Report, the Dawes Act–type of *assimilation solution* was deemed a failure. Congress ended the practice of taking reservation land and redistributing it. The notion of intact Native communities was now recognized as the best approach to helping build strong lives for Native Americans (Meriam 1928).

In 1934, the Indian Reorganization Act was passed in recognition that the Native American societies should be preserved as political cultures. Native peoples were asked to write constitutions, and new federal programs of support were instituted. A federal policy of protecting Native American arts and crafts soon followed. This admirable turnaround in U.S. policy had little impact, however, inasmuch as the politics of World War II soon dominated the nation's attention.

The Indian Reorganization Act, though representing a reversal of the Dawes allotment policy, also deprived Native governments of some measure of autonomy. In calling for the tribes to construct constitutions and political structures, the Act mandated that these constitutions and structures follow the patterns established by the non-Native American governments and reject some traditional governing patterns utilized by tribal organizations.

A new "Termination" policy took form during the Truman presidency (1945–1952) at the end of World War II. For example, the federal government's educational responsibilities to the tribes were now transferred to the states. Many federal schools on reservations were closed. The basic legislation behind Termination awaited the arrival of the Eisenhower administration in 1953. In that year, the United States was facing major budget cuts, and the administration saw fiscal benefits in cutting services to tribal organizations by eliminating the organizations. While the secretary of the interior, Fred Seaton, claimed that no tribal government would be dissolved without its consent, consent was loosely defined. In all, 109 tribal governments were dissolved as a result of the new policies of the 1950s. Included in these numbers were the Klamath, Siletz, and Grande Ronde of Oregon, the Menominee of Wisconsin, and several smaller tribes of Washington State (Churchill and Morris 1992, 15).

Accompanying the federal government's Termination policy was a return to an earlier policy—removal. This time the government decided that the indigenous peoples would be better off not on reservations but rather in the cities of the United States. Volunteers for removal were recruited and were given subsidies. The volunteers received moving expenses as well additional funds for food, housing, and vocational training (Cohen 1982, 169–170).

Other tribes were not left out of the Termination policy thrust. Without the consent of the Native Americans, Congress passed Public Law 280. This law transferred criminal and civil authority over the Native Americans in five states from the federal government to the state governments.

The Termination plans of the 1950s had many consequences: land-ownership patterns underwent fundamental changes; trustee relationships with the federal government were ended; special federal programs were discontinued; state legislative and judicial authority were imposed on Native Americans; and exemption from state taxation was ended in many cases (Charles F. Wilkinson and Eric Biggs, cited in Deloria and Lytle 1984, p. 20).

The Termination drive of the Truman-Eisenhower administrations was recognized as a failure even before the 1950s ended. The urbanization removal program merely resulted in urban Native Americans ending up on welfare rolls. Drawing together peoples from many tribes into concentrated geographical areas did, however, create a new Native American unity and awareness, with definite political consequences in subsequent years. People who remained on their own lands also suffered because much of the basis for economic welfare was taken away with federal budget cuts (Hagen 1961, 165).

The Kennedy administration (1960–1963) came into office with the promise that the United States would be seeking a "New Frontier." Facing southward, the new administration became the architect of an "Alliance for Progress" for Latin American nations, and facing inward, it endorsed the notion of economic development among the Native American tribes. The 1961 Area Redevelopment Administration Act allowed tribes to buy lands and facilities for industrial and commercial use. The notion that the tribes could expand the boundaries of their lands was a unique departure from policies dating back to the sixteenth century. The message conveyed was that tribes could and should develop their natural resources. A New Frontier or "Renaissance" for Native Americans had begun.

When Lyndon Johnson assumed the presidency in 1963 following the assassination of John F. Kennedy, he advanced the idea of tribes as autonomous entities. In a special message to Congress on March 6, 1968, Johnson spoke about "the Forgotten American." He proposed a new policy of self-determination that would erase "old attitudes of paternalism" and promote "partnership self-help" (1968–1969 *Public Papers*, pt. I, at 335; see Cohen 1982, 185). He assigned Vice President Hubert Humphrey the task of chairing a National Council on Indian Opportunity to review federal programs and to make recommendations for reforms. Johnson stressed the need for tribal leadership and involvement with the federal government to improve Native health, education, economic growth, and the strength of their community institutions. On April 11, 1968, the Indian Civil Rights Act was passed, which extended many liberties in the Bill of Rights to people in their relationships with tribal governments.

Political action groups, including the National Indian Youth Council and the American Indian Movement, were organized in the 1960s, in part as a consequence of the urbanization policies. A

March on Washington in 1972 was accompanied by workshops that developed a "Twenty Points" platform submitted to the White House (Deloria 1984, 236–238).

The Twenty Points were lost in a political melee that included an occupation of Bureau of Indian Affairs headquarters. They did not receive a serious hearing. Nonetheless, they remain one of the clearest articulations of what Native Americans wished in terms of their political and personal rights. The Twenty Points included statements on land control, religious freedom, oppressive state policies, and federal funding of programs. The main thrust of this platform was a call that relationships with the federal government be conducted on a government-to-government basis. Collectively, the document called for "restoration of a constitutional treaty-making authority," and a provision "that all Indians be governed by treaty relations" (Deloria 1984, 239).

President Richard Nixon (1968–1975) was in tune with the Native Americans' quest for more autonomy. His administration supported the preservation of the tribal governments, restoring the Menominee tribe to its former status in 1973. The Indian Financing Act was passed in 1974 providing funding mechanisms for business ventures. (The acts are reproduced in part in Prucha 1990, 263–270.)

The Indian Self Determination and Educational Assistance Act was passed in 1975, soon after Nixon left office (see Prucha 1990, 274–276). The Jimmy Carter administration (1976–1980) oversaw passage of the American Indian Religious Freedom Act, the Tribally Controlled Community College Assistance Act, and the Indian Child Welfare Act in 1978 (in Prucha 1990, 288–294). Cultural autonomy was recognized with the Archaeological Resources Protection Act of 1979 (Prucha 1990, 294–295).

Presidents Ronald Reagan (1980–1988) and George H. W. Bush (1988–1992) endorsed the notions of Native self-reliance, though their motivations were not necessarily always altruistic.

Both presidents, for example, guided budgetary policies that resulted in large cuts in federally funded programs, including programs for the tribes. In the 1980s unemployment rose to 40 percent on reservations (Baker and Rosenberg 1992, 29). A quick survey of reservations found that they lacked basic amenities such as electricity, plumbing, water, adequate housing, and medical care. All the policies of the 1960s, 1970s, and 1980s, though seemingly well intentioned, had done little to satisfy the First Nations' goal of self-determination and governmental autonomy. There was a simple answer to the question of "Why?": Money!

Vine Deloria, Jr., and Clifford Lytle, writing about the status of relationships between Native communities and non-Natives in the early 1980s, observed, "there is no good solution to the question of self-government today. Indians have few viable options open to them because they lack the substantial economic and social freedom to experiment with alternative ways of doing things" (Deloria and Lytle 1984, 263).

The Reagan administration's secretary of interior, James Watt, tiring of objections to the administration's budget cutting, told one group of Native Americans about his perceived solution to their problems: "Instead of depending on the Great White Father, why don't you start your own damn business?" (quoted in Connor 1993, 8).

And it was at this time that a business opportunity was almost miraculously placed at the doorstep of Native Americans. The tribes discovered that the gambling industry presented much hope for obtaining the resources needed to strengthen their communities.

As gambling enterprises spread across Native America in the 1980s and 1990s, other legislation designed to strengthen tribal communities was also enacted. The National Museum of the American Indian Act was passed in 1989, while the Native American Languages Act, the Native American Graves Protection and Repatriation Act, and the Indian Child Protection and Family Abuse and Protection Act became law in 1990. Yet, neither the new gambling industry nor these other federal programs have succeeded in making Native communities as strong as other groups in the United States.

Attributes of Contemporary Native American Communities

The population figures of Native American communities have fluctuated greatly throughout the years that tribes have existed alongside nonindigenous peoples in America. Table 4 in Chapter 7 indicates census figures for Native peoples since records were kept. The Census of 2000 lists a person as a Native American if that person makes a self-declaration of being in that demographic category. Because prior Census definitions have varied considerably, it is somewhat difficult to track the growth of this population with much accuracy. Better comparisons can be made for the populations of specific tribal communities, that is, for on-reservation populations.

The lowest population figure for the Native Americans was recorded in 1890 when the census of that year showed that the Native population was only 273,607, with 25,354 of these people living in Alaska. By 1990, the numbers had increased to 2,044,932, with 85,698 residing in Alaska.

The notion of self-declaration drove the numbers up considerably for the 2000 Census. Today the reported number of Native Americans is 2,475,956.

Those living on reservation lands that are held in trust for Native Americans by the federal government number 512,032, with 57,964 of these people being in Alaska (2000 U.S. Census). In 1990, there were 437,771 Native residents on 236 federally recognized reservations, with 47,280 in 198 Alaskan Native villages.

There are 52 million acres (82,000 square miles) of trust lands for Native peoples. This constitutes 2.2 percent of the land mass of the United States. If all the lands were side by side, they would rank in size as the sixteenth largest state—just a bit larger than Nebraska or South Dakota but smaller than Kansas or Idaho.

Native peoples are among the poorest people in America. Of their reservation numbers, 50.7 percent fell below the poverty index in 1990, while 39.4 percent were in poverty in 2000. The latest census indicated per capita incomes of $7,958, up from $4,478 in 1990, while family incomes climbed from $13,489 to $23,966 in 2000.

Unemployment rates on reservation lands were 21.9 percent in 2000, with many tribal groups experiencing unemployment among a majority of the working eligible population. Entrepreneurship is also very low among Native Americans, a natural consequence of poverty. There are fewer Internet connections, telephones, and roads on Native lands than are found elsewhere. Few of the reservations have reasonable access to banks for most of their populations.

Poverty is connected to lower educational attainment. Only 11 percent of Native adults hold bachelor's degrees, while 71 percent are high school graduates. This compares unfavorably with the general population, over 25 percent of whom are college graduates and 83 percent hold at least a high school diploma (*Statistical Abstract of the United States* 2000, Table 249).

Poverty impacts both housing and health. In 2000 almost 12 percent of housing units on reservation lands lacked indoor plumbing, more than twice the national average. A report from the U.S. Department of Agriculture in the mid-1990s found that 22.2 percent of Native households were "hungry or on the edge of hunger." Again, this situation was twice as bad in Native areas as in the rest of America. Ironically, the obesity rates of Native peoples are significantly in excess of rates found in other population groups.

Diabetes is closely related to diet and nutrition, and it is linked to many other serious diseases. Over 15 percent of Native Americans have diabetes. On average, Indians are twice as likely to have this disease as others. Indeed, for selected age groups the incidence is even higher. Among Native American women over 45, one-third have diabetes. The death rates from the disease and complications such as eye disease are much higher among Native peoples. Native women also have excessive rates of heart and kidney disease. Native Americans also have a higher incidence of cigarette smoking and alcoholism.

Native men also experience substantially higher death rates from accidents, homicides, and suicides than men in the general population.

A report in the *American Journal of Public Health* ("Special Report" 2003) indicates that Native peoples are much less likely to seek out professional health service providers in dealing with this array of health problems, making the incidence of problems much more severe.

Government officials designed many programs to alleviate conditions of desperation and poverty among America's indigenous populations. The government even tried policies that then Senator Patrick Moynihan (D-NY) summarized as "benign neglect." Policies designed to remake Native populations in the image of other Americans were also attempted. If the results can be summarized by Census Bureau statistics, it can be suggested that, for the most part, all policies have failed to achieve their intended results. Native Americans have been "at the bottom of the heap" in America, and they remain there today.

However, a new policy initiative has surfaced in the past

two decades, and renewed promise for improved lives has resurfaced. Economic growth on Native American lands has been promoted by federal recognition of gambling enterprises operated by and for Native peoples. Is this the avenue toward greater viability for Native communities? The next chapter examines the possibilities of this economic tool.

References

Baker, James, and Debra Rosenberg. "Gambling on the Reservation." *Newsweek* (February 17, 1992): 29.

Churchill, Ward, and Glenn T. Morris. "Key Indian Laws and Cases." In M. Annette Jaimes, ed. *The State of Native America: Genocide, Colonization, and Resistance.* Boston: South End Press, 1992, pp. 13–21.

Cohen, Felix. *Handbook of Federal Indian Law.* 2d ed. Charlottesville, VA: The Michie Company, 1982.

Conner, Matt. "Indian Gaming: Prosperity, Controversy." *International Gaming and Wagering Business* (April 1993): 8–10.

Deloria, Vine, Jr. *The Nations Within.* New York: Pantheon, 1984.

Deloria, Vine, Jr., and Clifford M. Lytle. *American Indians, American Justice.* Austin: University of Texas Press, 1984.

Hagan, William T. *American Indians.* Chicago: University of Chicago Press, 1961.

Jackson, Helen Hunt. *A Century of Dishonor.* New York: Harper and Brothers, 1881.

Jackson, Helen Hunt. *Ramona.* Boston: Roberts Brothers, 1884.

Meriam, Lewis. *The Problem of Indian Administration.* Baltimore, MD: Johns Hopkins University Press, 1928.

Prucha, Francis Paul. *Documents of United States Indian Policy.* Lincoln: University of Nebraska Press, 1990.

"Special Report: Native American Health." *American Journal of Public Health* 93 (2003): 1–6.

Stiffarm, Lenore A., and Phil Lane Jr. "Demography of Native North America: A Question of American Indian Survival." In M. Annette Jaimes, ed. *The State of Native America: Genocide, Colonization, and Resistance.* Boston: South End Press, 1992, pp. 23–53.

U.S. Census, *Statistical Abstract of the United States 2000,* Washington D.C.: U.S. Printing Office, 2000, Table 249.

Laws

American Indian Religious Freedom Act of 1978, 92 U.S. Statute 469.

General Allotment (Dawes) Act of 1887, 24 U.S. Statute 388.

Indian Financing Law of 1974, 88 U.S. Statute 77.

Indian Reorganization Act of 1934, 48 U.S. Statute 984.

Indian Self Determination and Educational Assistance Act of 1975, 88 U.S. Statute 2203.

Major Crimes Act of 1885, 23 U.S. Statute 385.

Public Law 280 (1952), 67 U.S. Statute 588.

3

The Keystone Topic for Contemporary Native America: Gambling

In 1979, tribal leaders at a Seminole Bingo Hall in Hollywood, Florida, decided to raise their prize limits above those permitted by the state of Florida for charitable games. In that singular action, the leaders set into motion a one-way force that became manifested in a Native American gaming establishment that today realizes well over $10 billion in annual revenues, or almost 20 percent of all money gambled legally in the United States. Although the gambling enterprise as an economic tool for community development (or the opposite) was new, gambling activity among Native Americans was not.

The crew that sailed with Christopher Columbus on the *Nina, Pinta,* and the *Santa Maria* in 1492 very likely had playing cards with them on their voyage to the "New World." One rumor suggests that they threw their cards overboard because they thought their gambling activity might be causing God to be leading them astray—that is, away from land. After the cards were discarded, they sighted land, and at this point they quickly made new gambling cards. Apparently, the crew's fear of God alternated with their desire to play. One thing is for certain, however: the crew of the three small ships did not introduce gambling to the Americas.

The Native population was no different than other populations have been since the beginning of time: they had games and they participated in gambling activities.

21

Stewart Culin has classified hundreds of Native games into two categories: (1) games of chance, including dice games and guessing games, and (2) games of dexterity, encompassing archery, javelin and darts, shooting, ball games, and racing games. The games continued when the Europeans arrived, although the Native Americans did adopt the use of playing cards and certain board games from non-Native settlers. On the other hand, there is little evidence that Native games of chance were transferred to the settlers. The Europeans did, however, adopt certain of the Natives' ball games, particularly the game that would become known as "La Crosse" (Culin 1992, 31–32, 809).

Culin relates some harmful effects of tribal gaming, especially from a bowl and stick-dice game played by the the Assiniboin of the northern plains:

> Most of the leisure time, either by night or by day, among all these nations is devoted to gambling in various ways, and such is their infatuation that it is the cause of much distress and poverty in families. For this reason the name of being a desperate gambler forms a great obstacle in the way of a young man getting a wife. Many quarrels arise among them from this source, and we are well acquainted with an Indian who a few years since killed another because after winning all he had he refused to put up his wife to be played for. (Culin 1992, 173–174)

Culin's account continues, "Women are as much addicted to the practice as men, though their games are different, and not being in possession of much property their losses, although considerable for them, are not so distressing" (Culin 1992, 173–174).

Other accounts of Native American games have been more positive. The Aginskys's found that among the Pomo of California, gamblers were a highly honored group, and that a family would happily welcome an apprentice gambler as a son-in-law. The tribal religion sanctioned gambling, and the full society participated in games. Tribal members were cautioned against winning too many possessions from one another as this would cause "hard feelings" (Aginsky and Aginsky 1950, 110).

Lesieur and Custer reviewed several studies and found patterns of activity that mitigated the pathological gambling behaviors: (1) games were formalized rituals with many spectators, (2) players could not go into debt as a result of the games—they could wager only those possessions they brought with them to the games, and (3) individuals had to have their family's permission to make wagers (Lesieur and Custer 1984, 149; *see also* Devereux 1949).

The lack of a general cross-fertilization of game development among tribes and non-Natives is evidenced in the almost complete lack of such controls in non-Native games in North America. Indeed, today there is little attachment of tribal gaming operations to such practices, or even to early types of Native games. Today's Native American gaming is an outgrowth of non-Native gaming.

With the beginning of the New Hampshire Sweepstakes in 1964, the United States fell under what has been called "The Third Wave" of gambling in our history. Lotteries began to proliferate, as did charitable gaming. Natives took notice of the commercial possibilities of gaming, with tribes stepping forth like other charities and establishing bingo games. Many Michigan tribes offered bingo games after the state law authorized charity gaming in 1972. The tribes purposely followed all the state guidelines governing the games. Similarly, tribes in California, Wisconsin, and Florida held charity gaming events in accordance with all the state rules. But the Native American games did not compete with other charity games on an "equal footing." The church and charity bingos invariably were able to operate in cities or towns—where large numbers of people lived. Most reservation lands were outside of cities. They could not compete equally.

Operators of a Native American bingo facility on Seminole lands near Hollywood, Florida, almost a one-hour drive out of central Miami, figured that the best way they could compete with bingo games in Miami was to offer big prizes. They ignored the state rule that jackpots could not exceed $100 per game. Therefore, on December 14, 1979, the Seminole facility permitted jackpots for some games to equal or exceed several thousand dollars. The idea of flouting state rules on the size of jackpots and games and on the number of days or hours of game operations was soon copied across the country.

Local law enforcement officials challenged the tribes' right to disregard state regulations. The tribes' actions precipitated a series of lawsuits in federal courts. A key factor in several major cases was a ruling by the U.S. Supreme Court in *Bryan v. Itasca County* (1976). In that case, which involved taxation, the Court interpreted the reach of Public Law 280 of 1952. That law had given certain states jurisdiction over criminal and selected civil matters on reservation lands. However, the Court ruled that the activities covered by Public Law 280 had to be activities that were prohibited for all members of the citizenry of a state as a matter of general policy of the state. The Court found that taxation did not pertain to such a prohibitory activity. The ruling suggested that future courts would have to examine prohibitions of activity such as gambling in the same light. Was the prohibition general, applying to all citizens in all circumstances as a matter of general state policy?

When the sheriff of Broward County, Florida, sought to close down Seminole bingo, the tribe responded by seeking to enjoin his activity in the federal district court of southern Florida. They challenged Sheriff Robert Butterworth's claim of jurisdiction under Public Law 280. The federal district court ruled on behalf of the tribe, but the sheriff appealed. In 1981, the court of appeals upheld the district court saying in essence that the state lacked the authority to impose its rules. The court invoked the reasoning presented in *Bryan v. Itasca County*. Since bingo was legal in the state of Florida, the rules regarding the way games were to be operated were not criminal prohibitory rules but rather were regulations of a civil nature not covered by Public Law 280.

The Seminole interpretation was followed with similar cases. In California, the 9th circuit upheld a federal district court ruling giving a tribe injunctive relief against enforcement of county and state laws regulating bingo games (*Barona Group of Capitan Band of Mission Indians v. Duffy* 1982). Similarly, Wisconsin and Connecticut federal district courts reasoned that state pull-tab and bingo game regulations were not applicable to tribal lands (*Oneida Tribe v. Wisconsin* 1981; *Lac du Flambeau band v. Wisconsin* 1986; and *Mashantucket Pequot Tribe v. McGuigan* 1986).

The Native gaming spread rapidly throughout the country. Whereas at the end of the 1970s, only a handful of tribes had any gaming operations, the situation quickly changed. By 1985, the number was over 80 (*Charlotte Observer* July 28, 1985). Two years later the first "official" statistics were issued. A Bureau of Indian Affairs survey revealed games among 108 tribes. Estimated revenues from all the games exceeded $100 million a year (Ryan 1986).

Soon, concerns were raised. State officials as well as rival gaming interests—both commercial and charitable interests—expressed fears that the unregulated Native American gaming was an invitation to criminal involvement as well as a new form of unfair competition. So the officials turned to Congress for a remedy.

While the tribes denied that crime was an issue, they recognized that certain problems needed to be addressed. Many of the tribes that had rushed into gaming for the economic rewards it would bring also embraced non-Native entrepreneurs to run the games. It was becoming apparent that the major flow of gambling moneys was moving toward these outsiders.

The views expressed to a congressional committee on August 24, 1987, by Mike Rumboltz, chairman of the Nevada Gaming Control Board, were representative of those of many state and local officials across the country. As the chief regulator of America's "gambling state," Rumboltz spoke with a special degree of authority.

> Our concerns involving Indian gaming, therefore, are focused on preserving the image Nevada has built . . . that gaming can be a fair and honest industry. With more than a half-century of sometimes painful experience, Nevada can attest that the single most important element for the future success of Indian gaming is the *immediate* implementation of a comprehensive system of strict gaming regulation. (Rumboltz 1987)

He added that law enforcement agencies in several states had reported that Native bingo had "provided a shelter for illicit activities such as skimming, money laundering, fraud, suspended political corruption, and embezzlement by management company personnel" (Rumboltz 1987). But this suggestion that crime was attached to Native gaming was met with strong denials.

On October 7, 1988, *Newsday* carried national columnist Jack Anderson's assurance that "there is no evidence of any organized crime involvement" in Indian gaming.

Senator John McCain (R-AZ) added that "it [was] clear that the interest of the states and of the gaming industry extended far beyond their expressed concern about organized crime. Their true interest was protection of their own games from a new source of economic competition" (*Newsday*, October 7, 1998, A-33).

Nonetheless, there were cases of crime in Native American casinos before the Indian Gaming Regulatory Act was passed in 1988, and some of the persons associated with the gaming operations had indeed had contacts with organized crime figures.

The very first tribes that embraced high-stakes bingo gambling did not do so on their own. They were assisted by entrepreneurs seeking rewards not shared with tribes. Internal tribal disputes over just who was in charge of gaming also presented challenges to the integrity of the games. The disputes sometimes led to violence.

The Early Spread of Native American Gambling

The linkage of certain personalities and organizational names is a story that starts on the Florida Seminole lands and then extends to Minnesota, Arizona, Washington State, California, Oklahoma, North Carolina, and Ohio as well as other locations. First came the tribal chairperson Howard Tommie, followed by James Billie, then Jack B. Cooper, Seminole Management Associates, and Stephen Hennington Whilden, Pan American Management, New England Entertainment, Allen G. Arbogast, and Michael Frechette.

Stephen Whilden appears to have been the catalyst among a large cast of characters. He was the main driver throughout a process that exposed problems attached to the unregulated use of outside gambling management firms by Native American tribes. Whilden has variously been viewed as superhero, clandestine mystery man, and flim-flam artist. There are indications that he had been in the Central Intelligence Agency, that he was a State Department official, that he served two tours of duty in Vietnam, and that he was a White House liaison between two undefined entities during the last days of the Nixon administration. He also was reported to have been on the staff of the Office of Management and Budget. He left all of this excitement and high adventure in 1977 to try his hand as a tribal attorney on the Hollywood, Florida, Seminole reservation. The job ad offered a salary of $15,000. Persuading the tribe to use moneys from a Catholic Church grant to augment his salary, he accepted the position with a $25,000 stipend.

If Whilden was really the prominent operative that the media suggested he had been, he was taking a giant step backward when he joined the Seminoles. But he may have had good instincts and may just have been contemplating a major leap forward at the same time. Within just a few years he was called the "nation's leading impresario in the hot new growth business of high stakes bingo on Indian reservations" (*San Jose Mercury* August 28, 1984). By 1983, he was connected to fourteen of the twenty-one high-stakes Indian bingo games in the United States.

After becoming tribal counsel, Whilden sought to exploit the tribe's special status under the law. He considered expanding the tribal cigarette business, and he also thought of establishing a dog racing track. The notion of having a track brought him into contact with Jack B. Cooper, a part-owner of a race track. However, the tribal chief, Howard Tommie, and Whilden instead decided that a bingo hall would not be as expensive as a track and might even make more money. Tommie then entered into a partnership with Cooper just before his term as chief ended in 1979. Soon he was parlaying his $200 a week salary as chief into an income exceeding $25,000 a month. Their newly formed firm was called Seminole Management Associates (SMA).

Banks were very reluctant to lend money to tribes for commercial-type ventures, mainly because tribal assets (especially land and structures) could not be used for collateral. Therefore, the tribe made an agreement to borrow $1.4 million from SMA. The SMA also agreed to run the bingo games for 47 percent of the net profits, after the loan was fully repaid and all other expenses were paid (*Miami Herald* May 30, 1983).

While Whilden's past may have been mysterious, Cooper's certainly was not. Actually, it was checkered. Cooper openly acknowledged that he had been a partner of mobster Meyer Lansky in the ownership of a Miami hotel. He also had business dealings with Morris Lansburgh, a man who had been convicted of conspiring with Lansky to "skim" (steal) $14 million from the Flamingo Casino in Las Vegas. Cooper also assisted dictator Raphael Trujillo of the Dominican Republic in purchasing aircraft from Sweden. And when Cooper forgot to pay his federal income taxes, he served a short prison term for tax evasion (*Minneapolis Tribune* April 17, 1983).

As Whilden was guiding SMA into the Seminole bingo operations, he also capitalized on another opportunity. Around this time, glass beads and other artifacts were discovered in a Tampa, Florida, parking lot; further archeological work at the site resulted in the unearthing of the bones of 140 Native Americans. The location also matched historical records pinpointing the location of the site from which Seminoles had been shipped to Oklahoma in the 1840s. Whilden quickly moved into action. He won the support of Florida's congressional delegation to have the land purchased by the tribe and put into trust for the purpose of establishing an appropriate Native American museum. The local Bureau of Indian Affairs (BIA) director declared that the "tract will be used to preserve remains of Seminole Indians and artifacts of Seminole culture" (*Miami Herald* May 31, 1983).

The existence of the American Indian Religious Freedom Act (passed in 1978) allowed authorities to waive time-consuming procedures, and in July, 1980, the tribe bought 8.6 acres of land, which was given trust status. The tribe built a small museum, a gift shop, and a cigarette shop, and finally a 1,400-seat bingo hall. Before the land was put into trust, the new tribal chairman, James Billie, signed an agreement with Pan American Associates for a loan to build and manage the bingo hall for twelve years. Whilden became a principal in Pan American.

As the Seminole operatives were reaching outward for more opportunities, Whilden discovered that he had some legal problems. A federal organized crime strike force tried to subpoena bingo records to prove that the managers were stealing from the tribe's profits. The Seminoles seemed unconcerned, admitting that they knew nothing about what went on in the counting rooms. "Believe me, skimming goes on at all levels of my tribe without me worrying about skimming at the bingo hall too," replied chairman Billie. The manager of the Tampa games responded, "We have the strongest control system in the business." (This response is echoed by Native gaming operators to this day, expressing a thought that somehow the tribes have achieved a better level of casino control than Las Vegas casinos, which have been in operation for decades.) A federal grand jury, unable to get to the records, failed to offer indictments (*Miami Herald* May 29, 1983).

When the final court decisions in the Seminole case cleared the way for the spread of Native American gaming, Whilden had already charted his course. He sought out Norman Crooks of the tiny Mdewakanton Sioux Reservation in Shakopee, Minnesota, a Minneapolis suburb. Pan American arranged for a Boston firm, New England Entertainment, to finance a bingo facility for Crooks's tribe. The two companies then merged and took the new name Little Six, Inc., for the Minnesota project. They agreed to operate the bingo games for fifteen years in exchange for a 45 percent share of all net profits from bingo after a $1 million loan for the building was repaid. Little Six received $850,000 beyond the repayment of the loans and other expenses in the first year of operations.

Crooks was happy with the operation. He claimed that the bingo game profits allowed the 150 inhabitants of the 250-acre reservation to have paved roads for the first time. He also enjoyed the $80,000 he received from Little Six for the use of his land. The bingo hall was constructed on a reservation parcel that was assigned to Crooks. The tribal chair neglected to tell the tribal council and tribal members that he was taking this money from Little Six. He won council approval for the tribe to also pay him a monthly stipend for the use of his land. In 1984, the members ousted Crooks as their leader and went to court to void the agreement with Little Six. The new tribal leadership complained that the BIA officials had not approved the agreement. They also pointed out that the agreement violated BIA contract guidelines that such agreements not exceed five years. In addition, they noted that some unsavory characters were associated with Little Six. The federal district court of Minnesota voided the contract, and the tribe took over management of the games (*United States ex. rel. Shakopee Mdewakanton Sioux Community v. Pan American Management Company* 1985).

When Whilden reached out for financial help from New England Entertainment, he latched onto a group with a past. Two of New England's partners had criminal records. Under Whilden's direction, Pan American also lined up New England Entertainment to be its partner in establishing a blackjack casino in the state of Washington on the Lummi Reservation. The federal authorities acknowledged that the criminal involvement of the New England partners was a major factor in their closing down the operation in February 1983 (*Akron Beacon Journal* June 3, 1984).

In 1984, the other principals in Pan American sued Whilden, claiming he misrepresented his New England Entertainment Associates and had concealed their criminal records. Whilden severed ties with Pan American and formed a new group called the American Indian Development Company. Soon the new group had contracts with reservations in New Mexico and Oklahoma, as well as an agreement with the Pala band of California (*San Jose Mercury* August 28, 1984).

Stephen Whilden seemed to be ubiquitous, but actually he was but one of a cadre of entrepreneurs looking for opportunity in Native American gaming. The high-stakes bingo games on the Cherokee reservation in North Carolina provide an example of how tribal revenues were diverted to non-Native managers. An audit of 1983 and 1984 revenues revealed that bingo revenues in excess of $8 million resulted in tribal shares of $800,000 after the Cherokee Management group had deducted "expenses" (*Charlotte Observer* July 7, 1985; *Raleigh News Observer* July 28, 1985).

A very troubling case developed on the California lands of the Cabazon Band in 1981. The tribe consisted of 22 individuals—16 adults and 6 children, and they lived on a 1700-acre reservation in Southern California that President Grant had set up for the tribe in 1876. Since the land was quite unfit for habitation at the time, most of the tribal members lived in local cities off the reservation. Two hundred of the acres, however, turned out to be located adjacent to Interstate Highway 10. In 1978, the tribe hired John Paul Nichols to be its financial adviser. Nichols had an unusual past, having spent seventeen years in South America as a consultant before moving to Sarasota, Florida, where he was a social worker specializing in writing federal grant proposals. As the tribal financial adviser, Nichols's eyes turned immediately to the 200 interstate acres and "tax-free" commercial possibilities. He examined outlets for the sale of cigarettes, for liquor, and also for a bingo hall and card games casino. Nichols invited several of his friends to develop a gambling hall.

The Cabazon gambling hall opened in October 1980. In 1981, when the Cabazon security chief, Fred Alvarez, complained a bit too publicly that money was being skimmed out of the gaming operations, he was murdered along with two other gaming employees. The murder was never solved. However, during the police investigation of the homicides, irregularities regarding the games surfaced. One casino manager was Rocco Zangari, identified by the California Department of Justice as a "onetime mob enforcer and former associate of a crime family in Buffalo, New York." Other crime figures were identified as frequent visitors to the gaming hall. Later, Nichols himself identified Zangari as the culprit behind an embezzlement of $250,000 from the project—a theft that took the scheme into bankruptcy (*Arizona Republic* October 9, 1983). In 1989, a witness testified to a congressional committee that the mob was indeed behind the murder of Alvarez and the two other victims in 1981 (*Baltimore Sun* February 9, 1989).

The hooded witness, known only as "Marty," spoke to the U.S. Senate Select Committee on organized crime and indicated that he feared for his life. "Marty" claimed that he had run a bingo operation on Indian lands for the benefit of "the Mob." He also claimed that the crime family he worked for had received between $600,000 and $700,000 per year, while the tribe received less than $100,000. He suggested that twelve of the reservation gaming sites were infiltrated by the "Cosa Nostra." He indicated that the Cabazon lands as well as a tribal site in Oklahoma were controlled by the Mob. He also fingered the Buffalino and Lucchese crime families as partners in Indian gaming. Finally, he suggested that the games had been rigged (*Arizona Republic* February 9, 1989).

An agent with the California attorney general's office who testified to the committee on the same day claimed that there were three cases of organized crime activity involving California tribes (*Baltimore Sun* February 9, 1989). Rebutting this testimony, the agent with the Federal Bureau of Investigation's (FBI's) criminal division suggested that the "Mob" infiltration was not "currently a problem." However, he added, "There's a lot of cash, and wherever you find that, you're going to find La Cosa Nostra" (*Arizona Republic* February 9, 1989).

Where was the federal government while all these things were happening? Was the Bureau of Indian Affairs exercising its trust responsibilities to the tribes? The answer is Yes, and No, but mostly No. The tribes had on several occasions sought the help of the BIA in examining contracts that were being made with outside management firms. The help they received was minimal. The BIA might observe what was happening and then close their collective eyes when they felt that the tribal leaders wanted the agreements—as bad as they were. This appeared to be the case with the Mdewakanton Sioux Community. The federal authorities were consulted, but they did not sign off on the agreement in 1982. Nor did they intervene in the matter. In 1985 a federal judge voided the agreement because the agreement had not received BIA approval. However, for nearly four years, Stephen Whilden's Pan American and New England Entertainment associates reaped large sums of money from the tribal operation.

In Minnesota and elsewhere, tribal leaders called on FBI to investigate outside operators. In 1983, the FBI actually "cleared" the Pan American and New England groups so that they could run games on the Lummi Reservation in Washington. A *Seattle Times* headline declared, "Federal Probe Clears Main Consultant to Lummi Blackjack." The operatives were "cleared" of ties to "organized crime" (February 3, 1983).

Eight months later, the *Arizona Republic* reported (October 9, 1983) that "in fact, background investigations by the F.B.I. at the request of the B.I.A. have been little more than simple computer checks for prior felony convictions . . . the result is that there is little protection for the tribe and the public against the possibility of unscrupulous gambling managers." BIA officials said that because they "don't have the capability of doing security checks, they rely on the Justice Department and the F.B.I." According to Susan Barnes, assistant U.S. attorney in Seattle, "The F.B.I., U.S. attorneys and Department of Justice are not in the business of clearing people for this kind of thing. There really isn't anyone to do a thorough check." "Marty," the hooded witness at the Senate committee, simply offered that the FBI was "not getting correct information" (*Arizona Republic* February 9, 1989). Perhaps worse, when a criminal background was discovered by one of the federal agencies, the authorities were reluctant to share the information with tribal leaders.

The fiscal travails that guided state political leaders to accept new forms of gambling activity produced similar effects on tribal leaders. The Reagan administration had precipitated fiscal crises within state and local governments by withdrawing support of federal programs. The administration did the same with Native American tribal entities. The Reagan government wanted states to stand on their own, while they also advocated Native American self-determination and self-sufficiency. If the tribes were going to be able to take care of themselves, that meant they would have to do so without federal grants of money. Severe budget cuts affected many federal programs designed to help Native Americans. Gambling may have been fraught with problems, but tribes felt there was no other direction in which to turn.

At the same time, state officials began to pressure Congress to take action to assure that Native gaming was regulated. At first they sought legislation that would give state governments the upper hand in the regulation efforts. However, tribal interests and congressional voices responding to those interests wished to confine all regulation authority to either the tribes themselves (a status quo arrangement) or to the federal government without state involvement. Legislation was introduced in 1983 and in each congressional year through 1988. State government enthusiasm for legislation waned when a new court case emerged involving the Cabazon and Morongo Indian casinos in California. When the U.S. Supreme Court agreed to review lower court decisions favoring the tribes, those expecting a victory for state government control were close at hand. Accordingly, they stalled the effort to have new legislation.

The issue in the new Cabazon case was the same one that was litigated in the earlier cases involving the Seminoles and Baronas: Could the states impose their regulations on Native gaming whether or not the gaming violated criminal laws or the general policy of the state? While the interests of the state governments may have expected a change in judicial policy, they were sadly disappointed (*California v. Cabazon* 1980).

The Supreme Court shocked these interests when on February 26, 1987, by a six to three vote, it upheld the lower courts and the earlier federal court rulings.

While the Cabazon ruling reaffirmed the earlier Seminole and Barona cases, it added new interpretations to the issues of Native American gaming as well. The Court accepted the dichotomy test of civil-regulatory and criminal-prohibitory as first set forth in the Itasca case of 1976. But the Court used a basic balancing test as well. It inferred that gaming activities could fall under the criminal prohibitory category only if the state could show that its gaming rules were necessary to protect strong community interests and did not collaterally negate important advantages to Native Americans that could come from the gaming operations.

The Court opinion indicated that Native American gambling presented very important advantages. The gambling supported federal policy goals of self-sufficiency for tribal communities. The federal policy had been enunciated by President Reagan as well as by the Department of the Interior and the Department of Housing and Urban Affairs, both of which supported grants for construction of bingo and parlors. The Bureau of Indian Affairs had approved tribal ordinances and contracts for the operation of the facilities. Moreover, the tribal gambling had proven to be successful in achieving many of the economic goals of jobs as well as support of tribal social welfare programs. On the other hand, the opinion recognized that crime could be a concern. However, the concern was outweighed by the advantages. The Court felt that the state government's arguments about tribal gaming crime had little force because the state (California) had given widespread approvals for non-Native gaming, and indeed the state itself operated a lottery.

The Court suggested that a state that approved gambling as a matter of state policy would indeed have a difficult task justifying bringing Native gambling under state control absent congressional authorization allowing the state to do so. The Court did not say that the tribes had a sovereign right to conduct gambling operations. The opinion suggested that Congress could set forth specific rules for the regulation of Native gambling, and the rules could bring state governments into the regulatory process.

The shoe was now on the other foot. Tribal spokespersons were content to let the status quo continue. They resisted all legislation giving the state a voice in regulation. Nonetheless, the fact that the tribes saw their vulnerability vis-à-vis non-Native management companies left room for some form of legislation.

The congressional representatives who advocated state regulation conceded that tribes could conduct what was called Class I gaming—the traditional games tribes had had for many centuries. They also acquiesced in allowing tribal bingo games (Class II gaming) to be under the control of the federal government and the tribes. A National Indian Gaming Commission was included in the legislation and was given powers of oversight. The powers extended to regulating contracts between tribes and gaming management companies. The companies were limited in the amount of gaming revenue they could take from the operations. The critical issue that caused an impasse between February 1987 and late 1988 was how casino (Class III) gaming would be regulated. The states would not give up their desire to control Native casinos, while the tribes were not about to yield control to the states.

A separate intervening event in 1987 opened the door to compromise. A tribe in Nevada wanted to have casino gaming operations on its lands. The Mojave tribal lands near the bottom point of the state of Nevada were only 10 miles away from the casino gambling center of Laughlin. The Mojaves realized that their land had advantages. They had water rights, and they were located closer than Laughlin to highways leading to the metropolitan areas of Phoenix and Southern California.

Initially, Nevada balked at allowing any gambling on the lands, telling the tribe that any operators would have to go through the exact same licensing process as any other gaming interest in the state and would be subject to the exact same form of regulation and taxation. The Mojaves were not prepared to give up that much, so they talked and talked, realizing that they really did not have any financial muscle to make a project of any viable size happen. Then in the 1985, they joined forces with the MoVada

Group—three Las Vegas entrepreneurs, one of whom was a casino license holder and also lieutenant governor of the state. The partners knew that nothing would happen, at least while they were involved, unless the state of Nevada gave its full cooperation. They persuaded the tribe to hire attorney Paul Bible, the former chairperson of the Nevada Gaming Commission. The tribal officials had bought some inside influence, but some might say they may have only been taken by an inside route. Nevada authorities and the tribe's representative reached a settlement. The tribe would agree to follow all the state's regulations on casino gaming, and they would allow state regulators to come onto tribal lands to enforce the regulations. The tribe would pay the state the costs of regulation. In turn, the state would forgo its tax on gambling wins (Garcia 1990; Carlson 1990). The tribe signed the agreement on October 15, 1987.

While a Senate Select Committee on Indian Affairs was sitting on the legislation and the 1988 legislative year was moving toward its end, Senator Harry Reid (D-NV) began to sense panic developing within the gaming industry and among other interests representing state governments. He felt a compromise was immediately necessary. His feelings became entwined with thoughts about his own state's experience with the Mojave tribe. The state and the tribe reached a compromise through open negotiations. Nevada was certainly happy with the results. Reid saw the scenario as a win-win game all around. Things began to fall into line. Reid suggested: "State and local government officials and law officers felt that they had to have some role in saying that Indian gaming did not have detrimental effect[s] on their citizens. To deal with this problem I suggested to Chairman Inouye that we use the concept of Tribal-State compacts to determine the regulatory structure of Class III gaming" (Reid 1990, 18).

Reid influenced the Select Committee on Indian Affairs to adopt a compromise position for tribal state compacts to guide regulatory policy for Class III gaming. On September 15, the Senate gave unanimous consent to the bill. The bill was then sent to the House where on September 26, 1988, it passed 323 to 84. The bill was sent to the president, and on October 17, 1998, Ronald Reagan signed what now became Public Law 100-497 into law (the Indian Gaming Regulatory Act of 1988).

The Indian Gaming Regulatory Act culminated six years of legislative struggles. We can now make observations about the outcomes that have followed the implementation of the Act over a fifteen-year period of time. We can investigate outcomes to see if the opportunities have been realized. First, we should take a summary look at the law.

In the law, Congress found that a "principal goal of Federal Indian policy is to promote economic development, tribal self-sufficiency, and strong tribal government." The purpose of the Act was to do precisely those things, as well as provide a basis for "the regulation of gaming by an Indian tribe adequate to shield it from organized crime and other corrupting influences, to ensure that the Indian tribe is the primary beneficiary of the gaming operation, and to assure that gaming is conducted fairly and honestly by both the operator and players."

A tribe could offer the important Class III casino games if the games were "permitted for any purpose by any person, organization, or entity." However, before the games were offered, a tribe had to pass an ordinance indicating that it approved of the games. Then the tribe would have to negotiate an agreement with the state government to provide for the manner in which the games would be regulated. The negotiated compact could not allow the state to tax the gaming, but the state could participate in regulation and receive a fee to cover the cost of regulation. If the state refused to negotiate "in good faith," the tribe could ask a federal district court to order negotiations.

The chairperson of the National Commission on Indian Gaming was required to approve management contracts with non-Natives. The chair would also investigate all contractors to assure their personal integrity. Outside managers could not receive fees for services in excess of 30 percent of the net revenues from the operations over a five-year period of time. The fee could be extended to as much as 40 percent over seven years if the chair found that the management company was providing capital investment funds that required extra income in order to provide for their recovery. The law also addressed gaming on new tribal lands. Such gaming was permissible under the Act if the lands were adjacent to existing lands. However, if an existing tribe acquired noncontiguous lands, gaming was only permitted if the land became tribal trust land and if both the secretary of the interior and the governor of the state agreed that the gambling was consistent with the public interest. Section 21 of the Act provided that information regarding the operations of gaming on Native

American lands was not subject to the provisions of the Freedom of Information Act.

An Initial Hurdle Cleared

Initially, the Nevada gaming industry cheered the legislative results they had achieved. The first reaction from tribes was that they had been defeated again. The Mescalero Apache of New Mexico and the Red Lake Band of Chippewas of Minnesota initiated a federal court action challenging the constitutionality of the Act on sovereignty grounds. The court of appeals concluded that Congress had the authority to pass the Act and that it met the tests of constitutionality (*Red Lake Band v. Swimmer* 1990). The Supreme Court refused to hear the case on appeal, letting the lower decisions stand.

In February 1996, the U.S. Supreme Court did declare part of the section on the resolution of disputes regarding the negotiation of compacts to be unconstitutional. The Court ruled that the Eleventh Amendment of the Constitution precluded suits by tribes against state governments in the federal courts. However, the effect of the ruling has not been major. Most tribes desiring to have Class III gaming already had their compacts in place, and other tribes also successfully negotiated new compacts with states since February 1996 as if the ruling had not been made (*Seminole Tribe v. Florida* 1996).

While this Seminole case seemed to empower states to ignore tribal desires to have Class III gaming, an opposite effect occurred. Tribes in states such as Wisconsin, New York, and California entered into agreements with states that allow them to have gambling on an exclusive basis—that is, gambling not permitted to other persons—in exchange for payments of gaming revenues to the states. The law clearly makes such taxation agreements illegal. Nonetheless, the secretary of the interior permitted such agreements to take effect. In two states, the tribes pay states as much as 25 percent of their revenues from gambling machines in order to have exclusive use of the machines. Governors and others are persuaded to enter agreements not only because they want revenues, but also because tribes have become major contributors of funds to political campaigns. The law indicates the purposes for which the tribal gaming money can be spent—political contributions are not authorized under the law.

Can we offer a verdict on the law? Has it helped strengthen Native American communities? Consider the following list of positive and negative answers to the question (Thompson and Dever 1994).

First, the positive:

1. Gambling money means tribal survival. Survival means food, housing, and medical care. Money from gambling activities has been placed into programs meeting basic needs. Survival is threatened by substance abuse—drugs and alcohol. Gambling revenues are used for treatment and prevention programs.

2. Gambling money means economic opportunity. Without jobs in their homelands, peoples gave up their tribal communities by leaving. Gambling has brought jobs to Native lands. Jobs have given members of tribes an incentive to return home and renew native communities.

3. Gambling revenue is invested in other enterprises to gain a diversity of employment and secure a stable economic basis for the future.

4. Revenue allows tribes to choose the direction of economic development. Before gambling, many felt pressured to accept any economic opportunity. They allowed lands to be strip-mined, grazed, or timbered in nonecological ways, polluted with garbage and industrial wastes. One tribe explored the prospects of having a brothel.

5. Gambling money gives educational opportunities. Tribes use funds for books, computers, new desks, new roofs, remodeled halls, and plumbing for schools. Schools serve tribes with both cultural and vocational education.

6. Revenues allow tribes to make efforts to reestablish original land bases. They hire archaeologists to identify traditional lands. Lost lands must be the most vital symbol of lost community, and now through gambling money, a measure of that community strength is being returned as the lands are purchased.

7. Reservation gambling focuses on cultural restoration activities. Money is spent on museum buildings that chronicle Native history. Tribes are also channeling funds into educational programs to reestablish their languages.

8. Community strength is political. The money brought in by gambling allows tribes to assert all manner of legal issues in courts and in front of other policy makers. Gambling also provided a catalyst for the creation of the National Indian Gaming Association in 1983. The association has participated as a serious lobbying group within the American political system.
9. Economic power is directed at state and local government treasuries. Tribes bring several economic benefits to local and state governments. Gambling employment has resulted in reduced welfare rolls. Gambling tribes give state and local governments payments in lieu of taxes for services they would otherwise receive at no cost. This money is important, and the payments give the tribes a new measure of influence in relationships with these governments.
10. The Indian Gaming Regulatory Act has lent itself to a strengthening of communities by requiring state governments to deal one on one with tribes on an equal footing.

Gambling also poses a danger to Native communities. Consider these items:

1. Native gambling presents opportunities for exploitation of tribes. If non-Native peoples are not closely watched, they can become a force that will seize the gaming opportunity for community development right out of the hands of Native peoples. Exploitation did not stop with passage of the Indian Gaming Regulatory Act of 1988.
2. Native Americans must also be critically aware that any gambling enterprise can be a magnet for scam artists and thieves of all sorts. While the overall record of Native gambling is good, there is evidence that thievery has occurred at gambling facilities.
3. Gambling operations can mean weaker communities if tribes in their quest for economic resources willingly yield authority to non-Native governments.
4. Gambling has torn some tribes apart. It can be a divisive issue, as many Native Americans oppose gambling for a variety of reasons—economic, social, and cultural. One tribe found that members who lived in an area close to major highway access points tried to separate

and form a new reservation because they could reap a greater share of the casino benefits. The collective good of the tribe was being set aside because gambling placed a dollar sign in front of its individual members.

5. Internal divisiveness regarding tribal gambling some-times pervades the issue of how to distribute the gam-ing profits. Where tribes neglect collective concerns—education, health, housing, substance abuse—and instead direct the bulk of the revenues to per capita dis-tribution programs—that is, equal payments to all indi-vidual tribal members—they may not be building stronger communities.

6. Gambling can tear Native cultures apart. Several tribes have resisted having gaming operations because gam-bling itself violates religious beliefs and operations would be seen as desecrations of lands. Others share those attitudes but allow the gambling because they want the economic rewards it brings. Gambling opens up lands to outsiders. They come in buses and automo-biles that cause congestion and pollution. They bring drinking and drug abuse behaviors. They engage in gambling. These behaviors serve as bad model behav-iors for members of tribes, especially the young.

7. Gambling jobs may not be the best building blocks for communities. Many of the jobs don't require intensive training—which may be good; however, the skills may not be transferable. Unless revenues are utilized to de-velop a diversified economic base, the concentration on gambling jobs may only create trained incapacities.

8. Tribal community strength is diminished if the defini-tion of what is a Native American can be so inclusive as to remove the unique qualities of the tribes' political position. The quest for gambling opportunities has brought many strange folks out of the woodwork, claiming that they constitute a Native tribe.

9. Native gambling can invite a backlash. Non-Natives do have a five-century track record of taking resources they see in the hands of Native Americans away from them.

10. The downside: gambling presents an ultimate danger to communities if tribes see in their new economic power

a weapon for dominating their neighbors rather than a new opportunity to build cooperative relations on an international basis.

Evidence of the Impact of Gambling on the Economy of Native American Communities

Gambling has been touted as an economic tool that can restore self-sufficiency for Native American communities. But what evidence do we have for this claim? Certainly, the Native American Gaming Association points out great benefits for gaming tribes. But are these tribes representative of all Native America? Are the benefits pervasive, or are they unique to specific tribes?

Tables 9 and 10 in Chapter 7 present data for the twenty-five largest gambling tribes, as well as for the twenty-five largest tribes in terms of 1990 and 2000 populations. The information reported is drawn from the U.S. Census reports of 1990 and 2000 and from information collected in July 1997 by *Casino Executive Magazine.*

The twenty-five largest Native American casinos are on reservations with a collective population of 17,823 in 1990. They employed 50,619 at facilities with 2,889,151 square feet of gambling space. They had 54,947 gambling positions (one for each machine and six for each gambling table). At full capacity, the casinos could have 54,947 people gambling at one time. Based upon a reasonable average revenue of $75,000 per gambling spot per year, the twenty-five casinos realize gross gambling profits of $4.12 billion each year.

The biggest casino tribes gain annual gambling revenues of $231,219 per (1990) reservation member. Bottom-line net revenues are usually between 25 and 50 percent of these gross revenues. The bottom-line revenues go to the tribal organization.

The largest casino tribes employ 2.8 persons for each member.

Between 1990 and 2000, the tribal populations of the twenty-five reservations having these casinos rose 62.9 percent to 29,025. The casinos have not become tools to build reservation populations adding to tribal solidarity. Most of the money for the casino jobs seems to leave the reservations, as there are many more jobs than reservation members. Moreover, while income on the reservations rose 242.6 percent (median) from 1990 to 2000, not all of the revenues are reaching all the members. Median per capita income moved from $5,083 to only $17,413. Median per capita poverty rates fell from 39.8 percent to 11.4 percent for the twenty-five reservations. But why should these reservations experience any poverty whatsoever?

The effects of gambling operations on Native American communities as a whole become clearer when we contrast these statistics with those of the most populated tribes. In 1990, the twenty-five largest reservations had a collective population of 296,268. Fourteen of the tribes had casinos in 1997. The casinos employed 7,192 persons, or 0.024 per member. The facilities had 471,400 square feet of gambling space for players. There were 9,451 gambling positions. Accordingly, their annual revenues from gambling profits could be expected to be $708.8 million, or $2,392 per member.

Between 1990 and 2000, the tribal populations on these reservations grew 60.4 percent to 485,148, a growth rate not as large as that for big casino tribes. In actual numbers, the growth was much greater.

The per capita income on the twenty-five most populated tribes grew from $4,479 to $8,710, or 95.4 percent, while the median poverty rate fell from 47.4 percent to 34.5 percent.

The conclusion that casinos do not help all Native America but rather mostly the selected smaller tribes is supported by the data. The casino is not exactly a magic bullet for economic development for Native American communities. The bullet has reached a target for only some tribes. Whereas some tribes have experienced extraordinary benefits from gambling enterprise, the masses of Native Americans remain impoverished. Census data also reveals that poverty persists even on some of the small reservations with large casinos, an irony that needs more intense scrutiny. Revenues are not always filtering down to needy tribal members.

The economic future of Native American communities rests with enterprise other than gambling. This enterprise is dependent upon tribal resources—land, natural resources, and education—a topic that is explored in the chapters that follow.

References

Aginsky, Burt W., and Ethel G. Aginsky. "The Pomo: A Profile of Gambling among Indians." *Annals of the American Academy of Political and Social Science* 269 (May 1950): 108–113.

Arizona Republic, October 9, 1983.

Arizona Republic, February 9, 1989.

Baltimore Sun, February 9, 1989.

Carlson, Tim. "The Fort Mojave Project–2." In William R. Eadington, ed. *Indian Gaming and the Law.* Reno: Institute for the Study of Gaming, University of Nevada, Reno, 1990, pp. 91–96.

Charlotte Observer, July 28, 1985.

Culin, Stewart, *Games of the North American Indians.* Lincoln: University of Nebraska Press, 1992.

Devereux, E. C. "Gambling and Social Structure." Ph.D. Dissertation, Department of Sociology, Harvard University, 1949.

Garcia, Nora. "The Fort Mojave Project–1." In William R. Eadington, ed. *Indian Gaming and the Law.* Reno: Institute for the Study of Gaming, University of Nevada, Reno, 1990, pp. 87–90.

Lesieur, Henry, and Robert L. Custer. "Pathological Gambling: Roots, Phases, and Treatment." *Annals of the American Academy of Political and Social Science* 474 (July 1984): 146–156.

Miami Herald, May 29, 1983.

Miami Herald, May 31, 1983.

Newsday, October 7, 1998.

Reid, Harry. "The Indian Gaming Act and the Political Process–2." In William R. Eadington, ed. *Indian Gaming and the Law.* Reno: Institute for the Study of Gaming, University of Nevada, Reno, 1990, pp. 15–20.

Rumboltz, Mike. Statement to U.S. Select Committee on Indian Affairs, August 24, 1987.

Ryan, Frank. Statement to U.S. Select Committee on Indian Affairs, February 18, 1986.

San Jose Mercury, August 28, 1984.

Thompson, William N., and Diana Dever, "The Sovereign Games of North America: An Exploratory Study of First Nations' Gambling Enterprises." In Colin Campbell, ed., *Gambling in Canada: The Bottomline.* Burnaby, British Columbia: Simon Fraser University, 1994, pp. 27–55.

Cases

Barona Group of Capitan Band of Mission Indians v. Duffy, 694 F.2d. 1185 (9th Cir. 1982). Cert Denied 461 U.S. 929 (1983).

Bryan v. Itasca County, 426 U.S. 373 (1976).

California v. Cabazon, 480 U.S. 202 (1987).

Lac Flambeau Band v. Wisconsin, 742 F. Supp. 645 (W. Dist. Wisc., 1990).

Mashantucket Pequot Tribe v. McGuigan, 626 F. Supp. 245 (D. Conn., 1986).

Mdewakanton Sioux Community v. Pan American Management, 616 F. Supp 1200 (D. Minnesota, 1985), Appeal Dismissed, 789 F. 2d. 632 (8th Cir., 1986).

Oneida Tribe v. Wisconsin, 518 F. Supp. 712 (W.D. Wisconsin, 1981).

Red Lake Band v. Swimmer, 740 F. Supp. 9 (D.D.C., 1990).

Seminole Tribe v. Florida, 517 U.S. 44 (1996).

Laws

Indian Gaming Regulatory Act of 1988, 102 U.S. Statute 2467.

Public Law 280 (1952), 67 U.S. Statute 588.

4

Other Issues

Land Claims

"The Cheyenne and Arapaho tribes of Oklahoma filed a claim Wednesday for 27 million acres [about 40 percent of the state given the tribes in a nineteenth-century treaty] but said they would settle for 500 acres to build a casino in a symbolic return to Colorado" (*Rocky Mountain News* April 15, 2004).

Two tribes that resided in Colorado were forced to leave behind "some very important spiritual and cultural connections to the vast area we still refer to as our homeland" (*Rocky Mountain News* April 15, 2004).

Treaties were broken, and a territorial governor even ordered that Native peoples be killed if they did not leave. The equivalent value of their spiritual homelands was spelled out in their offer—give us our 27 million acres or give us 500 acres for a casino.

The notion of place is critical for strong communities. It is linked to communities' opportunities to gain the sustenance needed to support the health and well-being of their members. With regard to Native peoples specifically, place has been essential in both the historical course of their community life and their community life today. Yet the idea that "the land" is exchangeable for an opportunity to simply run a casino and make money must be considered antithetical to traditional values of Native peoples.

Before the arrival of the European explorers and settlers, as well as African slaves, the American continents were occupied exclusively by ancestors of today's indigenous peoples. These peoples, in turn, had ancestors who had migrated to the Western Hemisphere 10,000 to 60,000 years earlier. Their numbers were in the millions at the time of the European arrival in the fifteenth and sixteenth centuries. The numbers at their peak levels are subject to much debate, but beyond question is the fact that Native peoples were the only occupants of the Americas in the centuries immediately before the voyages of Columbus.

The Creation stories passed down by the Native tribes lend a religious significance to certain American lands and give them recognition as places of the birth of their peoples. Specific places and specific parcels of land are considered sacred. Cherokee leader Jimmie Durham, speaking before a congressional hearing in 1978 on the construction of the Tellico Dam by the Tennessee Valley Authority (TVA), couched his opposition to the dam in terms of the sacredness of Native lands:.

> Is there a human being who does not revere his homeland, even though he may not return? . . . It was there that we were given our vision as Cherokee people . . . there is a (Cherokee) word for land: Eloheh. The same word also means history, culture, and religion. We cannot separate our place on earth from our lives on earth, nor from our vision nor our meaning as a people. We are speaking of something truly sacred. (Quoted in Wright 1992, 311–312)

In the sense of tribal identities, it might be quite accurate to say that the tribes of today did begin in the Americas and that *their* lands are in the Americas. However, people from whom these tribes were descended sometime in the distant past migrated to the Americas from other places, and perhaps several other places. It is likely their origins were with migrations from the Pacific Rim. It is commonly accepted that peoples of Asia walked to the Americas across either an ancient land bridge or an ice bridge between present Alaska and Siberia. Others may have come by boat.

While they likely made their ventures from parts of Asia, not all the travelers were racially tied to Asian nations of today. Some of the oldest known American people could have included people who were Caucasians. Discoveries in the state of Washington of "The Kennewick Man," a man whose bones were carbon-dated as 9,300 years old, confuse the notions regarding the specific origins of the continent's indigenous peoples. DNA testing suggests that the bones were Caucasoid. Other findings in locations such as

Spirit Cave, Nevada, also point to the existence of early Caucasians in the Americas. This perplexing information is also tied to findings of northern Asian human artifacts from antiquity that suggests European incursions deep into Asia. The Ainu peoples, an indigenous group in Japan, are also thought to have Caucasian roots, although today they "appear" quite Asian as they have intermixed for many generations with other Japanese.

Biological origins are only part of the origin story. Whatever conclusions scientific evidence may eventually render, issues regarding tribal identities remain. It is almost certain that the ancestors of today's indigenous peoples were firmly entrenched as the only peoples in the Americas at the time of the latter-day European and African incursions.

The sparsely populated continent met the needs of peoples as they pursued livelihoods based on hunting and fishing economies and individual agricultural activities. These economic patterns were quite different from the patterns established in Europe at the time of the migrations across the Atlantic. The indigenous patterns did not require, nor were they totally compatible with, individual ownership of parcels of lands.

In a famous speech in 1855, Chief Seattle replied to an offer to purchase tribal lands. "The President in Washington sends word that he wishes to buy our land. But how can you buy or sell the sky? The land? The idea is strange to us. If we do not own the freshness of the air and the sparkle of the water, how can you buy them?" Deloria wrote that the "tribal elders laughed contemptuously at the idea that a man could sell land. . . . It was ludicrous to Indians that people would consider land that could be owned by one man . . . The land is given to all people" (1969, 182).

Nonetheless, tribes were recognized as the legitimate occupiers and possessors of vast areas of land. They held the land in common. Europeans, on the other hand, did not embrace the idea of communal land ownership. Indeed, influential political philosophers (e.g., John Locke) emphasized that individual property ownership (including land) constituted a basic human right bestowed upon humankind by the Creator.

The new populations saw territorial control as essential to their own economies, which were directed toward factory manufacturing as well as agricultural production of goods for commercial sale. Moreover, Europe had already witnessed massive growth of urban populations, and people sought more personal land and space as they ventured to America.

The clash of values over land inevitably saw numerically superior newcomers displacing Native people and restricting the Natives to much smaller expanses of land, which simply could not support the manner of their lives. The displacement process also witnessed the Natives pushed off lands that held sacred value in their history and even now continue to have this value.

A system of reservations was accompanied by the newcomers' promises to provide support for Native peoples in terms of supplies and foods. The first to apply the reservation idea in the Americas were the Puritans of Massachusetts, who in 1638 forced the Quinnipiac peoples onto 1,200 acres and prohibited them from leaving the land.

Before the notion of moving the Native peoples onto reservations took hold, a number of legal scholars espoused the view that the indigenous tribes had rights to the lands they occupied and that the lands could be taken from them only by proper purchase or as a consequence of just wars. One such spokesman for Native land rights was theologian Francisco de Vitoria of Spain in the sixteenth century. His view was advanced by Roger Williams in the Rhode Island colony in the 1630s, and it found some support among the English colonial authorities.

Shortly following the adoption of the United States Constitution, which provided that the federal Congress would regulate affairs with the Native peoples, an act was passed providing that all land transfers from the peoples to non-Natives would have to be under the authority of the U.S. government. The treaty process was used for eighty years. But treaties were quite often set aside as non-Natives persuaded the government that they wanted more and more of the land.

But most treaties that were enforced were repudiated by the Dawes Act of 1887. The Act destroyed reservations and distributed small amounts of land (up to 160 acres) to individual Native peoples, which then became individually owned land, and sold off much of the remaining land to non-Natives. This practice was stopped forty years later, but, as noted in Chapter 2, found a renewal in the Termination practices of the Truman and Eisenhower administrations. Termination efforts (that is, termination of reservation and tribal status) were again ended by the Kennedy, Johnson, and Nixon administrations.

The process of taking lands from Native peoples seems to have ended, and reversals of fortune have been set into place. However, Native peoples continue their long efforts to seek restoration of lands and to obtain payments for lands taken in the past.

Although some steps have been taken to meet the demands of tribes for the return of lands or for payments, grievances over seizures of lands remain. Many of those with claims have turned to the federal courts, but the solutions to the problems are essentially political, not merely legal (Getches, Wilkinson, and Williams 1993, 308–318).

The U.S. government cannot be sued without its permission, and this permission is granted through acts of Congress. In 1855, Congress created the Court of Claims and permitted some actions to be taken against the United States to settle grievances. However, this court excluded Native claims for lands wrongly seized. Instead, each time there was such a claim, Native peoples had to approach Congress with a specific request for a solution.

By the 1940s, Congress had passed 142 special acts for land claims. Congress, however, felt that this piecemeal process was cumbersome, and, in 1946, it passed a law creating the Indian Claims Commission (Prucha 1990, 231–233). The decisions of this commission were subject to review first by the U.S. Court of Claims and then by the U.S. Supreme Court. The Indian Claims Commission existed until 1978. Cases not heard by that date were then transferred to the Court of Claims. The Indian Claims Commission reviewed treaties and other evidence of seizures of lands or takings without full compensation. The Commission determined the value of the lands and requested that Congress appropriate funds to be given to Native Americans. In no case could the Indian Claims Commission, or later the Court of Claims, require that the actual lands in dispute be returned to the Natives.

The Indian Claims Commission Act had one unintended consequence. It was passed as Congress was also endorsing the policy of tribal termination. However, the Act encouraged Native Americans to seek legal remedies for a myriad of issues because for the first time the tribes were now permitted to hire private attorneys. Prior to 1946, the nations could make contracts for legal services only with the approval of the Bureau of Indian Affairs. The 1946 Act allowed tribes to select attorneys and to make arrangements for them to work on a contingency basis. The attorneys would not have to be paid until the tribe won a financial judgment from the Commission and received payment through a congressional appropriation. The attorneys would be given up to 10 percent of the award amount. Since this claims process began,

Native Americans have steadily increased legal pressures against the government on all fronts.

The Bureau of Indian Affairs also set up a revolving loan fund so that the attorneys could pay expert witnesses. Most of the claims being made involved old records, maps, and archaeological evidence that had to be evaluated by experts, including historians and anthropologists. After the awards were made for the claims, the expert witness costs would be deducted. In addition, the Indian Claims Commission fixed costs for commodities or services given to the tribes by the federal government since the time their land had been taken from them. These costs were considered "offsets" and were subtracted from the award amount received by the tribes.

Considerable controversy arose over the methods the Commission used to evaluate lands taken from the Natives. Attempts to fix fair market value were deficient simply because there was no market for most of the land at the time it was taken. Moreover the Act provided that the Native Americans would receive no interest on the value of the lands from the time they were taken.

An amount equal to or exceeding 20 percent of the award had to be dedicated to tribal programs supervised by the Bureau of Indian Affairs. Because the tribes had experienced some abuse in the Bureau's oversight of tribal programs, they did not care for this rule. Moreover, many tribes correctly predicted that the awards would become an excuse for reducing funding of BIA programs. Most Native Americans preferred to divide the awards among tribal membership on a per capita basis. By doing this, the members could realize an immediate tangible result for the claims fight. Realistically, however, this was not always an optimal solution. The division of money awards among tribes with thousands of members resulted in small shares for individuals. Per capita payments were a few thousand dollars or less. This money was often consumed within a short time.

More than 614 individual claims were presented to the Commission. Of these, 204 were dismissed as having no merit, justifying compensation to the tribes. Awards were granted for 342 claims. In September 1978, when the Commission ceased existence, sixty-eight dockets were transferred for resolution to the U.S. Court of Claims. For the cases decided, the Interstate Commerce Commission gave $818.2 million to the tribes—or an average $2.4 million per claim. Lawyers' fees, witness costs, and "offsets" were subtracted from these awards (Parker 1989, 132–133;

Getches, Wilkinson, and Williams 1993, 311–318; Canby 1988, 264–268).

The tribes that accepted the financial awards had to agree that their dispute over the loss of their lands was settled for all time. Some tribes, however, were not ready to agree to these conditions and were unwilling to see their claims settled with monetary awards. They wanted their lands back. They therefore pursued separate litigation and turned to Congress for relief.

The Indian Claims Commission made a $10 million offer for land taken from the Taos Pueblo of New Mexico. The Taos people refused the offer, claiming that the land in question was sacred, and they wished to have it returned. They took their case to Congress and they won a more acceptable settlement. The Taos Pueblo was given back 48,000 acres. The land included Blue Lake, which was a shrine, the place where the Taos people were given life and the place where the spirits of departed Taos peoples rested.

The Yakima Nation of Washington received 21,000 acres, while the Confederated Tribes at the Warm Springs Reservation in Oregon had 61,360 acres returned in 1972 legislation (Kellogg 1978, 24–27). Other legislation has resulted in a return of lands for Native Americans in Maine and Connecticut.

A protracted court case that traveled through the Indian Claims Commission as well as the regular federal courts involved Oneida lands in New York State. Several million acres of Oneida lands were lost as a result of treaties with state government officials after the Revolutionary War. Congress did not approve these treaties. More than 260,000 acres were lost in the 1790s after Congress wrote the Non-Intercourse Acts of 1790 and 1793, which provided that Native Americans could lose lands only with congressional approval, that is, not by state government action alone.

Attorneys for the Oneida Nation did not uncover the evidence of this illegal taking of lands until the 1960s. However, when they approached the Indian Claims Commission on behalf of the Oneidas, who then occupied only thirty-two acres of reservation lands, they were told that a settlement would be limited to the value of the land when it was taken and that no interest would be given. The Oneidas would have to go through the claim process and make proofs of their claims, and they would be limited to a $3 million judgment. This was not acceptable to the Oneidas. The attorneys struggled to establish a right to sue the state of New York in federal courts. Not until 1985 did the U.S. Supreme Court rule that they had a valid claim to both a financial award and the return of some of the lands taken (Shattuck 1991; Canby 1988, 260–261).

A continuing controversy centers on over 7.3 million acres in the Black Hills of South Dakota. Eight Sioux tribes claim that the U.S. government wrongfully broke the Fort Laramie Treaty of 1868. That treaty had pledged that the Black Hills would be set aside "for the absolute and undisturbed use and occupation" of the Sioux. No "unauthorized" person, in the words of the agreement, "shall ever be permitted to pass over, settle on, or reside" on the land. Unfortunately, a unit of the U.S. Army under the command of George Armstrong Custer discovered gold in the Black Hills in 1874. Almost immediately, non-Native prospectors besieged the federal government to open up the land.

The government made offers to the Sioux for the land, but the offers were refused. Hostilities ensued, as a series of skirmishes between the Sioux and the federal military began. Small battles led to larger battles, culminating in Custer's fatal defeat at the Battle of the Little Big Horn in 1876. The defeat of Custer in turn led to massive reprisals.

Renewed efforts to take the Black Hills were made in the form of an offer that was made to a group of selected Sioux chiefs. An agreement was then submitted to all the male adults of the tribes for approval. The government accepted a 10 percent favorable response as ratification. This sham purchase of the Black Hills was challenged before the Indian Claims Commission. The Commission ruled that the eight Sioux tribes in the controversy deserved a combined settlement of $17.5 million. However, this was not satisfactory to the tribes: they wanted land returned. When they appealed to the Court of Claims, the settlement figure was raised to over $100 million. The U.S. Supreme Court then set the figure at $122 million. However, by the time of the ruling on the appeal, six of the eight tribes decided to withdraw from the action. They fired their attorneys. Nonetheless, the same attorneys persisted in the case, and the Court allowed them to continue to represent the tribes. The six Sioux tribes refused to accept the financial reward, and the U.S. Supreme Court in turn refused to make a judgment requiring a return of the land. Only Congress has the power to do so now. Political negotiations offer the only chance for a reasonable solution (*United States v. Sioux Nations of Indians* 1980).

Other land claims—either for a return of land or for compensation—are now being placed in front of Congress. While it seems contrary to the historical reverence for the land, as expressed in the voices of leaders such as Chief Seattle, a contemporary motivation for land restoration is found in policies that will permit gambling activities on the land. Nonetheless, as demonstrated by the Sioux, the notion of justice in land claims must not be completely clouded by immediate quests for dollars.

Water Rights

Whether community or individual use of land is for hunting and fishing, agricultural, industrial, or residential purposes, the land's value is severely reduced unless it has access to water. The rules for access to water vary between the eastern and western parts of the United States. In thirty-one eastern states (the north-south tier of Minnesota, Iowa, Missouri, Arkansas, Louisiana, and all of the states east of the Mississippi River), all people holding land have an equal right to reasonable use of the waters running over land or underneath land. The applicable rule is called the riparian law of water. It is derived from the body of court decisions in England called the common law.

Whenever a person acquired land, that person also acquired the same access to water that others holding land in the area had. Because water is plentiful in the eastern part of the nation, and because there is no argument over which person or group can have water, all have rights to the water no matter when they acquired the land. The quantity of water is not an issue facing the Native peoples of these thirty-one states. The issue does not exist in Alaska, either, as water is plentiful. Nor is it an issue in Hawaii, as indigenous people there do not have the same status as Natives in the continental United States (Burton 1991).

The issue of water quantity and quality is a matter of major concern in seventeen western states, all of which have tribal communities. These states follow a water law called *prior appropriation*. Much of the western land of the United States is arid. Access to water is therefore crucial.

The early political leaders of the United States adopted a general policy encouraging occupation and development of these western lands by new settlers. Indeed, the blockage of westward migration by the English colonial authorities through the Quebec Act of 1774 was considered one of the "Obnoxious Acts" that had precipitated the Revolutionary War.

One of the first major acts of the new independent nation under the Articles of Confederation was to provide for the surveying of lands west of the Appalachian Mountains. A series of almost continuous acts of the new nation provided for the protection of settlers and the distribution of lands to settlers as they moved further westward. A major war was fought with Mexico to further westward expansion of new settlements. The Homestead Act of 1862 freely gave western land to those who would settle and use the land. National policy also encouraged the exploitation of western lands for minerals. In the twentieth century, the federal government sponsored the construction of major public works projects to facilitate use of the lands through effective water collection and distribution. Native peoples were generally neglected as benefits were designed for newcomers.

All of the political actions encouraging settlement and exploitation of lands required that those using the lands have guaranteed access to water. The law of prior appropriation was established by the state governments of the western areas precisely to guarantee that those coming to the lands would have access to water at the time of settlement and in the future. Under the law, the first developer on the land was given a right to all the water his purposes demanded as long as he (the miner, rancher, or farmer) actually used the water. Any subsequent person desiring to use the lands acquired rights only to waters not being utilized by and assigned to the first (prior) user (Burton 1991, 19–22; Canby 1988, 277–279).

In years of drought, the first user would get all of the water his rights required, before a subsequent settler received any water at all. Without a guarantee to future waters at the time of first settlement, no newcomers would undergo the difficulties of moving to the lands or starting mining or agricultural operations on the lands. Newcomers would not settle and develop the land if they had to fear a loss of water rights every time another person entered the land of the watershed area.

The quantities of water allocated to each landholder under the law of prior appropriation were crucial. It is not difficult to see that the Native peoples would eventually present problems under this legal arrangement. Many Natives were assigned reservation lands only after other peoples had already appropriated the waters of the region. Also, where the reservations were established before others entered the area, the Native peoples were not prepared to put the lands into uses that required large quantities of waters. At the time, they may have relied upon hunting, fishing, and gathering methods in order to receive their food and also items that they could use in trade.

Newcomers used waters for agricultural and mining purposes and staked a prior claim to the waters. However, the U.S. government also encouraged the Native peoples to develop their lands, as the government wished to see them give up traditional ways of hunting and fishing and accept agricultural lifestyles. This notion was incorporated into the reservation philosophy as well as into the Dawes Act for distribution of lands to individual Native peoples. The idea of taking Native children from their home communities and sending them to special schools for education in the "way" of the newcomer also envisioned that they would use the lands for modern agricultural or industrial pursuits. But when the Native peoples did turn to agricultural or other pursuits, they found the waters that they now needed were already appropriated to others.

A modification of water law was necessary. It was provided by the U.S. Supreme Court in the 1908 ruling in *Winters v. United States*. A Montana tribe was confined to the 600,000-acre Fort Belknap reservation as a result of negotiations with the federal government in 1888. The reservation was bounded by the Milk River. The 1888 agreement provided no water rights for the Native Americans. However, the tribe was given money, goods, and supplies, which were intended to be used in new agricultural pursuits in exchange for previously held lands. It was clearly intended that the tribe would support itself with agriculture. Soon new settlers occupied the lands across the Milk River, and they established their rights to river waters through the law of prior appropriation. When the Native Americans started agricultural operations, they found that there was not enough water remaining after the new settlers took their share. The tribe, in concert with the U.S. government, sought to establish a share for the reservation. Litigation ensued.

The Supreme Court ruled that the tribe had a right to water that superseded the rights of others. The Court reasoned that the federal government could not have urged the Native Americans to give up lands that supported their hunting and fishing lifestyle and settle on lands to be used for farming unless they were going to give the Native Americans water for farming. The

Court held that when the federal government decided to establish the reservations, it also implicitly reserved sufficient water for Native American use in the future. That reserved right to water would be superior to any water claimed by outsiders after the reservation began.

The Winters Doctrine of reserved water rights did not resolve all of the water issues. Courts still had to determine exactly how much water the Native Americans could use and how much of the outsiders' prior appropriations could be reduced. Litigation in federal and state courts continued. The basic premise accepted was that the Native Americans should have enough water to irrigate all the lands they could put into farming; but still the exact amount was debatable. It was also difficult to cut off supplies to prior users as Native Americans expanded their farmlands. Their property rights had been granted by government action. A reassignment of water would involve a measure of compensation (Canby 1988, 279–290; Getches, Wilkinson, and Williams 1993, 774–799).

Questions of water law were confused by the fact that cases were heard in two court systems—state and federal. Finally, in 1952, Congress decided that all claims for water should be heard in state courts. It passed the McCarran Amendment, which technically allowed the U.S. government, as guardian of Native American reservation rights, to be sued by other water users in state courts. The courts could then bring in all the people wishing to use the state's waters and make a single determination regarding amounts allowed to each. The lower federal courts could then tell the Native Americans that they, too, should take their disputes to the state courts (Canby 1988, 290–294; Getches, Wilkinson, and Williams 1993, 799–839; Western Conference of Attorneys General 1993, 177–182).

Although Native Americans have been very suspicious of state authority, the arrangement was accomplished in an atmosphere of cooperation that did persist in most situations. The tribes and other parties retained the right to appeal state court decisions to the U.S. Supreme Court. Also, there has been no demonstrable pattern to suggest that the state courts have made a practice of discriminating against Native Americans on water allotments. But the fights do go on.

To bring stability to the issue, tribes and private concerns as well as local and state governmental officials have frequently met and reached compromises that can then be ratified by Congress. In this way long, costly, unpredictable litigation is avoided. The idea of resolving the disputes through negotiated settlements underwritten by congressional appropriations offers an ideal solution to most situations. The Western Governors' Association has taken the lead in gathering together state officials, key actors in Congress, the Western Regional Council, and the Native American Rights Fund to develop policy in this area acting as the Ad Hoc Group on Indian Water Rights. They make many recommendations to Congress, especially that any funding for water settlements not be made by cutting other funding to the Bureau of Indian Affairs. Environmental Affairs professor Lloyd Burton of the University of Colorado–Denver (Burton 1991) proposed that Congress establish an Indian Water Rights Commission to make final settlements for the disputes.

Minerals and Natural Resources

When Christopher Columbus set sail for the Far East and India, he carried dreams of silk and spices. Within days of his landing in the West and his encounters with the Native peoples, his sights were raised considerably. He no longer thought of merchandising commodities for the homes of the Spanish wealthy. His biggest discovery was that the Native peoples possessed vast quantities of gold. By the end of his second voyage, he had forced Natives to reveal the location of their gold. Then his crews used force to make them mine the gold for him. Columbus's voyages involved many discoveries and led to widespread colonization efforts as well as efforts at religious conversions. But the voyages also converted many European dreamers into greedy gold-seekers. Lands occupied by Native Americans became lands to be exploited for quick riches.

As more Europeans arrived, they continued to exploit lands that had provided sustenance for Native communities. They formed settlements, and they sought to possess the lands. Whenever it was discovered that the land held by Native peoples had mineral worth, Natives were moved—again and again, one way or another, peacefully or forcefully.

Gold was quite often the culprit. As the Bible attests, it was not gold that was the evil but rather the greed for gold. The discovery of gold gave settlers in Georgia an ill-conceived reason to persuade state and national authorities to push Cherokees off their lands in the 1830s—even though a peaceful settlement by those governments had placed the Cherokees on the lands "forever." President Andrew Jackson acquiesced in a policy removing the Cherokees to Oklahoma, even though the U.S. Supreme Court had ruled that the tribe had a right to Georgia lands. The Cherokees were soon marching across the South and beyond the Mississippi on their "Trail of Tears." In the next decade, the Winnebagos, Kickapoos, and Sac and Foxes were moved out of their Illinois and Wisconsin homes because the white settlers discovered deposits of lead (Walman and Braun 1985, 118).

Native Americans were moved out of central and eastern Colorado during the Pikes Peak Gold Rush of 1858. Hostilities over gold provided an underlying rationale for the bitter massacre of Natives at Sand Creek. The earlier California gold rush resulted in the relocation of Native communities to smaller and smaller parcels of land. Today California's Native Americans have over 100 very small rancherias. It is little solace for the Natives who had their communities decimated 150 years ago that the small parcels of land now house casino facilities that rival the giant gambling houses of Nevada.

In 1877, the quest for gold forced Chief Joseph and the Nez Perce off their Idaho lands and into their noble but futile run for the Canadian border. Utes, Piautes, Shoshones, and Mohaves were also pushed off lands and squeezed onto smaller parcels at the behest of new state governments until the U.S. government seemed convinced that the Native peoples no longer had anything of importance to non-Natives (Walman and Braun 1985, 133). Nonetheless, newcomers to the area kept probing the lands for value, and they continued to find things on the remaining Native lands that they wanted. Even when all violent hostilities between newcomers and Natives ended and Native lands could no longer be taken away, the exploiters were not deterred from their efforts to take away the wealth that was within the lands.

Throughout the twentieth century, non-Native American companies worked to find ways to get at various kinds of minerals that were the new gold for society—coal, oil, and uranium. The companies worked in concert with the Bureau of Indian Affairs to win leases to the properties (Walman and Braun 1985, 203).

Often Native peoples have been left with lands that cannot be utilized for economic benefit necessary to support their communities. Typically, they have lacked funding necessary to develop viable industrial uses of their lands. This is one reason the opportunities presented by gambling enterprise has freed peoples for proper ventures to develop their lands. The situation of poverty and nonproductive lands had left them exposed to additional land exploitation. Native Americans often felt pressured to accept any economic opportunity. Accordingly, they had their lands strip-mined, grazed, or timbered in nonecological ways, polluted with garbage and industrial wastes. Efforts were even made to use the lands as dumping grounds for nuclear waste materials.

Lance Hughes, director of the Native Americans for a Clean Environment, based in Tahlequah, Oklahoma, said that 40 Nations across the United States had been approached by the waste disposal industry. "It's big money. It's the biggest money there is right now . . . They pick on the poorest of the tribes" (*Daily Oklahoman* February 10, 1991).

Gaming revenues permit a more reasonable consideration of good economic opportunities. In addition, where past choices forced by economic necessity have led peoples to accept business ventures that disturbed their lands, the moneys from gaming can be targeted to clean up past degradations of the lands.

Hunting and Fishing Rights

For millennia the fish and game on Native American lands provided the primary sustenance for many tribal communities. Even after many lands became agricultural, the natural food supply remained very important as items for economic exchange. Today major policy disputes have arisen involving the rights of Native Americans to hunt and fish on reservation lands and nonreservation lands held by their ancestors.

The legal resolutions of hunting and fishing disputes have paralleled in some ways the reasoning behind the *Winters* water rights doctrine. In general, Native Americans preserve the right to hunting and fishing that they possessed before they moved to reservations—unless they specifically gave up those rights in negotiations with the federal government. The rights extend to off-reservation as well as on-reservation lands. Congress, however, maintains the power to modify the rights.

Some controversy revolves around the fact that Native Americans retain essential control over hunting and fishing on reservation lands, and state governments may not with some exceptions impose their regulations on the activity. Moreover, the state governments cannot prohibit the off-reservation possession or sale of fish and game taken from the reservations under tribal regulations. The rights of Native Americans to hunt and fish are subject to some limitations.

On-Reservation Hunting and Fishing

Native American tribes have the power to regulate hunting and fishing on reservations subject to rules set forth by the secretary of the interior, acting in a trust capacity. Where the tribe chooses not to impose regulations, the U.S. government fills the void. In some rare cases, the secretary of the interior has banned commercial fishing on reservations. In other cases, federal trespass laws have been evoked to prohibit non-Native Americans from fishing or hunting on reservation lands. Federal statutes also prohibit possession and sale of game taken from the reservations by nonmembers in violation of either federal or tribal regulations.

Tribes may exclude nonmembers from reservation hunting and fishing privileges. They may also require specific licenses for nonmembers if they wish to hunt or fish. Tribal control of hunting and fishing on the reservations is confined to the actual lands that are held in trust for the tribe. It does not extend to privately owned (fee) lands within the outer boundaries of the reservation. State regulations may apply to these lands.

State governments do have some powers over hunting and fishing on reservation lands. They can regulate non-Native participation by requiring that these nontribal members possess state licenses as well as tribal licenses to hunt and fish. However, the state cannot permit the non-Native Americans to fish and hunt when the tribe prohibits such activity; nor can the state interfere with tribal regulations, which may differ from state rules. For instance, a tribe may permit a person to catch ten fish, while the state rules limit them to six. Or the tribe may permit hunters to shoot does, while state rules permit deer hunters to kill only bucks.

State governments can interfere with on-reservation hunting and fishing when the activity is shown to be adverse to good conservation. Disputes in this area are not typical as Native American gaming officials usually share the same conservation concerns as state game protection personnel (Western Conference of Attorneys General 1993, 210–262; Canby 1988, 295–318).

Off-Reservation Hunting and Fishing Rights

The major area of controversy pertains to off-reservation fishing in waters that are shared between Native and non-Native fishermen. Much agony and bitterness have resulted from efforts to determine the fishing rights of Native Americans in several states.

What became known as the "Walleye War" in Wisconsin is one case in point. Generations of Chippewa communities in northern Wisconsin used spear fishing techniques to kill walleye pike during springtime. Treaties signed with the federal government in 1837, 1842, and 1854 assigned them to reservation lands but also recognized their fishing rights on all lands they had occupied. No controversy occurred for over a century. Then in the 1970s when the state prohibited the spearfishing techniques for the Chippewas as they did for all fishermen, the Native peoples sought remedy in federal courts. In 1983, the appeals court ruled that they could use spears for off-reservation fishing, although others could not do so. Non-Natives protested with activities that progressed from peaceful demonstrations to violent confrontations. The war in various stages lasted twenty-five years. Finally, negotiations between tribal councils and state authorities resulted in lease payments going from tribes to the state to preserve the rights in a manner considered politically acceptable to competing parties. The state also used its opportunity to negotiate certain provisions of state compacts for casino gambling in order to win a peaceful resolution to the conflict (Nesper 2002).

The Washington controversy is perhaps the strongest (Canby 1988, 301–310). The state of Washington has strictly regulated the quantity of salmon fishing permitted in its waters. However, modern techniques are available that can enable fishermen to completely destroy the fish supply of certain areas. For this reason, the state has prohibited modern equipment such as gill nets and other devices.

In 1854, several tribes of the American Northwest—including the Puyallups, Nisqually, and Lummi—agreed to give up most of their traditional lands and to stay on reservations. The Native peoples were promised many goods if they gave up rights to lands—lands that include the present-day city of Seattle. Among the promises was "the right to take fish at all usual and accustom grounds and stations . . . *in common* with all the citizens of the territory." As the "usual" fishing places included sea waters as well as widely dispersed streams and rivers, the treaty certainly recognized a right to fish waters that were off-reservation lands.

As in Wisconsin, for over a century, life progressed without controversy. However, as more non-Native commercial fishing interests were attracted to the waters and to the salmon runs, permitted supplies of salmon were being depleted. The state, fearing that the salmon might disappear altogether, instituted stricter conservation measures. They banned nets, and they designated more severe limits for the salmon take. The commercial fishermen accepted the new restrictions. However, when the state attempted to apply the limits to the Native Americans, they objected. The Native Americans had been taking only about 10 percent of the catch while using nets, but they were not agreeable to the notion that the state could say their nets were forbidden. They resisted the new rules, and they sought a federal court injunction against the state enforcement. Much litigation ensued.

The cases regarding Washington fishing treaties have gone the full course in federal courts at least three times. The U.S. Supreme Court has ruled on the subject many times. The rulings have also been used as a basis for decisions in other states. Nonetheless, the controversy rages on, and it is likely that any final resolution of the matter will have to involve Congress, as that body alone can serve as the ultimate authority on the matter. As the controversy stands, the Native Americans certainly have the favor of the courts.

The final rulings of the Supreme Court held, first of all, that the state of Washington could set an overall catch limit for salmon in its waters, whether or not those waters run through reservations. The state also has authority to set limits for its coastal waters. The limits must be for the purpose of preserving the future fish population, that is, prohibiting its total destruction.

Second, it was determined that seven Native American tribes in Washington would be permitted to take up to 50 percent of the state's designated catch limit. The high court held that the words "in common with" meant "an equal share." In addition, the tribes were permitted to continue to use nets that were banned for use by non-Native commercial fishermen. The tribes were allowed to commercially sell their portion of the catch to off-reservation people. The proceeds of the commercial sales could be retained by the Native Americans for their personal support and benefit "at moderate levels." Because many members of the tribes had incomes below the poverty levels, it was unlikely that the members were going to become wealthy because of fishing advantages. Still, the phrase "moderate levels" had no real practical meaning. The court also determined that the tribes would have an exclusive right to fish the waters within their own reservation lands; however, the catch in those waters would be subject to the state-determined limits and counted against the tribe's share.

The Supreme Court justices, as well as lower court judges, made a logical legal argument for their findings. However, they were not commercial fishermen. Their livelihood was not an issue in their decisions. The commercial fishermen and non-Native sports fishermen as well have been enraged by the decisions. The new restrictions greatly reduced their catches and their livelihood. They had been enjoying 90 percent of the catch. Their profits have plummeted as they have been restricted to 50 percent of the catch. They have asserted that the decisions violate their equal protection of the laws and accordingly the Constitution of the United States. However, the courts have held that the 1854 treaties are also part of the supreme law of the land, and in these matters the treaties take precedence over the "equal protection" clause of the Fourteenth Amendment (*Puyallup Tribe v. Washington Department of Games* I 1968, II 1973, III 1977; *Washington v. Washington State Commercial Passenger Vessel Association* 1979).

Similar rulings have been made in Oregon, Michigan, and Wisconsin. In a Wisconsin action not involving walleyes, the courts held that a treaty with the Menominees permitted tribal members to have special off-reservation fishing privileges, even though the existence of the tribe itself had been terminated. The tribe has since been reestablished under an act of Congress (*Menominee Tribe v. United States* 1968).

The decisions of the courts may be modified by Congress or by the secretary of the interior. These political entities have been cognizant of the feelings of non-Natives. Many of those feelings have been expressed in protests and in some cases in violence directed against Native fishermen. When protests ensued after the federal courts overruled the state of Michigan's ban on the use of nets by Native Americans, the secretary of the interior imposed a temporary restriction on off-reservation fishing by Native Americans.

The federal government is very reluctant to enter into the area of fishing and hunting regulations. Generally, these matters have been under the control of state governments. However, it seems certain that some federal political intervention will be necessary to find a solution that can at least partially satisfy both Native and non–Native Americans.

Many non-Native commercial interests have been operating for decades. These people have invested their careers and their families' futures in fishing. They have purchased expensive boats and equipment with the reasonable understanding that they could use these as their fathers did, and as their grandfathers did. They have also invested moneys in fisheries and other means to replenish and expand the stock of fish from which they take their catch. The states have also done so, using fishing license funds in part for this function. To be sure, the federal government, as well as tribal governments, has also made investments in fisheries. The courts, however, have not recognized these costs in their decisions. They have focused almost exclusively upon the treaty provisions and the necessity for overall conservation measures. Yet the commercial fishermen were not a party to the treaties. They were not around in 1854, nor were most of their ancestors. The controversy over fishing rights is likely to continue until political entities work out another compromise. Perhaps the opportunity to trade off concessions in the area of casino gambling compacts offers the best area for exploration.

The Bill of Rights, Religious Freedom, and Native Americans

Bills of rights protect people against actions taken by governments. In fact, constitutions are contracts between people and governments. The only provision of the U.S. Constitution that speaks directly to actions between people and other people is the Thirteenth Amendment, which prohibits any person from holding another in slavery.

When the American colonies existed under the sovereignty of England, the colonists enjoyed the protections of an English Bill of Rights (passed in 1689) as well as other protections such as those afforded in the Magna Carta and by legislation guaranteeing rights to habeas corpus. Actually, it was the English government's abuse of many of these rights that incited the Americans' move toward independence. After the colonies became independent, state governments held authority over the people. Therefore, various states, leading with Virginia, incorporated bills of rights into their constitutions.

There was no Bill of Rights under the Articles of Confederation government, for that document did not establish national powers over the people; rather, it only described relationships between the national government and the states. However, when territories were established in the northwest, the national government did exercise control over individuals through the courts and through matters such as taxation. Therefore, the Northwest Ordinance of 1787 included a Bill of Rights protecting the people from improper exercise of national powers. The new Constitution was also a document providing for relationships between the people and the national government. Indeed, the Constitution begins with the phrase "We the People." Therefore, the Constitution was well criticized during the ratification campaigns for not having a Bill of Rights. After the Constitution was adopted, Congressman James Madison immediately set about to write a Bill of Rights, and as the first ten amendments, the Bill of Rights was adopted in 1791.

Nonetheless, the Bill of Rights did not apply to relationships between citizens and state and local governments. However, starting in 1925 (*Gitlow v. New York,* a free speech case), the U.S. Supreme Court began to apply specific parts of the Bill of Rights to state and local government actions on a one-by-one basis. They did so by making the provisions part of the notion of due process, which the states had to guarantee in accordance with the Fourteenth Amendment, adopted in 1868. By the end of the twentieth century, almost all the Bill of Rights, with certain exceptions, did apply to actions by the state government.

There is a saying, "falling through the cracks," and that is where the members of the tribal governments as well as others dealing with tribal governments found themselves. The Fourteenth Amendment and its "due process" clause spoke directly to relationships between people and states. In an 1896 case, *Talton v. Mayer,* the Supreme Court specifically ruled that because the tribal governments were not part of the national government (disregarding the trust relationship) and were not states, the Bill of Rights did not apply to relationships between people and tribal governments, whether or not those people were tribal members.

There is some confusion over the meaning of this blind spot in government-people relationships. Critics of non-Native powers have been quick to suggest that the federal government through such cases was saying that Native Americans were "second class" in not having the rights of other Americans. They were wrong in this criticism. Native Americans did have the same legal protections of other Americans as individuals in relationships with state governments and as individuals in relationship with the national government. They just did not have the rights, as other Americans did not have the rights, afforded by the Bill of Rights in their relationships with tribal governments. The Native American Bill of Rights was *not* about protections from potentially abusive actions of states (and local governments) or the national government. It was about protections from potentially abusive actions of tribal governments—actions taken by Native American leaders of tribal governments. The passage of the Native American Bill of Rights Act of 1968 was designed to afford protections against abuses by Native American holders of power. To be certain, the Native Bill of Rights was not needed for all tribal governments. Of 435 recognized tribes and bands in 1968, 247 had formal constitutions and, of these 247, 117 contained bills of rights (Wunder 1996, 132).

Because the Native American Bill of Rights was slanted directly against abuses by Native leaders, many tribal leaders opposed it in Congress.

The charge in Congress for an Indian Bill of Rights was led by Senator Sam Ervin (D-NC), considered a liberal champion of civil liberties and the Constitution, especially through his later investigations of the Watergate scandals. However, in this case he may have been trying to "cover his tracks" as he had also been a Southern senator who had opposed civil rights for African Americans. He wrote the bill that would have incorporated the entire U.S. Bill of Rights into relationships between individuals and tribal governments. As the bill proceeded through Ervin's committee, tribes objected. So, too, did the Department of Interior. It was felt that the bill went "too far."

Part of the Bill of Rights requires the right to counsel. Tribes and the Department of the Interior felt that many tribal governments could not afford to provide lawyers to defendants in their courts. The provision was therefore scrapped. So, too, the Second Amendment protection of a right to bear arms was also eliminated. Also, the phrase in the Fifth Amendment (and the Fourteenth), that no government shall deprive a person of "life, liberty, or property" without due process of law, was altered. The

Indian Bill of Rights states that tribal governments may not deny persons "liberty or property" without due process of law.

The Ninth Amendment of the U.S. Constitution states that the other parts of the Bill of Rights are not totally inclusive. It also affirms that in no way does the listing of rights imply that the people do not have other rights also. This phrase was left out of the Indian Bill of Rights. But most telling was Senator Ervin's acquiescence to pleas from certain tribes that the prohibition on government-established religion, an essential part of the First Amendment, not be included. Several New Mexico tribes (Pueblo tribes) insisted that their governments were theocracies and that the United States should respect their establishment of government support for specific religions of the tribes (Wunder 1968, 136–137).

And so the bill was passed as it had been modified. Because of pressures from tribes and their supporters in the Department of the Interior, the full force of the American Bill of Rights is not being felt on many tribal lands today.

Ten years later, in 1978, Congress felt a further need to support the official quality of traditional Native American religion. Congress "affirmed" that "traditional religions" were an "indispensable and irreplaceable" part of Native American life.

By resolution of the two houses—the House of Representatives and the Senate—Congress proclaimed that tribes would have religious freedom. As this was a two-house resolution instead of an act, the matter did not require presidential action. The president could not veto the resolution. President Jimmy Carter had indicated that he had major difficulties about having the U.S. government endorse particular types of religious activities. Whereas the 1968 Indian Bill of Rights had left the door open for tribal governments (supported in part by all U.S. taxpayers) to declare financial and other support for their specific religions and the specific manner in which they worship their deity or deities, the new action of Congress declared that the U.S. government itself would give recognition to the establishment of tribal religions.

The resolution directed all federal government agencies to explore their policies and actions to assure that they did not deny Native Americans full access to religious sites and sacred lands. Agencies also had to guarantee that no policies were impeding the free practice of religions by Native Americans. Senator James Abourezk (D-SD) sponsored the resolution. He felt it necessary to give Native Americans a statutory basis for lawsuits, which could protect their religious sites and ceremonies. Supporters of the resolution argued that the U.S. government could give special treatment to Native American religions without violating the constitutional prohibition against the establishment of religions. By some manner of logic, they suggested that the prohibition might not apply because Native American religions were not "proselytizing" religions. We did not have to fear crossing over the wall between church and state because Native Americans did not seek to spread their religions the way Christians did. By the same strange logic, Congress might appropriate funds for Jewish synagogues or any new wave sect or cult that merely decreed that it did not wish to have converts.

Opponents worried that the resolution would require giving Native Americans access to sacred sites on private lands, allow Native Americans to use peyote, and limit the protections of the Endangered Species Act.

Abourezk and the other supporters misinterpreted the resolution. The opponents' worries have not reached fruition. Several law cases have thus far taken much of the "teeth" out of the resolution that the supporters might have wished it to have. Cherokees tried to stop the construction of a dam that would have flooded burial sites and sacred lands. In the case of *Sequoyah v. T.V.A.* (1980), the U.S. Supreme Court ruled against Native peoples because they did not own land in the area.

Another case arose after the National Park Service permitted private companies to have excursion boats to the Rainbow Bridge near Lake Powell, Arizona. Tourists visited the area, and many of them drank alcoholic beverages in excess. They would become loud and abusive, and would throw beer cans under the natural rock formation. The Rainbow Bridge was the home of gods worshiped by the Navajo Nation. The High Court recognized that the actions of the tourists impeded the Navajos' right to practice their religion. However, if the tourists were to be stopped by federal action, that action would in the eyes of the Court amount to an establishment of religion. It would be prohibited by the First Amendment. As with the *Sequoyah* case, the tribe lost the dispute because the land was outside of their reservation (*Badoni v. Higginson* 1981).

In the 1988 case of *Lyng v. Northwestern Indian Cemetery Protective Association*, the Supreme Court again ruled against the Native Americans. The Court gave its blessings to the construction of a logging road by the U.S. Forest Service. The project in the Six River National Forest of California disturbed the sacred burial sites of three different tribes. The issue of burial sites was given special attention in separate legislation.

The sanctity of the dead is an essential element in almost all religions. However, many of America's new settlers who had European origins did not always put a high value on the sanctity of the remains of Native peoples and their burial places.

The lead group of Pilgrims who got off of the *Mayflower* at Plymouth Rock purportedly raided the burial places of Native peoples. They took corn from Native storage pits, and they removed items from graves. According to the journals of these early settlers, they "brought sundry of the prittiest things away with (them), and covered up the corpse again" (Trope and Echo Hawk 1992, 35).

Two hundred years later, the federal government developed a new rationale for grave robberies—scientific investigation. Anthropologists wishing to study the physical qualities of different races apparently did not need the remains of non-Native bodies for studies, but instead sought out only Native bodies. In fact, the U.S. surgeon general issued an order in 1868 directing the Army to collect Native American remains for the Army medical museum. Parts from bodies were taken from battlefields and other places where the Army was engaged in violent confrontations with Natives. Native burial grounds were raided, and corpses were sold to the museum.

Every state in the United States has laws protecting cemeteries from desecration. Only rarely, however, were these laws enforced with regard to Native American graves. Courts often refused to define Native burial sites as "graves" because they did not have individual markers. A 1906 "Antiquities" law defined dead Native peoples buried on federal lands as "archaeological resources" and therefore federal property.

In the second part of the twentieth century, several states had revised laws to specifically include protection of Native American grave sites and bodily remains. However, not all state laws provide this protection. In 1986, many tribes inaugurated a lobbying effort directed toward Congress. In that year Northern Cheyenne officials discovered that the Smithsonian Institution possessed 18,500 human remains and asked that those remains be identified. Where found to be of indigenous origins, they asked that the remains be returned to their tribal homelands. The movement ended in the passage of two acts—the National Museum of the American Indian Act (1989), and the Native American Grave Protection and Reparations Act (1990).

The Museum Act created a special branch of the Smithsonian Institution. A $214 million facility has been constructed on the mall in Washington, D.C. The five-story 250,000-square-foot building was financed with $95 million coming from private sources, much of which was generated by tribal casinos. The grand opening of the museum was held on the autumn equinox, September 21, 2004. Although the collection displayed has been drawn from many sources, the core of 800,000 artifacts was brought together by George Gustav Heye a century ago. Formerly, his items had been on display in a very cramped building in New York City; now five million visitors a year are expected to view 10,000 years of history in the new location (*New York Times* March 28, 2004; *Washington Post* January 16, 2004).

The Museum Act of 1989 also required that the Institute make an inventory of all of the human remains and funeral objects in its possession. As they were identified, they had to be returned to the appropriate tribes.

The Grave Protection Act went much further. All Native remains held by federal, state, or local agencies had to be repatriated. The law also provided penalties for tampering with Native grave sites (Utter 1993, 96–98). As indicated in the land claims discussion, however, proper assignment of remains to specific existing tribes today is at times difficult, as migrations of peoples have been continuous. In addition, DNA-type evidence suggests that remains from antiquity in locations populated in recent centuries by Native peoples may be genetically of races unrelated to today's tribes, ergo Caucasians. This is not the case with remains from the past millennium.

Of ancillary importance to these Acts was legislation passed a decade before, in 1979. In that year Congress passed the Archaeological Resources Protection Act requiring the consent of tribes before outsiders could conduct archaeological explorations on their lands.

Sacred Sites and Religious Practices

The first Spanish conquistadors to come to the Americas justified military conquests of the Native peoples on the basis that they were not "Christian." Missionaries such as those who came to California at times sought to strip indigenous peoples of their cultural identities and even reduced individuals to slavery and peonage in efforts to make them "Christians." To be sure, there were also conversions to Christianity that were won with love and genuine concern for the people.

Some cultural conflict sprang in part from the notion that Christian institutions were not as focused on specific places and specific people as many indigenous belief systems. Religious leaders felt it necessary to spread the belief system to all peoples everywhere. They may have interpreted the absence of Christianity among Native Americans as an absence of all religions. However, Native peoples did have developed religious belief systems and rituals well before their contact with Europeans.

Traditional Native religions shared attributes that set them apart from Christianity. But there were also religious distinctions among the tribes. Natives who relied upon hunting and gathering for their sustenance often utilized animal ceremonialism, in contrast to agricultural nations, which featured rain and fertility rituals in their religions. The hunting groups focused on a male supreme being, while the agricultural societies worshiped both gods and goddesses. The agricultural nations saw creation coming out of the ground and spirits returning to the earth after death and burial. For this reason burial places are of central importance. Hunting societies looked toward the sky as the source of both the Creation and the heavenly afterlife (Hultkrantz 1993, 257–282).

Modern and historical Judaism and Islam give prominent recognition to certain places (Jerusalem, Mecca) in their faith structure. The traditional Native religions also were often tied to specific geographical places—even if they migrated as seasonal hunters or gatherers. Therefore, we find a much more place-specific context in their religions than in Christian sects. Christianity assigns sacred meanings to locations such as Bethlehem and Jerusalem; however, the places are less the object of worship than are specific mountains or lakes or woods, which might represent the place where a people was created or ended a long migration. Just as the Jewish nation considers Israel to be sacred land given just to them by God, the Navajo Nation believes that their Arizona and New Mexico lands are sacred. The boundaries of their home are provided by four sacred mountains: the Big Sheep Peak to the north, Mount Taylor to the south, the San Francisco

Peaks to the west, and Peludo Mountain in the east. To have these mountains near and to be able to worship in the mountains are critical factors in traditional Navajo religion—much as the Wailing Wall of Jerusalem is a critical place for the Jewish faithful (Deloria 1994, 267–282).

Non-Native settlers recognized Native rituals not as religious ceremonies, but as elements in a power struggle for a continent. The federal government's misreading of a religious ceremony, in which it was confused for a desire for a political uprising against the settlers, led the government officials—reservation agents and military commanders—into one of the most tragic episodes in the history of the United States.

On the first day of 1889, the Paiute prophet Wovoka had a vision in which he saw the Creator and was told to instruct Native peoples to live in peace with non-Natives and to participate in a "dance in a circle." If they did so, they would be able to travel to the other world where they would be reunited with their friends and relatives. Wovoka's teachings quickly spread, and they became known as the "Ghost Dance religion." Although a ritual of peace, the federal government attempted to suppress the Ghost Dance. When a band of Lakota Sioux persisted in the ceremony, a series of miscommunications and blunders culminated in disaster. In December 1890, federal troops opened fire on the band, killing over 150 men, women, and children (Walman and Braun 1985, 158–159).

Yet other Native American ceremonies and rituals were banned or suppressed by the government. The Sun Dance involved flesh piercing and long periods of gazing into the sun during which time a tribal member would experience visions. The dance was included in a general ceremony of friendship and thanksgiving, but the government saw it differently. The dance was made a punishable offense in 1883. Tribes engaging in the ceremony could have supplies promised in treaties denied to them. Northern Pacific nations had a ceremony called the Potlatch. The ritual promoted tribal solidarity as individuals would give away their possessions to other members. Some nineteenth-century Christians however, saw the Potlatch as antithetical to their capitalist value system, a system that had been successfully merged in some denominations with their biblical teachings (for example, "the Protestant Ethic"). In Canada, the government made the practice of the Potlatch a criminal offense (Walman and Braun 1985, 192; Champagne 1994, 230).

Native Americans also utilized the peyote plant for religious and medicinal purposes. Peyote ceremonies became widespread among western and southwestern Nations in the late nineteenth century. The active ingredient in peyote is a mind-altering stimulant called mescaline. During all-night prayer sessions, the peyote is either chewed or ingested as a tea. Participants in the ceremonies may have visions, hallucinations, or even out-of-body experiences. They also may experience nausea.

As the peyote ceremonies became popular among tribes across the country, opposition to the use of peyote developed. Traditional tribal religious leaders—shaman and medicine men—opposed it. Some tribes even passed rules against peyote ceremonies. Government officials considered peyote to be an illegal substance. Several states passed laws against its use, and general federal drug laws were interpreted at times to include bans on its use. In an attempt to have its use brought under the protection of religious freedoms, members of several tribes established the Native American Church in 1918. Only Native Americans (however defined) could belong to the church. Peyotism was incorporated in its beliefs. In other beliefs, the church was Christian. It advocated self-respect, brotherhood among Native Americans, morality, sobriety, and charity. Today the Church has about 400,000 members (Stewart 1987).

In 1954, a court ruling repudiated the notion that peyote use could be covered by the First Amendment's protections of the free exercise of religion. In 1970, the substance was classified as a hallucinogen under the Controlled Substance Act. However, at the same time, the Native American Church began to win support for its position. Several states recognized the ceremonies as proper religious activities and exempted them from their drug enforcement concerns. By 1990, twenty-eight states allowed peyote for Native American religious exercises, while twenty-two states did not.

The uneven treatment of the ceremonies became a matter of serious debate after the Supreme Court ruled in *Employment Division, Department of Human Resources of Oregon v. Smith* (1990) that a state could fire a civil servant for simply having participated in such a ceremony. Pressure on Congress was successful, and in 1994 the Native Americans' religious use of peyote won a general exemption from all drug enforcement activities (Getches, Wilkinson, and Williams 1993, 752–767; Peregoy 1995, 1).

Native Americans also utilize eagle feathers in religious ceremonies, and they revere them as sacred objects. To get feathers, however, birds usually must be killed. The Bald Eagle Protection Act (1972) prohibited the killing of the birds. However, in recognition of the religious nature of the feathers, the secretary of the interior can issue permits to Native Americans that allow them to selectively kill eagles as long as the overall conservation mandate of the legislation is met. The killing of the eagles must be strictly and solely for the purpose of gaining religious feathers for Native peoples (Getches, Wilkinson, and Williams 1993, 765–766).

Native American medicine men have also won an exemption to customs searches of their sacred medicine bags. The medicine men would travel to Canada to gather herbs, rocks, shells, arrowheads, and other objects for their bags. The bags would then be used in healing rituals. However, if a bag was opened by a nonholy person (such as a government customs official), its religious powers would be wasted.

Issues remain to be decided by policy makers in the future. Religious practices and government endorsement of religious establishments, the opposition to which are so much a part of the mantra of certain political factions in the United States, will be matters of confusion for the same factions as they support greater autonomy and community sustenance among Native Americans.

Stereotyping Native American Cultures

Native American communities are weakened when Native Americans are subjected to stereotypes that do not recognize them as autonomous human beings and that perpetuate notions that can destroy self-respect. Some non-Native cultures have portrayed Native Americans and their activities in offensive and degrading ways. Books, films, and other popular media present a multitude of stereotypical images.

Historian Jack Utter offers this list of descriptive patronizing and offensive images, which he has found in the literature: "innocent children of nature, subhuman demons, untrustworthy thieves, noble savages, bloodthirsty murderers, royal princesses, human curiosities, unfeeling stoics, natural born warriors, innately inferior humans, shiftless wanderers, vanishing vestiges of the stone age, wild animals, devil worshippers, completely democratic egalitarians, loyal 'Men Friday,' born bearers of wisdom, magical healers. Born mystics, automatic knowers of nature, super naturals, favored 'pets' of the government, the enemy, the antithesis to 'civilization,' and the bearers of a holy message to mankind." They were either "nobles" or "savages," but rarely were they just "human beings" (Utter 1993, 74).

One of the most well-known names used for a Native American in popular media is "Tonto." The name of the Lone Ranger's "trusted sidekick" is a Spanish word that means "stupid." On the other hand, some of the images would be considered positive, but all lack a genuine and accurate quality. Attempts to portray Native Americans as possessors of "total goodness" also label them as being "less than human" (Utter 1993, 75).

Many Native Americans also find the use of some mascots and nicknames by schools and professional sports teams very offensive. Although Native Americans themselves use many of the same names (Chiefs, Warriors, Indians, Braves), the names and mascots may carry different meanings when they are imposed by outsiders.

Similarly, symbols that have special meaning to many Native Americans are bantered about freely when used as tools to capture money from non-Natives at gambling casinos controlled by tribes. For instance, there are tribal casinos named "Seven Feathers," "Soaring Eagle," "Spirit Mountain," "Lucky Eagle," and "Inn of the Mountain Gods." What this writer found to be offensive to his own "adult taste" and what he would consider offensive to anyone asserting the dignity of Native American peoples were the costumes of the cocktail waitresses at the Foxwoods Native American casino in Connecticut. The women wandered around in very scanty "Native" outfits revealing their posteriors rather prominently while their headbands displayed feathers. The "authenticity" of the feathers I observed was very dubious.

Non-Natives should be criticized, and their conduct corrected (especially when the conduct is tied to public authorities such as public schools and universities), but stereotypes and offensive imaging should be attacked wherever it is found. There is only one public domain, and if tribes and Native peoples themselves choose to publicly (and officially) use words and symbols thought offensive when used by others, they too must reflect on the images they are projecting onto that same public domain. It is problematical to suggest that members of any minority group can use language in public that contains words demeaning to that minority without impugning the dignity of the people. The notion that we can insult our own ethnic groups publicly carries further burdensome overtones when it is realized that sizable portions of the public, perhaps one quarter of the population or more (certainly almost all Hispanic peoples), have a heritage linked to indigenous ancestors. As many Americans have some indigenous heritage, the insults should not be acceptable, regardless of who the speaker is. I should find it as offensive to hear a "white" person publicly use the word "honky" as I would if I heard a nonwhite person use this derogatory term; similarly, as a person with French heritage, I should find the word "frog" offensive as applied to another person, regardless of whether the speaker is French.

Non-Natives may not intentionally offend or demean Native Americans when they use the nicknames. They may even argue that the team names portray Native Americans in a positive manner. Native Americans counter with the idea that a stereotype is offensive whether or not the user means to offend, and that their use rarely results in positive portrayals of today's Native Americans.

The issue of team nicknames came to national attention in the 1990s, when three teams won prominent professional championships. The Atlanta Braves won two National League baseball championships in addition to a World Championship. Their fans cheered for the Braves by doing the "tomahawk chop": They waved toy tomahawk hatchets up and down with their arms as they chanted what they considered to be Native American "war cries." The "leading fan" of the Braves was Jane Fonda, wife of team owner Ted Turner. Jane had a long-standing reputation as a champion of minority peoples' causes, but she too was caught up in "Brave Fever" when the games were played. In 1995, the Braves played the American League champion Cleveland Indians in the World Series. The Indians' mascot was a smiling caricature of a Native American with a feathered headdress.

Superbowl appearances and victories by the Washington Redskins football team put the spotlight on what has to be the most offensive team name—a name referring to race and skin color.

Indian Country Today editor Tim Giago believed the use of the name "Redskins" to be illustrative of a national "insensitivity" to the values of Native American culture (Giago 1991). Amazingly, the owner of the team, Jack Kent Cook, responded to the criticism with the suggestion that his use of the name was "complimentary" to Native Americans. Giago then described how fans of the football team used "peace pipes" and painted their faces red. He asked how members of the Catholic faith would respond if fans of the New Orleans Saints football team carried crosses and waved them at games. (Some no doubt did so.) He did not think the public would accept a mascot dressed up as the Pope throwing incense into the air, painting foreheads with ashes, and holding mock communions at halftime. And certainly African Americans and Asian Americans would not accept teams called "Black skins," or "Yellow skins" (see Leiby 1994).

Native Americans have attacked symbolic caricatures used by the Cleveland Indians baseball team, the Kansas City Chiefs football team, the Golden State Warriors basketball team, as well as dances by mascots for college teams such as the University of Illinois—"The Fightin' Illini," and the Florida State University "Seminoles." In recognition of the Native Americans' sensitivities, many schools have changed their nicknames and stereotypes.

The state legislature of Wisconsin passed the American Indian Studies law in 1989, which provides for instruction in "culture and value system differences and human relations." In 1992, the state assembly passed a resolution urging schools to review policies toward use of Native mascots. In Minnesota, forty-four high schools made changes in school nicknames.

At the college level, Stanford University and Dartmouth College dropped the nickname "Indians" and instead became, respectively, "The Cardinal" and "The Big Green." The Marquette University "Warriors" became the "Eagles," and the Eastern Michigan University "Hurons" also became the "Eagles." St. John's ceased being the "Redmen," and are now the "Johnnies." Oklahoma University dropped "Little Red" as its mascot. On the other hand, Illinois has refused to drop its "Fighting Illini" mascot "Chief Illiniwick," who performed his version of a "war dance" at football and basketball games. However, the University of Iowa informed officials of the University of Illinois that "Chief Illiniwick" and his dance would not be welcome in Iowa City whenever the "Illini" played games with the "Hawkeyes." In 1993, the Wisconsin Indian Education Association along with the Oneida tribe resolved to work with the Athletic Board of the University of Wisconsin at Madison to develop a policy that would stop the university athletic teams from competing with other teams using tribal mascots, symbols, and logos. They still play Illinois (www.pages.prodigy.net).

Several newspapers, including the Portland *Oregonian*, have made editorial decisions to drop all Native American nicknames and other nicknames offensive to any ethnic group in references to teams in sports stories. Atlanta's baseball team is now the Atlanta baseball team, and the Cleveland Indians are the Cleveland baseball team (Stein 1992, 15).

Not all Native Americans are upset with team nicknames. Washington Redskins' jackets are very popular—and very obvious—on reservations, although their display is subject to ambiguous interpretations. There is no ambiguity behind the support the Washington Redskins and Atlanta Braves have received from one tribe. The chief of the Eastern Cherokee reservation of North Carolina indicates that his tribe has made considerable profits by selling 300,000-feather headdresses to Washington fans and tens of thousands of toy tomahawks to Atlanta fans. It was good business. Others in the tribe saw the commercial venture as an insult to their own culture.

Surveys of Native Americans reveal that team nicknames are not offensive to most respondents. A 2003 opinion poll determined that only 37 percent of Natives found "Redskin" offensive. Less than 10 percent found the names "Indian" and "Braves" offensive as professional team names. In 2002, a Peter Harris poll for *Sports Illustrated* magazine found that 83 percent of Natives did not want teams to stop using Native nicknames; while 67 percent did not object to use of the name "Redskins" (www.deckerjones.com/a_mantoothlz.htm; www.mtechacademy.org/web2002/etubb/si-poll.htm).

There are limits to government policy in the area of stereotypes and mascots. The free speech guarantees of both the U.S. Bill of Rights and the Indian Civil Rights Act of 1968 do allow people to offend one another. Restrictions are allowed where the offenses are personally delivered in a "face-to-face" or other direct manner, which would excite violence, and the use of nicknames in most occasions would not meet the test needed for legal restrictions. On the other hand, the spirit of the Indian Religious Freedom Act as well as common human civility should lead individual government officials and other community leaders such as newspaper editors and television executives to urge schools and professional teams to drop clearly offensive symbols and activities.

On the other side of the equation, Native Americans might choose to focus their attacks on displays that are clearly offensive, and particularly on those that carry some intentional offense. There should be a common awareness that many portrayals of ways of life are artistic and deserve the protections of freedom of expression—protections that are essential parts of the freedoms all peoples enjoy. When non–Native American modern dancers choreograph a routine that uses drums and feathers that may be viewed as similar to Native American drums and dances, the dance interpretations should not be censored for that reason alone. Even private groups should hesitate to interfere with such portrayals unless they are obviously or purposely done in ways that mock specific people. Objections to the use of drums and chants in artistic portrayals should also be selective, for drums, chants, and even feather dress outfits have been used by many societies across time and across the world. Native Americans have not been the only people to use drums. They are not the only peoples who have used feathers in ceremonial dress. They are not the sole guardians of authenticity regarding regalia. Whether or not legalities are involved, all people should be sensitive to the dignity of others.

Political Jurisdiction

A leading political scientist of the 1960s, David Easton, defined *politics* as "the authoritative allocation of values for a society." Strong communities must have a large degree of control over the politics within their borders. Strong Native American communities must have strong political systems. The bottom line for determining whether a community is a viable political system involves an assessment of the extent to which the community has the capacity to oversee and mandate the distribution of valuable resources (including power and status) within its boundaries (its society). Native American communities have populations, and they occupy lands. The issue is how much political control do they have over the lands and over the actions of people on those lands. Sometimes the answer is "a lot," and sometimes the answer is "a little," but always the answer contains elements of confusion (Easton 1966, 96–100).

The occupation of lands—in many cases an occupation occurring over several centuries—has brought with it certain inherent powers that may remain even in the face of contemporary policy decisions. For example, the Indian Civil Rights Act (Bill of Rights) was written and adopted in 1968 by Congress and provided for "equal protection of the laws." Nonetheless, the U.S. Supreme Court has held that a tribe can use discriminatory criteria to define its own membership. In the particular case the Court held that the tribe could treat men and women differently in determining membership. Making such a determination regarding who is in or who is out of a tribal community was recognized as an inherent power of a tribe that could not be altered by law (*Martinez v. Santa Clara* 1978).

No political control system, however, can be total, whether based on inherent powers or man-made edicts. Cities share powers with states, and both share powers with the federal government. Tribal governments also share power, but to what extent? Citizens of states are also U.S. citizens. So, too, are Native Americans. This was not always the case. The Fourteenth Amendment provides that "all persons born or naturalized in the United States and subject to the jurisdiction thereof, are citizens of the United States and of the states wherein they reside." The words seem plain and direct. Nonetheless, prior to 1924, all Native Americans were not citizens. Congress chose to imply that Native peoples somehow were not under the jurisdiction of the United States. This notion would severely contradict the idea that Congress had authority over the people, or that the Natives were "dependent" upon the federal government. This contradiction was changed in 1924 with an act of Congress that granted citizenship to all Native peoples, although some have declined the offer. As a practical matter, all Native Americans are now U.S. citizens (Prucha 1990, 218).

Two areas of political control deserve special discussion—judicial jurisdiction and regulation and taxation. Judicial power is a special kind of political power in that judges—as opposed to other political officials—have the *final* word in dispute resolution. Taxation involves the mandatory seizure of private property by governments. Accordingly, it is one of the primary indicators of the exercise of political power. Regulation is a matter of major concern in that its imposition may place boundaries on the liberty within a community.

Problems of definition have to be mentioned before jurisdictional and regulation and taxation issues can be approached. Native American reservations and lands consist of a variety of property, some owned by tribes as units, others owned by individuals—Natives and others. First of all, the Congress of the United States has recognized that Native Americans have an interest in what happens within reservations, no matter what the nature of the land ownership is. Therefore, Congress has designated as "Indian Country" all lands that are within the outer boundaries of a reservation, no matter who owns the lands. The Dawes Act of 1887 and various allotment acts since that time resulted in a loss of tribal ownership of many of the reservation lands. Some of the land was allotted to individual Native Americans and later came to be owned by these Native Americans as private personal land. Some of these Native Americans accordingly sold their land to non-Natives. Much of the land within reservation boundaries remained in trust status for the entire tribe. Some of the land was assigned to individuals but still retained its trust designation. The tribe as a whole repurchased some of the privately owned land, but it was not held in trust by the federal government. A jurisdictional maze that cannot easily be described has resulted from a "checkerboard-type" distribution of lands in "Indian Country"—that is, lands within the outer bounds of reservations.

Judicial authority is generally divided into criminal and civil jurisdiction. *Criminal jurisdiction* involves major crimes (felonies) and minor crimes (misdemeanors). *Civil jurisdiction* involves governmental regulations as well as disputes among individuals. Our concern should be with just what judicial authority the tribal community has and what authority the tribe does not have.

The exercise of full criminal judicial authority requires that governments have law enforcement structures in place—police, attorneys, judges, and corrections personnel. Traditionally, many tribes would settle both civil and criminal disputes through the consensual actions of councils in accordance with past practices. In today's complex world, matters totally of internal concern for tribes may be resolved in the same way, but many actions involve difficult questions and also outside concerns. More formalized methods of dispute resolution are often required. Jurisdiction is a theoretical question but is also a practical question of resources.

Congressional actions dating back to the 1820s assigned some criminal jurisdiction over matters arising on Native lands to the federal government. An "assimilative crimes" provision made violations of state criminal laws federal offenses. Treaties with Native tribes also specified how some criminal disputes would be resolved. In some circumstances, Congress and treaty provisions may let tribes handle criminal matters.

The U.S. Supreme Court resolved a critical case in the development of criminal jurisdiction in *Ex Parte Crow Dog* in 1883. Crow Dog, a Native American, murdered a fellow Native American on reservation land. He was tried, convicted, and sentenced to death in federal court. The Supreme Court narrowly interpreted legislation and failed to find any federal jurisdiction. The conviction was set aside. However, Congress was not content to let tribal authorities handle murder cases. Therefore, in 1885 Congress passed the Major Crimes Act whereby jurisdiction in the case of seven major crimes (the list of crimes was later expanded) occurring on Native lands was placed in the hands of federal courts.

During the Termination era of the 1940s and 1950s, the federal government sought to get out of the business of tribal oversight. In addition to its efforts to get tribes to "disband" as community political units, Congress passed Public Law 280 in 1952. The law assigned both criminal and civil jurisdiction over occurrences on Native lands to state courts in several states. At first this law was meant to apply only to criminal cases in California. However, the special nature of the legislation changed in committee, other states were added, and as an afterthought, Congress added "civil" jurisdiction—without defining what it meant. Ever since that time the intended meaning of "civil" has been left rather "up in the air." Tribal governments felt that their concerns were being abandoned by a sometimes supportive federal government and were being handed over to hostile state governments. The federal motivation included the notion that less federal money would have to be spent on these law enforcement concerns. But the states were not all that comfortable with having to expend resources in these new criminal law duties. An unintended result was that the volume of law enforcement efforts was reduced in Indian Country.

The thrust of Public Law 280 was later modified as states were permitted to return this criminal law authority to the federal government, and also Congress required tribal approvals before additional tribes (or states) were affected by the law. Native Americans have continued to oppose the imposition of Public Law 280. The tribes originally covered by the law were given no voice in its application (in whether or not they would be included); when the law was changed, only the states were given a voice in determining who possessed criminal law jurisdiction over the Native lands.

Public Law 280 has not stripped all tribes in the covered states of their ability to exercise criminal law powers. Tribes in these states do have courts and judicial systems that handle minor criminal actions. The criminal jurisdiction of tribal courts may even extend beyond Indian Country in cases involving tribal members. Moreover, Public Law 280 has been rather limited in its civil jurisdiction scope. More definitive answers to the matter of jurisdiction have been forthcoming from recent decisions of the Supreme Court (Canby 1988, 176–200; Getches, Wilkinson, and Williams 1993, 478–493). The litigation on permissible tribal gambling, as mentioned, suggested that states even in Public Law 280 jurisdictions could not impose "civil" limits on tribal gambling, unless all such gambling was prohibited throughout the state (*Cabazon v. California* 1987).

In another ruling, the U.S. Supreme Court held in *Oliphant v. Squamish Tribe* in 1978 that tribal courts could not impose even misdemeanor jurisdiction over non-Natives for criminal occurrences on trust lands. The Court did acknowledge that criminal acts by non-Natives were a law enforcement concern of the tribes. However, the Court offered that Congress had to resolve the matter. Only that body could determine whether the tribes were to possess the jurisdiction, and then Congress could address the question with specific legislation. Because there was no such legislation, the criminal jurisdiction remained with the outside federal authorities, or in Public Law 280 states, with state authorities.

In 1959, the Court rendered a more favorable civil jurisdiction ruling from the standpoint of Native America. The Court found that a non-Native who operated a store on Navajo trust lands and sold goods to a Native family on credit could not go to Arizona state courts to seek a judgment for payment from the buyers. The Court recognized that the Navajo tribe had a court system that was capable of making rulings in cases involving Native people and others. It was reasoned that an assignment of jurisdiction to the state would undermine self-government among the Navajo people (*Williams v. Lee* 1959).

Although Public Law 280 spoke of civil jurisdiction, the notion of civil authority contained in the Act of Congress did not extend far into matters of regulation or taxation. Decisions in these regards have been made in accordance with treaties and other pieces of legislation.

A wide variety of taxes may apply to Indian Country. Like other Americans, Native Americans are besieged by taxes at every turn. Native Americans are subject to federal taxes, to tribal taxes, and, in some cases, to state and local (non-Native) taxes as well. Tribal governments, on the other hand are, as a general rule, exempt from taxes. Profits that are derived from tribal lands or from tribally run businesses—which are run on trust lands—are not subject to federal income taxes. This same immunity from taxes is given to enterprises owned by state or local governments. The casino profits of tribal gaming facilities are not subject to Internal Revenue Service collections. Similarly, states may not tax these businesses. It can be noted that, even though the Indian Gaming Regulatory Act of 1988 specifically prohibits state taxation of Native gaming operations, many tribes have agreed to give large sums (as much as 25 percent) of their gaming receipts to states, usually in exchange for some extra benefits or services. In addition, to the critics who falsely claim that "the Indians don't pay taxes," it must be added that Native Americans in conceptual terms pay the *largest casino taxes* of any gaming operation in America. They pay a tax that represents 100 percent of their net profits. The money goes to the tribal government and as such must be considered a "tax."

The federal government cannot levy capital gains taxes on tribal lands, and it cannot tax timber cut from the trust lands. The matter changes considerably if the tribe is conducting business outside of Indian Country. Then taxes are paid by the tribe the same as if the tribe were any other business entity. The situation involving tribal business on private lands (even if tribally owned) that are within Indian Country is somewhat confusing (*County of Yakima v. Yakima Indian Nation* 1992).

Individual Native Americans pay federal taxes. Employees of Native American casinos pay income taxes on their wages. Tribal members who may benefit from a "per capita" distribution of casino profits must pay federal income tax on those moneys. The courts have also ruled that the salaries of tribal officials are subject to federal income taxes. If the Native Americans live outside of Indian Country, they also are subject to all state taxes—income taxes, sales taxes, and property taxes (*Superintendent of Five Civilized Tribes v. Commissioner* 1935).

The tribes pay social security taxes for their own employees, even if the employees are tribal members. They also pay unemployment insurance taxes, as authorized by Congress, even though the insurance system is administered by states. The tribal governments can issue tax-free "municipal bonds," as may state and local governments, but only for on-reservation projects. Also, the Courts have upheld the imposition of a federal automobile excise tax on vehicle sales to a tribal police force. The courts reasoned that the tax was levied against the automobile supplier, not the tribe. State and federal taxes on gasoline sold on tribal lands must be paid because these taxes are levied on distributors before the gasoline comes into Indian Country—and in a sense the tax is "passed on" through pricing mechanisms.

State governments possess some taxation authority over matters occurring within Indian Country and on trust lands. The U.S. Supreme Court upheld the state of Washington in its application of cigarette sales taxes on tribal lands when the purchaser of the cigarettes was a non-Native person. The Court ruled that the tribal business had to collect the taxes for the state in the same manner as any other business. Sales to tribal members were exempt from the taxes (*Washington v. Confederated Tribes of Colville* 1980).

In 1924, Congress specifically authorized states to levy taxes on mineral production on trust lands. Accordingly, the taxes were considered legal. However, a comprehensive mineral leasing act for Native lands passed in 1938 omitted the issue of taxation (Indian Mineral Leasing Act). The courts held that the omission meant that the states could no longer tax the mineral production.

That tribes may tax is uncontested, but as with any other taxes, disputes do arise regarding the appropriateness of particular tribal taxes. One case involved the application of a new severance tax on a private company that held a lease for taking oil and natural gas from trust lands. The company argued that the lease took precedence over the tax. However, the courts agreed that the tribe could impose the new tax. The tribe's role as a government was as important as its role as a lessor of property (*Merrion v. Jicarilla Tribe* 1981). While the secretary of the interior often becomes involved in the tribes' business matters—approving contracts, for instance—the secretary need not approve tribal taxes.

The federal government may impose regulations upon tribes. The applications vary according to various laws. Tribes are not subject to all U.S. labor laws on tribal lands for tribal employees. However, private businesses on tribal lands are covered by labor laws. Some courts have ruled that federal work safety laws apply to the lands, whereas others have found that tribes are exempt from the laws. Provisions of treaties have been evoked to support either application or exemption from laws. In general, the National Environmental Protection Act applies to trust lands (*Davis v. Morton* 1972). However, the specific application of environmental standards is not as clear.

Environmental regulations pose a unique problem. The federal government can clearly impose these regulations on all lands within reservations. However, many environmental provisions are enforced by states or tribes if they agree to carry out the enforcement activities and follow standards that are at least as rigorous as those of the federal government. Tribes may enter into contracts with the Environmental Protection Agency to do such enforcement throughout Indian Country. Tribes may thereby enforce pollution standards of their own design on privately owned non-Native lands within their boundaries. The courts have reasoned that it would be impractical for states, tribes, and the federal government to divide regulation over such areas. In the same vein, if tribes do not negotiate for enforcement powers, and the state does, the state may enforce its regulations (which may be different—but must be at least as strict as federal regulations) on the reservation lands— even those lands held in trust for the tribe (Western Conference of Attorneys General 1993, 263–300). The rationale behind this policy is that environmental protections must be continuous, as the harms of pollution and degradation of lands extend beyond immediate political jurisdictions.

A similar line of reasoning was offered by courts upholding state enforcement of quarantine as well as compulsory school attendance laws on trust lands. The state activity, however, was authorized in advance by the secretary of the interior (Canby 1988, 226). It is also recognized that the problems of liquor sales and consumption cannot be dealt with in a "checkerboard manner" (*Rice v. Rehner* 1983). Therefore, Congress has given states the authority to impose their liquor laws on people—Natives and non-Natives alike—within Indian Country. And if a tribe adopts a liquor ordinance that is more restrictive than a state's law, that ordinance is operative throughout Indian Country. States and tribes may also impose their respective zoning laws on certain Indian Country lands where it is shown that a consistency of development rules and their enforcement is necessary for an area (*Brendale v. Yakima* 1989).

Is there an answer to all this confusion? There is, but it is unlikely that it will manifest itself soon. Congress has the power to resolve all of the difficulties and give strong definition to the wavy, blurred fine lines present in the discussion of jurisdiction, but Congress is unlikely to do so. First, as important as the matters are, they impact only a very small part of the population— less than 1 percent. Second, a definitive resolution of jurisdictional questions of necessity will involve much acrimony and emotional debate. Third, everyone, with the possible exception of the few people involved in the specific instances, seems content to let the courts argue over the fine points and to make ad hoc and reversible (not irreversible) decisions.

Other than recognizing that the ultimate—though unexercised in most cases—power resides with Congress, we can conclude that Native American communities exercise considerable powers by exercising jurisdiction over Native American lands—albeit in a shared manner.

The Canadian Perspective

The Native Americans who reside in Canada share many of the same political concerns of their brethren in the United States. They seek better lives for themselves, and they seek stronger communities. While the issues—poverty, land claims, religious freedoms, gambling, and economic development, to name a few—were dealt with above in context of the United States, it is hoped that a Canadian overview summarizing many of the common issues will show a recognition that indigenous peoples of North America experience a common place in the broader political arena.

It is difficult to neglect the 1.3 million Canadians, or 4 percent of the national population, who claim some indigenous heritage. For a more detailed account, the reader is referred to the definitive treatment of Native Americans in Canada provided in Olive Patricia Dickason's *Canada's First Nations* (2002).

We will retain much of the same terminology used earlier—Native Americans, Native peoples, tribes, and so on—although variations of the terms are used in Canada. Tribes in Canada are typically called "First Nations," and tribal communities are called "bands," which often live together on "reserves." One accepted term for Canadian Indians is "Amerindians." One American term for a category of indigenous living in the North ("Eskimo") is considered derogatory in the Canadian context (although a professional football team in Edmonton proudly uses the name as its mascot), so here these people will be referred to as "Inuits."

Numbers Today

The 2001 Census of Canada indicates that 1.3 million Canadians consider themselves to have an indigenous heritage; however, fewer indicate that their "identity" is with these peoples. There are 704,851 who identify themselves as Amerindians. They are associated with 614 bands that live on more than 2000 reserves with over 10,000 square miles of land. Actually, just over half of this population lives on reserve lands. Another 292,310 persons have identified themselves as "Metis," described later. There are 45,070 Inuits.

The Natives are subdivided into so-called status Indians, and others are called nonstatus Indians. Some are also referred to as "Treaty" Indians, a term that overlaps other categories. However, the term "Treaty" Indians does not apply to Native peoples in British Columbia and other reaches of the land not covered by a treaty process that ended in 1921. The designations have relevance for eligibility for some government benefits, and for the most part the designations follow the series of treaties (beginning in 1871) that assigned Natives to specific reserves in exchange for promised benefits. As in the United States, the assignments were not always negotiated by equal partners on each side of the bargaining table, and often the government of Canada did not fully deliver the promised benefits (e.g., food, housing, clothing).

Native peoples in Canada utilize ten different language groups with 58 dialects. Inuits share the same language but have various dialects. Metis use French and English, as well as indigenous languages (Champagne 1994, li, 492).

Reserves are found in all Canadian provinces except Prince Edward's Island and Newfoundland, as well as the territories. Seventy percent of the Natives live on reserves. There are no reserves for the Inuits or Metis; however, the Province of Alberta does recognize Metis communities (Champagne 1994, li–lii).

Similarly, the Inuits are not organized into "reserve" communities. The Inuits did win a monumental political agreement that has given them control of vast northern lands along with a new government authority to conduct public affairs by themselves for themselves. Throughout the 1980s and 1990s, the Inuits negotiated for a new territory of Nunavut. The formation of Nunavut is discussed later in this chapter.

Early History

By the time of the European Contact, over a million Native peoples may have been settled in the Canadian area. Their ancestors had sought their sustenance from the resources of Canadian soil and waters for thousands of years. The most advanced in terms of community living were in the Pacific coastal areas. They lived in villages in large wooden houses and took much of their food supply from the ocean and its tributaries. Pacific Coast tribes had about 40 percent of the Native peoples of Canada. Iroquoian Nations of the midcontinent region had also developed complex agricultural societies and lived in semipermanent villages. To the north were the Inuit peoples and Athabascans who lived in small bands that moved frequently in search of game. East Coast Natives belonged to small bands tied together by Algonquian languages and customs. Extensive trade networks existed among many diverse Natives (Champagne 1994, xxiv–xxviii; Long and Chiste 1994, 334–346).

The first era of Contact between indigenous American and European peoples occurred in the Atlantic coastal region of Canada. Nearly 500 years before Columbus, Europeans from Norway landed in Newfoundland. These Vikings sought relationships with Native peoples, and they even built villages. However, the relations were not good, and hostilities led to a withdrawal of the Europeans. After Columbus, the same Atlantic coastal areas were visited by other European ships from England, Holland, and France. The most extensive European explorations of Canada were made by the French and English, and soon the two nationalities were vying for dominance in a profitable fur trade with the Native peoples. The French also sought permanent communities in Canada for agricultural settlers and also bases for activity by Jesuit priests who wished to convert the Natives to Christianity (Champagne 1994, 20–36).

The French and English saw the Natives as essential commercial partners as well as people available for religious conversion. For these reasons, relations with Natives were somewhat different from those experienced in the United States, where from the time of the first contacts, Europeans were in competition with Natives as they both desired to occupy the same lands. In the north, Native peoples were valued, and a measure of goodwill and cooperation was highly desired. Among the French (and English too) were many trappers who moved among the Natives as individuals and soon came to become part of Native communities. Intermarriage was endorsed as a way to establish good relationships. The close contacts of trappers and Native peoples led to distinct communities of peoples of mixed heritage. These new peoples took on a distinct identity—they became known as the Metis (Long and Chiste 1994, 351–357).

The era of good relationships was somewhat illusory and certainly could not be permanent, as England and France spread their long-held mutual hostilities to the Canadian soil. Natives were drawn into military alliances with either the French or English, and they often suffered when they were on the losing side. In the grand scheme of things, they had to lose as the British and then the Americans (of the United States) took command of the continent. After the French and Indian Wars (1754–1763) and the American Revolution (1775–1781), persons of European heritage both north and south of the border desired to occupy land for permanent settlements. On both sides of the border, the Native peoples stood in the way of "progress."

The Canadian Confederation

The British in London had a more sympathetic view of Natives than did the settlers, but British dominance of policy was phased out as Canada gained dominion status in 1867. Prior to that date, in 1850, the era of treaties began in Canada.

British authorities in Canada began a process of securing Native lands for white settlement in 1850. Two treaties (Robinson-Superior and Robinson-Huron) were negotiated with tribes occupying large regions of land. Native peoples were required to give up lands in exchange for guaranteed smaller parcels on which they would receive various commodities and payments from the government. The parcels were designated as reserves. Tribes were broken up into bands that occupied the reserves. Often bands from different tribes occupied the same reserves of lands (Champagne 1994, 176).

The process of treaty writing established in 1850 was continued after new Canadians achieved autonomy from the British with passage of the British American Act in 1867. The Act created the Canadian Confederation—a union initially comprising Ontario, Quebec, Nova Scotia, and New Brunswick. It provided that authority over relationships between Natives and those of Canadian heritage would be controlled by the central government. In 1876, the Canadian Parliament passed the Indian Acts, which was aimed at assimilation by authorizing parcels of land for individual Native families and providing for citizenship for certain Natives. The Act restricted alcoholic beverages for reserves of land. Traditional Native political structures were eliminated as the Indian Act of 1876 imposed an elective council system for local band government.

In 1871, the Canadian government negotiated the first of eleven "numbered" treaties along the model set forth in 1850. Treaty Number Eleven was negotiated in 1921 (Champagne 1994, 209, 280). The first reserves were set up in Manitoba (which joined the Confederation in 1870), and annual payments were given to Natives along with seeds and farm implements. Subsequent treaties covered the new provinces of Saskatchewan, Ontario, Alberta, and the Northwest Territories. Later treaties provided for education and medicine for Natives. The numbered treaties did not cover Natives in British Columbia and certain northern reaches of Canada. In these areas, land was secured from Natives by legislative agreements or other means.

The Metis People

Native peoples identified as Indians were given new band statuses and received reserve lands. However, the Metis, who lived mostly in the Prairie Provinces of Manitoba, Saskatchewan, and Alberta, were generally ignored by the treaties (with minor exceptions), and there are no nationally recognized Metis reserves. The Province of Alberta did give legal recognition to Metis communities in 1938.

Although Canadian Natives escaped the ravages of lingering wars with the central government, there were some armed conflicts, most of which involved the Metis peoples. The roots of the Metis peoples can be traced to the 1600s—specifically to members of ongoing communities of descendants of both European traders and trappers (mostly French but also English and Scottish) and Indians. They settled specific lands and acquired land rights under French legal principles. They spoke the French language as well as Native dialects and adhered to the Catholic religion. Their Red River community in present-day Manitoba was established in the early 1800s. The private Hudson's Bay Company, which had a grant for the land, gave permission for the Metis settlement. However, after establishment of the Confederation, the Canadian government sponsored non-Metis settlements by eastern Canadians (mostly English-speaking Protestants but also Germans and others). The Canadian government purchased the land from Hudson's Bay, surveyed the land (on the basis of English land law), and sought to redistribute the land to both the Metis and new non-Metis settlers. The Metis resisted the actions by forming a government of their own. Canada refused to recognize the government. When Canada sought to impose its land system, the Metis revolted. They were led by Louis Riel, who sought some allegiances with other Native peoples. Riel was also opposed by other Natives who had been involved in territorial disputes with the Metis for generations. An 1870 Metis revolt failed in the face of over a thousand British and Canadian military troops. Riel and most of the Metis fled westward.

Eventually, Riel moved to Montana. He actually won three elections for a seat in the Canadian Parliament—which he held in absentia fearing his arrest if he went to the national assembly in Ottawa. When a repeat of the Manitoba experience threatened new Metis settlements in Saskatchewan in 1884, Riel felt a call (almost in the religious sense) to "lead" his peoples in a second revolt. In 1885, the Metis, again hopelessly outnumbered, were defeated by Canadian armies, and Riel was hanged for treason. He remains a martyr among both the Metis and many French Canadians who feel alienated within the Canadian national community (Long and Chiste 1994, 351–357).

Contemporary Relationships: The "White Paper"

Throughout the early decades of the twentieth century, the Native peoples of Canada were quiet. A 1927 amendment to the Indian Law of 1876 had stipulated that they were not to engage in political activity in any collective manner. (General citizenship rights and Canadian national voting rights were not granted until 1951.)

The quiet posture of Inuits, Metis, and other Natives belied major social concerns and concerns for justice. As with Natives of the lands to the south, the peoples suffered hardships; their suffering has continued in recent times. The indigenous are the poorest of Canadians. One-fourth live in unheated houses, and one-half in houses without running water. One-third of family units are headed by single parents. One-half of the Native Canadians receive the greatest share of their income from federal subsidies. Only 20 percent of Native peoples complete their high school education compared with 75 percent of others.

Native Canadian life expectancies are ten years shorter than life expectancies of other Canadians. Infant mortality rates are double those for the rest of Canada, with over 50 percent of total health problems alcohol related. The Native communities experience the highest suicide rates in Canada—two-and-a-half times the average. Violent death rates are three times as high (Long and Chiste 1994, 343–344).

Individually, many Canadian Native people observed and participated in the civil rights protests that swept the United States in the 1960s. Native Americans and Canadians identified with the grievances being expressed by African Americans. However, as a collective force, Canadian Native peoples needed their own "wake-up call." They got it on June 25, 1969.

In 1963, the federal government appointed Harry B. Hawthorn, an anthropologist, to study the social conditions surrounding Native Canadians. His report suggested that the government modify aid given to reserve Indians and increase incentives for Natives to seek their economic futures off-reserves in cities through the process of assimilation. While Hawthorn documented many of the deprivations of Native peoples, his call for tribal members to join the non-Native economy seemed to resonate with the top political leadership of the country (Hawthorn 1966).

Canada's Minister of Indian Affairs Jean Chrétien (who became prime minister of Canada in October 1993, serving until 2003) issued a "White Paper" entitled "Statement of the Government of Canada on Indian Policy, 1969." Under the political leadership of Prime Minister Pierre Trudeau, the Canadian government determined that special status for reserves and for Native bands and tribes was to cease. The Indian Act was to be repealed, and the Indian Affairs Ministry abolished. Reserves were to be broken up, and their lands given to individual Native people. The White Paper seemed to mimic the failed—and repudiated—Termination polices of both the 1887 Dawes Act and the Truman and Eisenhower administrations in the United States.

Native Canada was shocked into action. The White Paper gave Native Canadians a sense of unity unrealized up to that point in history. Collectively, they rejected the White Paper, and they responded with wave after wave of demands. They became politicized as they had never been before. One organizing force was Harold Cardinal, leader of the Indian Association of Alberta. Cardinal penned *The Unjust Society,* which repudiated the Trudeau-Chrétien policy initiative and called for a national Native movement. In 1970, Cardinal orchestrated the writing of *Citizen Plus*, which many called the "Red Paper." This statement called for a reorganization of the Ministry of Indian Affairs as well as a new recognition of land claims (Champagne 1994, li–liv).

The protests hit their mark. On March 17, 1971, the Trudeau government withdrew its White Paper policies. The protests did not end. Continued pressure by Native groups reaped many rewards. The first obvious reward was a total reversal of the 1927 policy prohibiting collective political activity by Native peoples. Instead, the Canadian government agreed to sponsor and fund different groups that would be recognized as official voices. The Native Council of Canada was reorganized in 1971 as the official body representing Indians and Metis peoples. The Metis were also represented by the Metis National Council. The Inuit Tapirisat of Canada was formed in 1971 to represent peoples of the north. The National Indian Brotherhood was designated as the voice of indigenous Natives of the rest of Canada. It later was renamed the Assembly of First Nations (Long and Chiste 1994, 357–359; Mawhiney 1993).

The Land

Although the legal basis for most land acquisitions from Native peoples was secured through treaties or legislation, some lands were taken without legal authority. Moreover, many of the provisions under the treaties were not implemented. Native peoples were not always given required services or commodities. Natives interpreted provisions for "medicines" as being provisions for medical care, while provisions for education were recognized as including college education. Natives wanted the promises to be kept. As a result, a string of legal controversies have arisen seeking fulfillment of treaty obligations and demanding either the return of lands improperly taken or compensation for the takings.

Native Canadians headed for the courts and won a critical victory with the case of *Calder v. Attorney General* in 1973. As a result, Canada created the Office of Native Claims in 1974 (Long and Chiste 1994, 372–375). The major land claim involved the Inuit peoples (see below). Besides claims for ownership and use of lands, Native Canadians expressed a disdain for the degradation of lands caused by industrial activity, mining, and power projects. Lands have been damaged, and fish and game supplies killed. The health of the people has been threatened by pollution, and ways of life have been greatly disturbed. Inadequate funding of national programs to guard against environmental abuses has transformed these matters into ongoing issues of major concern. In the North a new Nunavut Territory for the Inuits is empowered to take action in this area; however, matters of expertise and funding such efforts remain outstanding.

The Inuits

For most of Canada's history, the Inuits were simply ignored. However, the Supreme Court ruled in the 1939 case of *In Re Eskimos* that the Inuits were covered by the provisions of the Indian Act. Whereas they had been bypassed by the treaty process, much of their land base had been used by others for various purposes—mining, power projects, military use. They had not been consulted, nor had they been compensated for the taking of their land. Their small numbers and dispersed and wandering communities led many to think that they did not exist. But they did exist, and with the collapse of the fur trade in the 1940s—a trade that gave them their economic livelihood—they turned to the national government for relief.

In the 1970s, their new national organization asserted a claim for full control of their lands. In 1975, they won an agreement granting them ownership of lands in northern Quebec on a basis similar to Native ownership of reserve lands. They won a settlement for east Arctic lands in 1976, and in 1984 they made an agreement to take possession of 240,000 square kilometers of west Arctic lands along with a $45 million settlement.

Another 1975 agreement upheld their rights to fish and hunt the lands without interference from outside governments. Claims to the ownership of additional lands continued to be discussed throughout the 1980s. Difficulties arose as other Native Canadians, specifically the Athabascan Dene peoples, also registered claims on much of the same land. Slowly a boundary settlement was engineered. The population of the Northwest Territories held a successful referendum in 1982 to approve a boundary that would be used to create the territory of Nunavut.

In 1991, the Canadian government agreed to separate off the eastern portion of the Northwest Territories and make a new territory to be called Nunavat. This 350,000-square-kilometer territory would have a civilian government, and its affairs would be conducted like those of the other territories, with a legislative council and an executive authority. The fact that 22,720—nearly 90 percent—of the population of Nunavut is Inuit means that the governmental structures are essentially controlled by these Natives. In addition, the 1991 settlement provided that the Inuit peoples would receive a grant of $580 million to support the governmental activities and to help establish new business enterprise. The new territorial government began operations in 1999 (Purich 1992; Long and Chiste 1994, 346–351; Dickason 2002).

Other Issues

The national government of Canada opened the door for charitable as well as provincially run gambling operations with passage of the Gambling Act of 1969. As a result, every province as well as the territories established lotteries and authorized charity bingo games. Several also authorized casino gambling either by charities or the provincial government. Native peoples reasoned that they should be permitted the same opportunities to have gambling enterprises.

In the United States, Congress passed an act that provided a method for establishing Native gambling. Canada's Parliament did not do so. However, in 1985 the prime minister and the premiers of the provinces entered an agreement for trading $100 million of provincial funds for a federal stipulation that they would not have a national lottery. The funds were used to replace a national sports lottery started to finance the Winter Olympic games held in Calgary, Alberta (Osborne and Campbell 1989).

The agreement was made without Native participation. However, as a result of the 1985 action, many Natives were left in a kind of "no man's land." Provinces told the Native bands that gambling was covered by federal law. Federal officials refused to grant bands authority to gamble on the basis that they had transferred all gambling authority to the provinces. In some cases, provincial police stopped Native gambling. In other places, the Royal Canadian Mounted Police moved to close down Native gambling operations.

Some provinces, however, have allowed Natives to have casinos. They include Ontario, Manitoba, and Saskatchewan. It appears that future gambling issues will be argued out on a band-by-band and province-by-province basis (Thompson and Dever 1994).

The Central Issue:
Strong Indigenous Communities

Although the Trudeau government had repudiated its own White Paper and had reversed its Termination policies in favor of self-government for Native Canada, its actions seemed hollow as it prepared for a constitutional conference of national and provincial leaders in order to amend the basic law of Canada in 1982. The associations representing the collective voices of Native Canada were completely left out of the conference. After the government heard protests from the groups, they offered to let the groups attend "as observers." This patronizing gesture was rejected, and Native Canada boycotted the 1982 conference.

Nonetheless, the conference did produce some favorable results for Native Canada. The new constitution (a revised British North American Act) provided that "The existing aboriginal and treaty rights . . . are . . . recognized and affirmed" (Section 35–1), and "aboriginal peoples . . . includes Indian, Inuit, and Metis . . ." (Section 35–1).

The 1982 conference also agreed that the provincial premiers and prime minister would confer each year with Native organizations on issues of concern to Native peoples. Such annual conferences were held for five years, but no major decisions were made. In 1987, at another national conference, the government leaders agreed to a statement of constitutional principles known as the Meech Lake Accord. The Accord recognized Quebec specifically as a "Distinct Society" and ignored Native peoples.

Native Canada was again incensed that the prime minister and premiers could recognize the special condition of a European settled province, but ignore the special existence of the indigenous peoples. The Accord was to take effect after being approved by all ten provinces. Native groups were not included in the ratification process. A deadline of June 23, 1990, was set for completion of the ratification process. As the date approached, all provinces but Manitoba had indicated approval for the Accord directly. Only Manitoba stood in the way.

The issue in Manitoba needed a special legislative rule in order to be debated and resolved before June 23. The special rule required unanimous consent. Native Canadian Elijah Harper was the only Native member of the Manitoba legislative body. His singular act of refusing to grant unanimous consent to debate and resolve the ratification process for the Meech Lake Accord meant that the Accord could not be ratified in Manitoba. That killed the Accord. Efforts to resolve national constitutional issues continued.

A 1992 meeting of the Canadian prime minister, provincial premiers, and the major Native association leaders drew up what became known as the Charlottetown Accord. The Accord promised cultural protection for all Native Canadians as well as "inherent" rights of self-government and autonomous control of natural resources. The rights were to be protected by Canadian courts. The Accord also brought the Metis directly under the provisions and programs authorized by the Indian Act. The Accord was endorsed by the leaders of the Native groups, but its approval was contingent upon the favorable vote of the entire Canadian electorate.

The main thrust of the Charlottetown Accord was directed toward the status of provincial-national relationships and, of course, the special demands of Quebec's special recognition. These provisions were not warmly embraced by non-French Canada, although the general electorate did indicate in opinion polls that they favored provisions for Canadian Natives. Those provisions were lost in the campaign rhetoric. On October 26, 1992, the electorate soundly defeated the Accord. Metis and Inuit voters had approved the Accord by large numbers. And while the Assembly of First Nations was enthusiastic about the Accord, over 62 percent of the Natives living on reserves said "No" with their votes (Champagne 1994, lii–liv; Long and Chiste 1994, 359–377).

The defeat of the Accord leaves the constitutional status of Native Canadians along with their pleas for special community rights up in the air. This status of "limbo" continues into the twenty-first century. Had the Quebec voters voted "Yes" for a modified separatism in 1995, the issue of Native sovereignty would be a priority concern in Canadian national politics. Indeed, several bands within Quebec Province had indicated that they would exercise their inherent sovereignty and declare independence from Quebec if Quebec sought any degree of independence from Canada. However, in a very close contest Quebec said "No" to separatism. That question will never be dead, nor will the quest for Native sovereignty ever disappear. A national consensus—even a consensus among Native Canadians—on questions of constitutional status and sovereignty remains elusive. One thing is certain, however. Native Canadians will continue to participate in the Canadian national system both as individuals and as collective units with an identity separate from that of other Canadians but with a desire shared with others for a better life and stronger communities than they have heretofore had within the Canadian system.

Concern for Native communities has increased immeasurably during the past decade. In 1991, the national Parliament appointed a Royal Commission on Aboriginal Peoples (RCAP). The Commission met over a four-year period expending a budget of $50 million and producing a five-volume, 3,537-page report that presented 440 recommendations. The theme of the report was oriented toward past wrongs done to Native peoples. The thrust of the recommendations was that there should be a threefold power relationship in Canada—among the national government, the provinces, and the Native peoples. At the onset of the report the Commission wrote, "at the heart of our recommendations is the recognition that Aboriginal peoples are peoples, that they form collectives of unique character, and that they have a right to governmental autonomy" (v. 1, p. 1).

Among the recommendations was a call to merge over 1,000 bands of Indians, Inuits, and Metis into sixty to eighty nations. The Commission also suggested that voluntary governments of Natives be formed among those that live within cities. Greater federal aid was suggested for the entire array of programs already serving Native people, as well as for many new programs.

The major findings lingered without action. Where there was extra funding of programs, the moneys were moved from other programs. However, Parliament did appropriate $350 million as a "healing fund," and the minister of Indian Affairs and Northern Development "apologized" for all manner of the past wrongs done to Native peoples.

As the report seemed to speak most directly to Indians, both Metis and Inuits were critical of its recommendations. So, too, were others who felt that the report emphasized a separateness for a nation already divided greatly over issues involving French-speaking Canadians in Quebec. The strongest critics of the Commission and the reaction to its report suggest that a wave of sentimental "political correctness" had descended upon the land. It was pointed out that many other Canadian groups had suffered grievous wrongs at the hands of both governments and other groups in society, yet they had been able to rise above their conditions of degradation and subjugation through individual hard work and an enterprising spirit. The critics claim that the solution to problems facing Native peoples will similarly be resolved through an independent spirit within individuals and their communities (see especially Flanaghan 2000).

References

Books and Articles

Burton, Lloyd. *American Indian Water Rights and the Limits of Law.* Lawrence: University Press of Kansas, 1991.

Canby, William. *American Indian Law in a Nutshell.* 2d ed. St. Paul, MN: West Publishing, 1988.

Cardinal, Harold. *The Unjust Society.* Edmonton: Hurtig, 1969.

Champagne, Duane. *Chronology of Native North American History.* Detroit: Gale Press, 1994.

Deloria, Vine. *Custer Died for Your Sins: An Indian Manifesto.* New York: Macmillan, 1969.

Deloria, Vine, Jr. *God Is Red.* 2d ed. Golden, CO: Fulcrum Publishing, 1994.

Dickason, Olive Patricia. *Canada's First Nations.* Oxford: Oxford University Press, 2002.

Easton, David. *The Political System: An Inquiry into the State of Political Science.* 2d ed. Chicago: University of Chicago Press, 1971.

Flanaghan, Tom. *First Nations? Second Thoughts.* Montreal: McGill-Queen's University Press, 2000.

Getches, David, Charles Wilkinson, and Robert A. Williams Jr. *Federal Indian Law.* 3d ed. St. Paul, MN: West Publishing, 1993.

Hawthorn, H. B. *A Survey of Contemporary Indians of Canada.* Ottawa: Indian Affairs Branch, 1966.

Hultkrantz, Ake. "Native Religions of North America." In H. Byron Earhart, ed. *Religious Traditions of the World.* San Francisco: HarperCollins, 1993, pp. 257–372.

Kellogg, Mark. "Indian Rights: Fighting Back with White Man's Weapons." *Saturday Review* (November 25, 1978): 24–27.

Leiby, Richard. "Bury My Heart at RFK." *The Washington Post* (November 6, 1994).

Long, J. Anthony, and Katherine Beaty Chiste. "The Canadian Natives." In Duane Champagne, ed. *Native America: Portrait of the Peoples.* Detroit: Visible Ink Press, 1994, pp. 331–377.

Mawhiney, Anne-Marie. *Towards Aboriginal Self-Government: Relations Between Status Indian Peoples and the Government of Canada 1969–1984.* New York: Garland Press, 1993.

Nesper, Larry. *The Walleye War: The Struggle for Ojibwe Spear Fishing and Treaty Rights.* Lincoln: University of Nebraska Press, 2002.

Osborne, Judith, and Collin Campbell. "Recent Amendments to Canadian Lottery and Gambling Laws: The Transfer of Power from Federal to Provincial Governments." In Colin Campbell and John Lowman, eds. *Gambling in Canada: Golden Goose or Trojan Horse?* Burnaby, BC: Simon Fraser University, 1989.

Parker, Linda S. *Native American Estate: The Struggle over Indian and Hawaiian Lands.* Honolulu: University of Hawaii Press, 1989.

Peregoy, Robert M. "Congress Overturns Supreme Court's Peyote Ruling." *NARF Legal Review* 20, no. 1 (January 1995): 1, 6–7.

Prucha, Francis Paul. *Documents of United States Indian Policy.* Lincoln: University of Nebraska Press, 1990.

Purich, Donald. *The Inuit and Their Land: The Story of Nunavut.* Toronto: Lorimer, 1992.

Royal Commission on Aboriginal Peoples. *Report.* Ottawa, Ontario: RCAP, 1991.

Shattuck, George C. *The Oneida Land Claims: A Legal History.* Syracuse, NY: Syracuse University Press, 1991.

Stein, M. L. "Change in Policy Draws Some Reader Complaints." *Editor and Publisher* (March 21, 1992).

Stewart, Omer C. *Peyote Religion.* Norman: University of Oklahoma Press, 1987.

Thompson, William N., and Diana Dever. "The Sovereign Games of North America: An Exploratory Study of First Nation Gaming Enterprise." In Colin Campbell, ed. *Gambling in Canada: The Bottom Line.* Burnaby, BC: Simon Fraser University, 1994, pp. 27–55.

Trope, J. T., and W. R. Echo Hawk. "The Native American Graves Protection Act: Background and Legislative History." *Arizona State Law Journal* 24 (Spring 1992): 23–40.

Utter, Jack. *American Indians: Answers to Today's Questions.* Lake Ann, MI: National Woodlands, 1993.

Walman, Carl, and Molly Braun. *Atlas of the North American Indian.* New York: Facts on File, 1985.

Western Conference of Attorneys General. *American Indian Law Desk Book.* Boulder: University of Colorado, 1993.

Wright, Ronald. *Stolen Continents.* Boston: Houghton Mifflin, 1992.

Wunder, John. *The Indian Bill of Rights.* New York: Garland, 1968.

Court Cases

Badoni v. Higginson, 638 F.2d (10th Circuit, 1980); cert. denied, 452 U.S. 954 (1981).

Brendale v. Yakima, 492 U.S. 408 (1989).

Bryan v. Itasca County, 426 U.S. 373 (1976).

Calder v. Attorney General of British Columbia, 1973 Supreme Court Report 313 (1973).

California v. Cabazon, 480 U.S. 202 (1987).

County of Yakima v. Yakima Indian Nation, 502 U.S. 251 (1992).

Davis v. Morton, 469 F.2d 593 (10th Circuit, 1972).

Eastern Band of Cherokee Indians v. U.S. and Cherokee Nation, West, 117 U.S. 288 (1886).

Employment Division, Department of Human Resources of Oregon v. Smith, 494 U.S. 872 (1990).

Ex Porte Crow Dog, 109 U.S. 556 (1883).

Gitlow v. New York, 268 U.S. 652 (1925).

In Re Eskimos, 1939 Sup. Ct. Reports 104 (1939)

Lac Flambeau Band v. Wisconsin, 742 F. Supp. 645 (W. Dist. Wisc., 1990).

Lyng v. Northwestern Indian Cemetery Protective Association, 485 U.S. 439 (1988).

Martinez v. Santa Clara, 436 U.S. 49 (1978).

Mashantucket Pequot v. Connecticut, 737 F. Supp. 169 (Dist. Ct. Conn., 1990).

Menominee Tribe v. U.S., 391 U.S. 404 (1968).

Merrion v. Jicarilla Tribe, 455 U.S. 130 (1981).

Oliphant v. Squamish Tribe, 434 U.S. 191 (1978).

Puyallup Tribe v. Washington Department of Game, I 391 U.S. 392 (1968); II 419 U.S. 1032 (a.k.a. *U.S. v. Washington*) (1973); III 433 U.S. 165 (1977).

Rice v. Rehner, 463 U.S. 713 (1983).

Roff v. Burney, 168 U.S. 218 (1897).

Seminole v. Butterworth, 658 F.2d. 310; cert. denied, 455 U.S. 1020 (1982).

Sequoyah v. T.V.A., 449 U.S. 953 (1980).

Superintendent of Five Civilized Tribes v. Commissioners, 295 U.S. 418 (1935).

Talton v. Mayes, 163 U.S. 376 (1896).

United States v. Rogers, 4 Howard 567 (1846).

United States v. Sioux Nation of Indians, 448 U.S. 371 (1980).

Washington v. Confederated Tribes of Colville, 447 U.S. 134 (1980).

Washington v. Washington State Commercial Passenger Fishing Vessel Association, 443 U.S. 658 (1979).

Williams v. Lee, 358 U.S. 217 (1959).

Winters v. United States, 207 U.S. 564 (1908).

Statutes

American Indian Religious Freedom Act of 1978, 92 U.S. Statute 469.

American Indian Religious Freedom Act Amendments of 1994 (Peyote Use Act), 108 U.S. Statute 3125.

Archaeological Resources Protection Act of 1979, 93 U.S. Statute 721.

Area Redevelopment Administration Act of 1961, 75 U.S. Statute 47.

Bald Eagle Protection Act of 1972, 86 U.S. Statute 1064.

General Allotment (Dawes) Act of 1887, 24 U.S. Statute 388.

Indian Child Welfare Act of 1978, 92 U.S. Statute 3069.

Indian Claims Commission Act of 1946, 60 U.S. Statute 1049.

Indian Financing Law of 1974, 88 U.S. Statute 77.

Indian Gaming Regulatory Act of 1988, 102 U.S. Statute 2467.

Indian Mineral Leasing Act of 1938, 52 U.S. Statute 347.

Indian Reorganization Act of 1934, 48 U.S. Statute 984.

Indian Self Determination and Educational Assistance Act of 1975, 88 U.S. Statute 2203.

Major Crimes Act of 1885, 23 U.S. Statute 385.

The National Museum of the American Indian Act of 1989, 103 U.S. Statute 1336.

Native American Grave Protection Act of 1990, 104 U.S. Statute 3048.

Public Law 280 (1952), 67 U.S. Statute 588.

Tribally Controlled Community College Assistance Act of 1978, 92 U.S. Statute 1325.

5

Chronology of Native America

The Origins of Native American Peoples

Native American religions, like almost all other religions, have stories about the Creation. Anthropological evidence of modern-day "scientific" standards do not verify religious origin stories—whether in the Garden of Eden or stories of people emerging out of the soil or descending from the sky. Rather, modern science demonstrates the existence of peoples at various places at various times and presents evidence of movements of peoples over the face of the earth. However, such evidence does not negate origin stories as reference points for interpreting events in the life of a people.

Native peoples are related to others who moved great distances over millennia of time. The movements were usually not constant, and they were generally not part of the history of single generations. That history was not reflected in written documentation. Much of it was lost as oral traditions of record keeping were built up by generations after generations of peoples who remained in singular locations and found references to a creator in specific places on the face of the earth. Before the physical evidence of origins is presented, a brief reference to the origin stories is appropriate.

Ake Hultkrantz's study of Native religions discerns two patterns of creation. Exemplifying the first pattern were Plains societies such as the Shoshone, which revolved around the hunt. Animals were central to the spiritual life, and their creator took a male form. He resided in the sky from where he sent animals and gave life to the people. In the second pattern, societies such as the

105

Zuni and Pueblos relied upon agriculture. Their spiritual life emphasized fertility and a quest for rain. The Creator was female, symbolizing "Mother Earth." Life came out of the soil, as did the people. Both kinds of society considered specific places as sacred. In these places, people first came to life. These places were on the American continents (Hultkrantz 1993).

Although there is physical evidence of movements between Asia and the American continents, this does not mean that it is totally accepted by everyone on scientific grounds. Cato Sells, the commissioner of Indian Affairs under President Wilson, ruled in 1914 that textbooks that classified Native Americans as part of the Asian races could not be used in boarding schools for Native Americans. The commissioner claimed that he was "advised by the best authority that the Indians are classed by the anthropologists as a 'distinct race'" (*New York Times* December 28, 1914).

50,000 BC– 3000 BC	Physical ancestors of Native Americans cross a land bridge called Beringa linking North America with Asia. The migration of peoples is probably motivated by the food supply tied to large animals that are moving in search of vegetation. Emerging and receding "Ice Ages" are responsible for changing the locations of food sources. There is also evidence that some Asian peoples used boats to make journeys in Pacific waters. Carbon dating techniques lead to conclusions that people may have been on North American soil as long as 50,000 years ago. Some evidence has also suggested that some of the early people on the continents may have been Caucasians.

Native Americans in the Western Hemisphere

25,000 BC– 15,000 BC	Tribal groups thrive in the American Southwest. Stone pointed weapons exist in New Mexico. The early era is called the Clovis era as many stone points are discovered near the town of Clovis.
10,000 BC– 6000 BC	Implements and artifacts are discovered in places throughout the continent. Technologies advance.

6000 BC– AD 1000	Settled agricultural communities become prevalent. Ceremonial mounds present evidence of permanent sites. The Anasazi emerge in the Southwest, as do the Mogollon and Hohokam peoples. The Adena, Hopewell, and Mississippian develop in the central region. Athabaskan peoples migrate from northern Canadian regions to the Southwest. Their descendants include the Navajo.
AD 1000 – AD 1492	Contacts are made between Native Americans and Norwegian explorers. The contacts are not friendly. Thorvald Erickson is killed in conflict. His brother Leif documents visit to the Americas but soon abandons notion of settlement (1004–1007). Mound-builders of the Midwest abandon communities, as do Anasazi of the Southwest. Hunger, disease, or struggles among tribes may have caused breakup of societies. Modern tribes develop. Dekanawidah and Hiawatha (or persons who take on their identities) conceive of the Iroquois Confederacy of Five Nations.
1492–1494	Under the Spanish flag, Christopher Columbus sails to the Western Hemisphere. He reaches the island of San Salvador and makes contact with the Arawak people. He calls these people "Indios" or "Indians," thinking that he has reached Asia. He starts a quest for gold. He sails back to Spain, while part of his crew establish a community called "Navidad." They mistreat the local people, and they are killed before Columbus returns on his second voyage in 1493. By 1494, Columbus enslaves the Arawak, forcing them to find gold. He takes 500 back to Spain as slaves, as Spanish colonization of the Americas begins.
1512	Spanish Law of Burgos is initiated by Bartholome de las Casas seeking justice for Native peoples. Slavery is forbidden, and Native rights are recognized if they obey a *requerimiento* stipulating sovereignty of the Church of Rome. However, the Spanish use the Na-

tives' ignorance of the *requerimiento* as an excuse to continue mistreatment and subjugation of the peoples.

1539   Francisco de Vitoria establishes philosophy that the Natives have ownership rights to lands. Spanish *conquistadors* in the Americas do not always agree.

1607   English settle Jamestown Colony and establish relationships with Natives in Virginia. Good relationships disintegrate, and wars continue from 1616 to 1631.

1620   Pilgrims land at Plymouth. Before they have arrived, the Natives in New England suffer from a smallpox epidemic due to contact with Europeans who land sporadically along the Atlantic Coast. Pilgrims are greeted by friendly Natives whose numbers include Squanto and Massasoit. Squanto had previously been kidnapped by English sailors and taken to Spain where he escaped and miraculously was able to find passage back to New England where he joins Massasoit's Wampanoag tribe. Massasoit makes a treaty of friendship with Pilgrims (1621). Peace lasts until his death in 1661.

1626   Dutch settlers purchase Manhattan Island from the Shinnecock. Dutch leader Peter Minuit engages in the first of continuing misunderstandings over acquisitions of lands, as he later purchases parts of the island from another tribe that claims hunting rights on the lands.

1629–1640   In 1629, the Puritans colonize Massachusetts Bay. They seek religious domination over Native peoples. They consider the smallpox epidemics to be a sign from God that the Puritans are entitled to rule Natives. The Puritans seek military domination as well. In 1637, the Puritans ally with other tribes and with Pilgrims to destroy most of the Pequot tribe in battle. The Puritans establish the first reservations in 1638 by making the Quinnipiac peoples move onto 1200 acres of their original lands, forbidding them either to leave or sell the lands or buy weapons or whiskey. However, Roger Williams protests the mistreatment of Native peoples. He establishes Rhode Island in 1636 and insists that settlers respect Native peoples and that they purchase any properties they utilize.

1640–1700   European settlers along the Atlantic Coast engage in fighting with Natives. The son of Massasoit, Metacom (called King Philip), objects to the Puritans' reservation policies. He instigates major battles in 1675 and 1676, but he is defeated.

Natives in the South also rise up against dominating English settlers only to be subdued in Bacon's Rebellion, 1676–1677. Spanish armies engage in years of conflict with the Pueblo peoples in the Southwest, conquering the Natives in 1692.

1700–1763   The English and the French vie for control of North America. Natives are allied with each side. Conflicts between English settlers and Natives continue. The Yamasee War occurs in Georgia between 1715 and 1717.

Colonists show concern over education of Native youth, as they establish the first Native school at William and Mary College in 1723.

As the final English-French war in America approaches, Benjamin Franklin creates the Albany Plan for uniting the British colonies in a common American government. His plan uses structures present in the Iroquois confederation. It is rejected at the Albany Congress in 1754. The War for America (French and Indian War) lasts from 1754 to 1763.

1763–1774   The English Parliament prohibits the colonists from moving across the Appalachian Mountains to form new settlements. In 1774, the western lands are put under the control of Quebec Province. The English hope to use the Native occupation of the lands as a control over the growth of the Colonies and their desires for independence. English law is violated by settlers who seek to push the Natives off their lands. The English control of the Great Lakes area is resisted by Pontiac. The chief creates an alliance among the Delaware, Ottawa, Ojibwas, Seneca, Pottawatomie, and Hurons. During hostilities in 1763, English General Jeffry Amherst is alleged to have authorized that smallpox-infested blankets be given to Native peoples. An unrelated smallpox epidemic weakens Pontiac's alliance, and the chief agrees to peace in 1765.

1769   Spanish priest Junipero Serra begins missions in California. By 1835, there are eighteen mission-fortresses from which the Spanish work to convert the Natives into Christian farmers. Many are captured and held in peonage while they are being "civilized" and "Christianized."

1775–1783 The American Revolution finds Native peoples fighting on each side. The Iroquois Confederacy is divided. The Oneida ally with the Americans, hoping to win the right to maintain traditional lands after the war. They are disappointed as the independent United States shows no gratitude. General John Sullivan leads the Americans in a campaign against the other Iroquois Nations. Native villages and crops are burned. The new Continental Congress divides the Colonies into districts. Each is given a commissioner who is empowered to negotiate treaties with Native peoples. The Articles of Confederation (written 1777, ratified 1781) places Native American affairs in the hands of the new national government.

1786–1787 Congress places Native American affairs into two departments—one for Northern states and one for Southern states.

           The government also establishes the first federally recognized reservations. The Northwest Ordinance of 1787 pledges national assistance for the education of Natives and indicates that lands will not be taken from them without their consent.

1787–1789   The U.S. Constitution is written and ratified. Congress is given powers to make laws involving Native Americans.

1790–1824   The first Trade and Intercourse Act is passed. This and subsequent acts passed from 1792 through the 1820s forbid persons from trading with Native Americans without permission of the national government. The government establishes twenty-eight trading houses to ensure that Natives receive fair dealings in trade, as well as to defeat commercial competition from the Spanish and English traders. Trading houses are abolished in 1822.

From 1803 to 1806 Meriwether Lewis and William Clark lead an expedition to explore the newly purchased Louisiana territories. Sacajawea, a Shoshone, acts as their interpreter, as they meet fifty tribes on their journey.

From 1806 to 1813, Shawnee brothers Tecumseh and "Prophet" Tenskwatawa organize Natives in the Northwest Territories against white settlers and the U.S. Army. Tribes reject treaties that seek to move them off their lands. However, the actions of Tecumseh in raising a Native military force and of Tenskwatawa in providing a spiritual message—"follow the traditional ways and you cannot be conquered"— only encourage the hostility of the United States. In 1811, General William Henry Harrison engages the Shawnee and allied forces under Tenskwatawa at Tippecanoe Creek in Indiana while Tecumseh is away recruiting his own forces. The Natives are forced to withdraw. Upon his return, Tecumseh finds that his allies have deserted him. He regroups and joins British forces (War of 1812) but is himself defeated and killed in 1813 at the battle of the Thames in Ontario.

1820s   The Cherokee in the Southeast represent everything that the United States desires among Native peoples. They embrace "civilization"; they become farmers; they dress as non-Natives. In 1821, the Cherokee Sequoyah develops a written alphabet of the Cherokee language. A newspaper is printed in the language. The Cherokee adopt a constitution, and the Bible is printed in their language. Unfortunately, gold is discovered on Cherokee lands, and the gold is pursued by non-Natives. The Cherokee are forced to leave their lands.

1823   The U.S. Bureau of Indian Affairs is created and placed in the War Department by order of the president. The action is formally recognized by an Act of Congress in 1834.

1830s   In 1830, President Andrew Jackson enunciates his policy of removing Native Americans from the eastern part of the United States to lands west of the Mississippi. Congress passes legislation supporting his policies. While he desires a voluntary removal, many tribes resist. Resistance is futile. In 1838 and 1839, 16,000 Cherokee are compelled to walk a "Trail of Tears" from Georgia to Oklahoma. Over 4,000 die during the winter march.

1846–1848   The Mexican War is successfully fought by the U.S. military. As a result, large areas occupied by Natives as well as Mexicans—Colorado, Utah, Nevada, California, Arizona, and New Mexico—come under the jurisdiction of the United States.

1848   Gold is discovered in California. The rush of non-Native gold-seekers into the state effectively destroys many Native communities. Gold rushers are willing to kill Natives to get to the gold. Native attempts to defend lands are considered "hostile" by American military, which intervenes. In a few brief decades, a population once as large as 100,000 is reduced to less than one-fifth that number.

1849   The Bureau of Indian Affairs is transferred from the War Department to a newly created Department of Interior.

1850   The British government negotiates treaties with Ojibwa in Canada. Natives agree to give up lands north of Lakes Huron and Superior in exchange for promises of hunting and fishing rights, supplies and goods, lump-sum payments, and annual payments. Native Canadians agree to settle on twenty-one reserves of land. The agreements (known as the Robinson-Huron and Robinson-Superior treaties) set the pattern for future treaties negotiated by the Canadian government and tribes between 1867 and 1921.

1854–1855   Washington and Oregon tribes yield lands to settlers who have pushed into their territories. Treaties guarantee their right to continue to fish and hunt in their traditional manner. These guarantees become major matters of contention in lawsuits over a hundred years later.

1861–1865   The Civil War years are years of tragedy for Natives. Many tribes in "Indian Territory" (in present-day Oklahoma) side with the Confederacy (particularly the Cherokee under leader John Ross). In 1862, Sioux warriors in Minnesota react to Indian Agents' corruption and failure to provide promised food by going on a rampage. Over 600 settlers are killed. The Sioux are held responsible collectively, and most are driven from the state. As many as 1,700 are taken prisoner, and thirty-nine of these are hanged.

            In 1863, Army forces under Kit Carson use a scorched earth policy, driving Navajos out of their Arizona homelands and forcing 8,000 on a "Long Walk" to New Mexico. Many die along the way. Others are allowed to return "home" in 1868. Carson's "war" tactics serve as a model for General William T.

Sherman's policy of burning a path through Georgia toward the end of the Civil War.

In 1864, U.S. Army troops in Colorado kill hundreds of Natives at Sand Creek. Gold-seekers had urged the government to subdue the Natives.

1867   The United States purchases Alaska from the Russian government. The sale brings many Native Alaskans—including Inuit (Eskimo) and Aleut—into a relationship with the U.S. government.

The British North American Act is passed creating the Confederation of Canada, which at first consisted of the provinces of Nova Scotia, New Brunswick, Quebec, and Ontario. The central government in Ottawa is given jurisdiction over relationships with all Natives in Canada.

1869–1870   The Metis peoples (of mixed Native and European heritage) resist the Canadian authority in their Manitoba communities. In 1869, the Red River Settlement of Metis (near present-day Winnipeg) rallies behind leader Louis Riel to oppose the intrusion of non-Metis settlers emigrating from eastern Canada. Riel creates a provisional government, but he is confronted by Canadian armed forces supporting the new settlers. Violence erupts in 1870, and the Metis are subdued. Many flee to lands further west. Riel moves to Montana.

1870   President Ulysses S. Grant institutes policies giving various Christian denominations control over the administration of specific reservations. Army officers are forbidden from holding positions as "Indian Agents." Within two years religious groups control seventy BIA agencies serving 200,000 Native Americans.

1874–1877   Dakota Sioux are subdued. Following the Minnesota uprising (1862), many Sioux are banned to Dakota Territory. Gold is discovered in 1874 in the Black

Hills. Non-Native settlers ignore treaties guaranteeing lands to Natives. The Army seeks to keep peace but inevitably finds itself in conflict with the Sioux. General George Armstrong Custer seeks to control the Natives. He misreads the strength of the forces of Crazy Horse and is killed along with 225 men at the Battle of Little Big Horn in Montana in 1876. The defeat mars the nation's centennial cerebration and leads to massive retaliation. Along with 900 Sioux followers, Crazy Horse surrenders in 1877 and is later killed while in federal custody.

1876   The Canadian Parliament passes the Indian Act. The Act asserts national authority over Native nations and defines the status of Native peoples. It forbids alcoholic beverages on reserves and restricts non-Native access to lands.

1877   Chief Joseph ignores a treaty banning his Nez Perce tribe from Idaho homelands. The U.S. Army is led on a 1,700-mile chase before capturing Joseph's small band. Exhausted and fearful for the women, children, and elderly of his tribe, he declares: "I will fight no more forever." The Nez Perce are allowed to return to a small portion of their homelands in Idaho in 1885.

1879   Captain Richard Pratt, who had served with the military in battles with Native Americans on the Plains, and later as a warden guarding Native prisoners, wins federal support for opening the first "Indian School" at Carlisle, Pennsylvania. A system of boarding schools is developed, and within ten years over 10,000 Native children are enrolled. Many of the children are removed from tribal homes against their will. Discipline is very strict, and the children are forced to speak English only, given English names, and required to dress as non-Natives. Pratt is convinced that these steps are needed in order to "civilize" Native peoples. Many children run away from the schools; others become despondent and homesick; many succumb to diseases.

1881–1883   Reform elements coalesce. In 1881, Helen Hunt Jackson's book, *A Century of Dishonor*, is published. A scathing condemnation of government policies toward Native peoples, it leads reformers to call for investigations and changes. The Women's National Indian Association is founded in Philadelphia, followed by the creation of the Indian Rights Association. In 1883, Quakers sponsor conferences on reform at Lake Mohonk, New York. The "reformers" embrace the policy of "assimilation."

1884   The Canadian Parliament passes a law forbidding the Potlatch ceremony by Native peoples. The ceremony is one in which tribal leaders give property away to demonstrate their community spirit. The law is not repealed until 1951.

1884–1885   Louis Riel returns to Canada to lead the Metis community of Saskatchewan in a new uprising against intruding settlers from the eastern part of Canada. Many of the events of 1869 and 1870 are repeated. Riel leads a provisional government of his peoples, but its authority is challenged by Ottawa. In 1885, Riel's Metis group skirmishes with the Royal Canadian Mounted Police. Several police are killed. The Canadian Army sends troops to Saskatchewan. The Metis are subdued, Riel is captured, and in November 1885 he is executed.

The 1884 decision in *Ex Parte Crow Dog* holds that Natives cannot be tried in federal courts for crimes committed on reservations. This leads Congress to pass the Major Crimes Act of 1885.

1886   Apache Chief Geronimo resists army suppression of his peoples for over a decade. He avoids capture by going across the Mexican border and hiding. Over 5,000 troops capture the leader in 1886. Geronimo and 500 of his followers—including women and children—are taken to prisons in Florida. They are released in 1894 but not allowed to return to their San Carlos, Arizona, lands until many years later.

1887   The General Allotment (Dawes) Act is passed as the achievement of reform forces demanding that Natives assimilate with other Americans. Tribal lands are broken up. Some are distributed to Natives, and others are sold to non-Natives. Natives are urged to become farmers, but much of the land given to them is not good farmland.

1889–1890   Wovoka, a Paiute from Nevada, experiences a vision and leads a religious movement called the Ghost Dance. He tells Native Americans that if they take up traditional ways and participate in the Ghost Dance, all of their lands will be returned to them and outsiders will leave them alone. Fearing that his message will cause the Native populations to rise up with arms against the U.S. authority, the Bureau of Indian Affairs bans the dance in 1890. Nonetheless, the Ghost Dance movement continues in Dakota Territory, where an attempt to break up a dance ceremony results in a melee. In the confusion, the U.S. Army attacks Wounded Knee—a basically unarmed Native community of men, women, and children, killing over 300.

1917–1918   Twelve thousand Native Americans—almost all volunteers—serve with the armed forces in World War I. In 1919, Congress recognizes their service with an act granting them U.S. citizenship.

1924   All Native Americans are given U.S. citizenship. Some states, however, continue to deny them the right to vote. Arizona does not grant the right until 1948.

1928   U.S. Senator Charles Curtis of Kansas is elected vice president of the United States on a ticket with Herbert Hoover. Curtis is a Native American raised with the Kaw Tribe.

            The *Meriam Report* is published. The report finds that living conditions for Native Americans are "deplorable." Rates of diseases are very high, poverty and hunger are rampant, and educational levels are low. The study provides a basis for the reform programs of John Collier in the 1930s.

1934–1936   John Collier serves as the head of the Bureau of Indian Affairs and seeks to implement policies of self-sufficiency and autonomy for Native Americans. Policies of assimilation (Dawes Act) are ended with the Indian Reorganization Act and the Johnson O'Malley Act (both 1934). Collier helps Native business ventures with the passage of the Indian Arts and Crafts Board Act (1936).

1941   Felix Cohen publishes the *Handbook of Federal Indian Law*. Considered a monumental work, it brings together laws, administrative rulings, court cases, and much historical detail from the first days of European Contact to the contemporary era. Updated versions are published until 1982.

1941–1945   Over 25,000 Native Americans serve in the military during World War II. Particularly distinguished service is given by Navajo code talkers who use their Native language to disguise messages so that Japanese enemy forces cannot understand them. Pima Native Ira Hayes is distinguished as one of six Marines raising the American flag atop Mount Surabachi on the Island of Iwo Jima. Although celebrated as a "war hero," Hayes finds readjustment to the poverty conditions of his reservation homeland very difficult. He moves to Chicago as part of the relocation program but cannot adjust to urban life either. In despair and addicted to alcohol, he returns to Arizona and his tribal home, where he dies tragically in 1955 at the age of thirty-two. His story is told in "The Ballad of Ira Hayes," by folk singer Johnny Cash, and in the feature film *The Outsider* where he is portrayed by actor Tony Curtis.

1945–1953   President Harry S Truman rejects John Collier's policies of Native self-sufficiency and autonomy. A new "Termination Era" begins. Dillon Myer—the man who ran the Japanese American internment camps during World War II—is placed in charge of the Bureau of Indian Affairs. He initiates a program to relocate Native Americans from reservations to urban communities.

1946   The Indian Claims Commission is created. It continues to operate until 1978, handling claims for lands wrongfully taken from Native Americans.

1951   The Canadian Indian Act is revised. Religious and cultural ceremonies such as the Potlatch and Sun Dance are permitted. Voting rights are extended to new groups of Native Canadians. (The Inuit win voting rights in 1950.)

1953   The Eisenhower administration continues Truman's policies. Congress passes a resolution enunciating the policy of Termination, along with legislation terminating several tribal organizations—including the Klamath in Oregon and the Menominee in Wisconsin. Congress passes Public Law 280 transferring criminal jurisdiction over Native Americans in several states from the federal to state governments.

1959   Alaska becomes a state. Alaskan Natives formalize demands for land, as the federal government begins granting Alaskan lands to the new state government. In 1971, the Alaska Claims Act resolves disputes by creating twelve regional Native corporations, giving the Natives forty million acres in land and grants of $962,500,000.

1961   The Kennedy administration rejects the Termination policies of the Truman-Eisenhower era.

The Congress of American Indians sponsors a conference in Chicago. It prepares a Declaration of Indian Purpose, which calls for economic development, more educational programs, better housing, and medical care.

1968   The American Indian Movement begins in Min-
        neapolis. It is led by Clyde Bellecourt, Mary Jane
        Wilson, and Dennis Banks. The focus of AIM is the
        urban Native Americans and the special problems
        urban Natives face. AIM gains attention because of
        its confrontational style of politics. In 1969, members
        of AIM take over Alcatraz Island, in 1970 they
        protest showings of the film *A Man Called Horse,* in
        1972 they participate in the takeover of BIA offices in
        Washington, D.C., and in 1973 they are involved in
        an occupation of Wounded Knee.

        The American Indian Civil Rights Act is passed
        guaranteeing many of the same rights to persons in-
        volved in interactions with tribal governments as
        they have in interactions with the federal or state
        governments.

1969   Dartmouth College drops the "Indians" as its sports
        teams' mascot. The action leads many other institu-
        tions around the country to consider how such mas-
        cots may denigrate Native peoples.

        On November 9, Alcatraz Island, formerly a federal
        prison, is occupied by AIM, which demands that the
        island be designated a cultural center for Natives.
        AIM cites an 1868 Sioux treaty that states that unused
        federal property shall revert to Native possession.
        The occupation does not end until June 11, 1971.

        The Canadian government issues a "White Paper"
        expressing its recommendation that Native Canadi-
        ans cease having special status and be assimilated
        into the general population and the general structure
        of law. The White Paper immediately arouses oppo-
        sition from Natives.

1971   The Canadian government withdraws the White
        Paper of 1969.

        The Native American Rights Fund is founded as a
        vehicle for providing legal services to Native Amer-

icans. The fund has been very helpful in many successful court battles for Native rights.

1972   Native Americans march from the Rosebud Sioux Reservation in South Dakota to Washington, D.C. The "Trail of Broken Treaties" march draws several hundred, including AIM activists. In Washington, about 500 of the marchers occupy the BIA building, and they hold it from November 2 to November 8. They list a "Twenty Points" program as a set of demands. The main "demand" is that the federal government reestablish the process of making treaties with Native Americans. President Nixon rejects the Twenty Points.

1973   Two hundred Native Americans occupy the village of Wounded Knee, South Dakota, in what they call Wounded Knee II. The group seeks the ouster of the "traditional" tribal government, which they claim is corrupt. FBI agents seek to end the occupation. Two Native Americans are killed in a firefight between the FBI and AIM members. A negotiated settlement ends the sixty-seven-day occupation. However, the atmosphere of violence continues at Pine Ridge. Two FBI agents and another Native are killed in gunfights in 1975. Leonard Peltier is convicted of one of the killings. His imprisonment remains a point of protest for many Native Americans.

The Canadian Supreme Court issues a ruling in the case of *Calder v. Attorney General* holding that Native peoples had legal ownership of lands before the Europeans came to Canada. The lands could be given up only through legal processes. The ruling leads the government to establish a claims office for Natives who had their lands seized illegally.

1977   An Indian Policy Review Commission issues a report after two years of work. The report calls for Native sovereignty and for the creation of a cabinet-level Department for Indian Affairs. Although the essential provisions of the report are ignored, the position of director of the BIA is elevated to assistant secretary of interior for Indian affairs.

1978   Native Americans "discover" the gambling enterprise. A Seminole reservation in Florida begins offering bingo games with prizes in excess of those allowed by state rules. Federal courts support the Seminoles. Native American gaming rapidly spreads across the United States.

1979   The Lakota Sioux of South Dakota win a court judgment of $122 million as compensation for the loss of the Black Hills. The tribe refuses the money. They want the land.

The U.S. Supreme Court rules in *Washington v. Washington State Commercial Passenger Fishing Vessel Association* that a treaty negotiated in 1855 allows tribes in Washington State to have up to one-half of the annual allotted salmon catch in the state.

1980   Congress passes the Maine Indian Claims Act granting a financial settlement of $81.5 million to Passamaquoddy, Penobscot, and Maliseet tribes. Part of the funds are used to purchase 300,000 acres of land, which is put into trust for the tribes.

1982   The Canadian Constitutional Act gives official recognition to Inuits, Metis, and Indians as "Aboriginal peoples of Canada," and it also recognizes the rights gained by Native Canadians through treaties.

1983–1987 The Canadian government conducts annual constitutional conferences with representatives of Native Canadian groups.

1987–1988 The Supreme Court upholds previous court rulings on Native American gaming in the case of *California v. Cabazon* in 1987. As a result, Congress passes the Indian Gaming Regulatory Act of 1988 to ensure that Native gaming is operated under national guidelines.

1989   The U.S. Senate releases a report showing that the Bureau of Indian Affairs has mismanaged lands and moneys held in trust for Native Americans. Millions of dollars have been lost through oil, mineral, and forest leases. More than $17 million was missing due to poor bookkeeping. The report urges that tribes be given greater control over their own assets and programs.

1990   The Meech Lake Accord on constitutional relationships in Canada is defeated. The Accord had offered special society status to Quebec but ignored Native peoples. Passage required approval of every provincial legislative body by late June 1990. However, Elijah Harper, a Native Canadian and member of the Manitoba legislature, refused to agree to a unanimous consent motion that was required so that the Accord could be voted on in Manitoba by the deadline set for passage.

1992   The voters of Canada reject the Charlottetown Accord. The Native Canadian vote is divided. The Accord would have increased Native rights of self-government but not as much as some Native groups desired.

            Native American Congressman Ben Nighthorse Campbell of Colorado is elected to serve in the U.S. Senate—the first Native American to serve in the Senate since Charles Curtis. He begins his Senate term as a Democrat but in 1995 changes parties and becomes a Republican. He announces his retirement in 2004.

1994   In April, President Clinton invites all tribal leaders in the United States to a conference at the White House. He pledges to deal with the tribes on a government-to-government basis.

1996   The Supreme Court rules that part of the Indian Gaming Regulatory Act is unconstitutional. In *Seminole Tribe v. Florida,* the Court holds that tribes may not sue states in order to compel negotiations to permit casino gambling. Tribes change strategies to win casino gambling compacts with states by offering to share gambling revenues with state governments. They also seek compacts through initiative votes in elections.

1998   Tribes finance an election (Proposition 5) to win a compact from California to allow casinos. They spend over $75 million in the campaign, while Nevada casinos spend one-third that amount in a futile effort to stop the compacts. Proposition 5 wins in the election, but in 1999 the California Supreme Court rules that it violates the state constitution.

The U.S. Supreme Court rules in *Kiowa Tribe v. Manufacturing Technologies* that tribes enjoy immunity from civil lawsuits against their commercial ventures, even if those businesses operate off-reservation lands.

1999   Nunavut Territory officially begins operation as a new unit of the Canadian government, run by and for Inuit peoples of the north. The territory is carved out of the Northwest Territories.

The U.S. Supreme Court rules in *Minnesota v. Mille Lacs Band of Chippewa Indians* that treaty rights guaranteeing hunting and fishing privileges are not suspended when the tribal lands become lands within a new state government. The Court holds that its interpretation of treaties with tribes will be liberally construed in favor of the tribes.

2000   California voters approve a new measure (Proposition 1A) to allow Native American casinos.

2001   An Ontario court rules that the Metis are Aboriginal people who are covered by Canadian laws regarding Native bands.

The U.S. Supreme Court rules in the cases *Nevada v. Hicks* and *Atkinson Trading Company v. Shirley* that the civil authority of tribes does not extend to lawsuits against non-Native government officials or to the taxation of activities taking place off-reservation lands.

2002   Forest fires devastate the White Mountain Apache reservation in Arizona destroying $300 million worth of timber.

Federal courts rule that scientists may examine the 9,300-year-old remains of a skeleton called "Kennewick Man" found in Washington State in 1996. It is determined that the remains do not have modern Native features and that the remains may be those of a Caucasian.

2003   Federal courts order the government to pay tribes in excess of $100 million for BIA misuse of trust funds. The suit is filed by 300,000 tribal members.

Federal courts permit the National Football League franchise in Washington, D.C., to have a patent on the name *Redskins*.

In the California election for governor, one candidate is forced to return $4 million in illegal contributions received from Native tribes.

The U.S. government blocks plans to put nuclear waste on Utah's Gosh Ute Reservation lands.

2004   President Bush's budget includes an additional $44 million in funding for recalculating royalties owed to Natives due to government misuse of trust funds.

The Museum of the American Indian opens on the Mall in Washington, D.C. It is built around the collection of George Gustav Heye. It is partially funded by $30 million in contributions from Native American casinos.

Voters reject the expansion of Native gaming in Washington State and California but allow its expansion in Oklahoma.

References

Hultkrantz, Ake. "Native Religions of North America." In H. Byron Earhart, ed., *Religious Traditions of the World*. San Francisco: Harper-Collins, 1993, pp. 257–372.

New York Times, December 28, 1914.

6

Biographies

People of Native heritage in North America have distinguished themselves in many leadership roles over the millennia. While Native political officials often governed by consensus, whereby they led by following, they quite frequently distinguished themselves in ways deserving of special recognition. Of course, there were many outstanding Native American leaders in military roles, but they made their presence felt in domestic roles as well, working for the health of their peoples, engaging in hunting and gathering pursuits, in education, in economic development, in statesmanship, and in political activism. In these myriad pursuits, leaders were of vital importance in preserving Native communities and in bringing new strength to communities.

Space allows us to recognize only a few of the great leaders from the past and the present. A dismaying statistic must precede our listings, however. The American people can visit two monumental collective memorials to those deemed the greatest Americans who have ever lived, but only one of these memorials honors any Native American. One of these memorial collections, the Hall of Fame for Great Americans in New York City, was begun in 1901 by renowned architect Sanford White. White designed a circular pathway enclosed by hundreds of columns, between which busts of over 100 "Greats" were displayed over the next century. Actually, 106 individuals were selected, but only 102 statues were finished and put on display. Selections were made by private individuals working with New York University. The display was originally located on land owned by the university in the Bronx. The busts were commissioned and funded privately. Ownership of the land and display was transferred to the Bronx Community

College of the City University of New York in 1973. The display stands on the highest natural point in New York City. Sadly, not one Native American is honored in the display.

The other collection of honored persons is found in Washington, D.C., in the Capitol Building. Statues of these "greats" appear in the side rotunda of the Capitol, designated as the Hall of Columns and the National Statuary Hall. By official action of Congress in 1864, each of the states selects two individuals for inclusion in this collection. The selections are official ones, made by legislative bodies, and the states must finance the sculptors' work. The financial endeavor usually involves a cooperative public-private effort. Unlike the collection in New York City, this one does honor individuals with an indigenous heritage. Seven of the entries, in fact, are Native people: Hawaii's Kamehameha I; North Dakota's Sacajawea; Oklahoma's Will Rogers and Sequoyah; Wyoming's Washakie; Nevada's Sarah Winnemucca; and New Mexico's Popé, a statue that still remains to be installed.

As Nevada is my adopted home state, I want to confer special honor on Sarah Winnemucca for her exemplary accomplishments, which were often made in the face of adversity and amid much criticism. Not only does she merit prominence by being placed on the cover of this book, but she also leads the list of Native biographies in this chapter. Sarah Winnemucca's biography is followed by resumes of the other Natives in the hall of honor in the Capitol Building and then by other renowned Natives. Rounding out this chapter are non-Natives whose actions added strength to Native communities.

Native Americans Honored in National Capitol

Sarah Winnemucca (1842–1891)

Nevada's 2002 entry into the Statuary Hall collection is a notable individual whose life and life message bridged gaps between Native and non-Native cultures. She was a strong advocate for her Paiute people in their struggles with the American government, while at the same time she expressed much admiration for non-Natives. Twice she married non-Native men.

Sarah Winnemucca was in terms of "blood" quantum 100 percent Native American. Yet in today's world where political correctness is so pervasive some Natives of much less indigenous heritage are very critical of her activities and her writings. Others show only admiration for her accomplishments. In 2001, the Nevada legislature passed a law to raise funds so she could be honored as one of the two most notable persons who had lived in the state. Her autobiography, *Life among the Piutes* [sic]: *Their Wrongs and Claims,* was published in 1883 and was considered the first book written by a Native. Its publication earned her a place in the Nevada Writers Hall of Fame. She is also in the National Woman's Hall of Fame. She was the only woman to have been the chief of the Paiute people.

Sarah Winnemucca was born with the Native name of "Thocmetony," which means "shell flower." Her birth date has been listed as both 1842 and 1844 by different sources. She was born on Paiute lands near Pyramid Lake in western Nevada and became acquainted with non-Natives early in her life. Her grand-father was the Northern Paiute chief "Captain Truckee," who fought alongside of John C. Fremont as American settlers expelled Mexican troops from California. Truckee became a guide for new settlers coming to California. He brought his granddaughter to California and enrolled her in a convent school. She learned both English and Spanish, and she was able to write in both languages.

In California she worked with the U.S. Army as an inter-preter. Her first husband was Army Lieutenant Edward Bartlett. After that marriage ended, Sarah Winnemucca became a teacher for Paiutes who had been removed from Nevada to an Oregon reservation. In the late 1870s, she took up the cause of her wronged people and assumed the role of political lobbyist and ac-tivist. While she was always a peacemaker between Natives and non-Natives, she began to agitate for justice in a national speak-ing tour. Her abilities to articulate her cause took her on a lecture tour. She gave 350 speeches, and she won the friendship of many influential people, including Ralph Waldo Emerson, Elizabeth Palmer Peabody, and Mary Mann, widow of Horace Mann.

Mary Mann encouraged Sarah to write her book and helped publish it. Sarah's friends helped her with her most special pro-ject, a Native American school run by Native Americans. The school became a reality in Lovelock, Nevada, in 1884. After the failure of her second marriage, to Lieutenant Lewis Hopkins, she left the school to live with her sister in Idaho and died there in 1891, disappointed by her failure to help her people through national legislation. Earlier, she had befriended U.S. Senator Henry Dawes of Massachusetts and had worked with him to pass the 1887 Act, which sought to assimilate Native people with other Americans. The Act was soon seen as a failed effort; among the Act's failures was its requirement that her school no longer service Native children because it was not under national authority.

Kamehameha I (1758–1819)

The text of this book does not specifically discuss Pacific Island Natives or indigenous peoples; this is an oversight made for the purpose of text length. The oversight is admitted. Nevertheless, the indigenous of Hawaii and islands such as Samoa and Guam could be considered Native Americans; thus, the author would like to recognize one Pacific Islander who was selected by the state of Hawaii for a place of honor in the nation's capitol. Recognition is therefore appropriate for Kamehameha I for his leadership of people indigenous to Hawaii. This king of his peoples was born in about 1758 on the island of Hawaii. He was considered to have divine powers and to possess superhuman strength and courage as a warrior. His military skills also benefited from the arms he acquired from British Navy forces.

Kamehameha may have been exceedingly vicious and cruel on the battlefield, but nonetheless, his military actions resulted in the unification of all the inhabitants of the islands of Hawaii in 1810. In civilian roles he was recognized as a unifier who peacefully opened up Hawaii to international trade.

Popé (c.1630–c.1690)

Popé (pronounced Popay) organized his Pueblo peoples in what is now New Mexico and led them in a successful revolt against Spanish colonial rulers in the region. The Spanish were harsh and brutal against those indigenous peoples who would not comply with the requirement that they convert to Christianity and give their labor to the building of Catholic churches.

After three generations of oppression, the Pueblo armies attacked the Spanish on August 10, 1680. The attack continued until the Spanish were driven out of New Mexico to El Paso. Over 400 Spanish soldiers and civilians were killed. It was the first successful revolution against foreign rulers in North America. The Pueblos retained their self-rule until 1692 when a new invasion of a larger Spanish army force came to their lands.

Will Rogers (1879–1935)

Will Penn Adair Rogers was born of Cherokee heritage in 1879 near present-day Claremont, Oklahoma, which was then Indian Territory. He became a leading national figure as an author, lecturer, film actor, stage entertainer, and radio personality. His regular column of political and daily events of life appeared in 350 newspapers. He was also a cowboy performer. He was in fifty silent movies and twenty-one talking features. At the time of his death in 1935, he was considered America's premier humorist. A frequent traveler abroad, he was also world renowned. He died with pilot Wiley Post in an air crash in Alaska. His most well-known remark was simply, "I never met a man I didn't like."

Sacajawea (c.1787–1812)

Sacajawea, as interpreter for the Lewis and Clark expedition in the early nineteenth century, played a major role in the exploration of western lands in the United States. Sacajawea, whose name means "little bird," was born among the Shoshone people in Idaho, but as a child she was captured during hostilities with other tribes and sold into slavery to a French Canadian trader, who met the expedition as they traveled up the Missouri River. Through her skill with languages, she soon joined the explorers. Miraculously, during the expedition she was reunited with her Shoshone relatives, who proceeded to shower Lewis and Clark with gifts of horses, shelter, and food. The date of her death is a mystery, with some claiming she may have died on the Wind River Reservation in Wyoming in 1884. Clark's personal journals, written between 1825 and 1828, listed her as deceased.

Sequoyah (1770–1843)

Two Cherokee leaders—Sequoyah and John Ross (Ross is profiled later)—attempted to guide their people toward fulfilling the vision that Jefferson and others in the young American Republic set forth for them. They sought to become like the Americans who had settled near their lands.

Sequoyah was born in 1770 of mixed (Cherokee and European) parents and achieved notice as a skilled farmer and hunter. He willingly served under the command of Andrew Jackson in battles against the Creek. In the 1820s he invented a set of symbols (called a syllabary) for the Cherokee language. With this new written language he translated the Bible and also published a weekly newspaper for his peoples. Sequoyah also became involved in efforts to rebuild a united Cherokee people after migrations tore apart unity in the 1830s. He died in 1843 during a quest to find a lost band of his peoples.

Washakie (c. 1800–1900)

Washakie's bronze statue was placed among the Statuary Hall collection in 2000 by the state of Wyoming. His placement in a century year was quite appropriate, for he was reported to have been born and to have died in century years. He was the only known Native at the time of his death to have been given a full military funeral and burial.

Washakie was born among the Salish tribe in Montana. His father was a Flathead, and his mother a Shoshone, the tribe with which he later identified. By 1850, Washakie was renowned as a warrior, and he became the chief of the Eastern Shoshone people. Because the Shoshone were engaged in hostilities with the Sioux and Cheyenne, he sought allies with the U.S. Army. He claimed friendships with John C. Fremont, Kit Carson, and Jim Bridger (Bridger would became his son-in-law). Washakie built up his tribe with government grants for schools, churches, and hospitals. He was instrumental in establishing the Wind River Reservation as a permanent homeland for the Eastern Shoshone in Wyoming.

Other Distinguished Native Americans

Dennis Banks (1930–)

Dennis Banks was born in 1930 on the Leech Lake Chippewa Reservation in Minnesota. He was among the co-founders of the militant American Indian Movement (AIM) in 1968, the organization that was involved in the struggles for Native hunting and fishing rights and other causes. Banks was at the helm during the 1973 protest at Custer, South Dakota, which led to the seventy-three-day occupation of Wounded Knee. Banks has established himself as a credible actor, starring along with Native Russell Means in the 1992 film *The Last of the Mohicans*. (*See also* Russell Means.)

Clyde Bellecourte (1939–)

Clyde Bellecourte was born in 1939 on the White Earth Reservation in Minnesota. Along with Dennis Banks, he participated in the seventy-three-day occupation of Wounded Knee and also helped draft the "Twenty Points" presented to President Nixon after the occupation of the Bureau of Indian Affairs headquarters in 1972. (*See also* Dennis Banks.)

Robert La Follette Bennett (1912–)

In 1966, Robert La Follette Bennett became the second Native American to hold the post of commissioner of the Bureau of Indian Affairs. Bennett was born on the Wisconsin Oneida Reservation in 1912 and studied at the Haskell Institute in Kansas. After graduation, he became a clerk in the Bureau of Indian Affairs in Washington. He soon was serving as a field officer on the Navajo and Ute reservations. Returning to Washington, he received a law degree from Southwestern School of Law, after which he again returned to the Navajo reservation. He also served a tour of duty with the Marine Corps, coming back once more to the Bureau in Washington. In 1966, President Lyndon Johnson elevated him to the top post in the Bureau. In that office Bennett worked to dismantle Termination policies and to encourage the advancement of Native peoples in government positions. He left the Bureau in 1969 and subsequently established a Native American Athletic Hall of Fame, and he has directed the American Indian Law Center at the University of New Mexico.

Ben Nighthorse Campbell (1933–)

A member of the Northern Cheyenne tribe, Ben Nighthorse Campbell was elected to the United States Senate from Colorado in 1992. He served through 2004. Campbell was born in California in 1933. After service in the U.S. Air Force, he attended San Jose State College, graduating in 1957. He excelled in sports, becoming a three-time United States Judo champion in his weight class. He was on the 1964 United States Olympic Team that competed in

Tokyo. Campbell also had business interests, notably ranching and jewelry design.

Campbell was elected to the Colorado legislature in 1983 and to the U.S. House of Representatives in 1987. In 1995, after serving two years in the Senate, he switched his party affiliation from Democrat to Republican. As a member of Congress, he sponsored improvements in the Indian Arts and Craft Act, and he promoted the creation of the Smithsonian Museum of the American Indian, as well as the renaming of Custer National Battlefield Monument as the Little Bighorn National Battlefield Monument.

Harold Cardinal (1945–)

Harold Cardinal, a Cree Indian, was born in 1945 in Alberta. He achieved prominence as a young author. He wrote *The Unjust Society: The Tragedy of Canada's Indians* in 1969, when he was only 24 years of age. In the same year, the Trudeau government issued its "White Paper," and it was Cardinal who was selected to write the Native response. It was published in 1970 as *Citizens Plus* but is commonly known as the "Red Paper." This activity as a voice for Canada's Natives led to Cardinal's election to prominent positions with Native organizations. He has served as the president of the Indian Association of Alberta and as vice president of the Assembly of First Nations.

Matthew Coon Come (1956–)

Matthew Coon Come served as the grand chief of 12,000 Cree Natives of northern Quebec. He achieved considerable renown for challenging separatists in Quebec for their neglect of the traditional rights of indigenous Canadians while espousing an essentially French ethnic nationalism. Coon Come indicated that while the French of Quebec might wish to leave Canada, the Native people of Quebec intended to stay.

Coon Come attended residential schools as a child and went on to study political science at Trent University and law at McGill University. Later, when he became the leader of the Assembly of First Nations, he led the fight for Native fishing rights; he also urged a revision of the National Indian Act to include provisions of the Canadian Human Rights Act. He also encountered considerable criticism from other Natives for his outspoken attacks on alcohol and tobacco use by tribal leaders.

Nellie Cornoyea (1940–)

The self-educated Nellie Cornoyea was born in 1940 near Aklavik in the western Arctic region. She turned to public affairs after working with a Canadian Broadcasting Company radio station in the Northwest Territory town of Inuvik. Soon she was a leading spokesperson for the Inuit peoples. She actively pursued land claims on behalf of her peoples, and she was influential in gaining the agreement that has led to the creation of a new territory—Nunavut—which is comprised of mostly Inuit peoples. She is a leader in the Inuit Tapirisat of Canada, the group that speaks for her peoples at national constitutional conferences. For many years she has held an elected seat in the Northwest Territory legislative body and in 1991 was elected leader of that body.

Crazy Horse (1842–1877)

Among the leaders of the Native American forces at the Battle of Little Big Horn was Crazy Horse, a Sioux born in the Black Hills in 1842. The federal government responded to General Custer's embarrassing defeat by sending overwhelming numbers of military men to the Plains. The Native Americans could not match the superiority of the federal army. Crazy Horse surrendered in May 1877 and was murdered while in confinement four months later. (*See also* Sitting Bull.)

Crowfoot (1830–1890)

Crowfoot was born a Blood in about 1830 and gained fame as the leader of the Blackfoot Confederacy in Alberta.

The confederacy included his own Bloods, the Sarce, Peigan, and Blackfoot tribes. The chief represented the Native peoples of Alberta in negotiations for Treaty Seven in 1877. Crowfoot always sought peace. He therefore refused to join Sitting Bull in the Sioux wars against the U.S. Army, but he did give Sitting Bull refuge after the Army pushed him out of Montana. Crowfoot died in 1890.

Charles Curtis (1860–1936)

Charles Curtis was the consummate politician of his era. He was born in 1860 of mixed heritage, tracing his lineage back to a chief of the Kaws and also to members of the Osage tribe. While his blood quantum was probably only between one-quarter and one-half Native, he openly identified with that heritage, using it for his political advantage. His political positions were not designed to appeal to Native voters; rather, they were calculated to appeal to whatever combination of voters he needed to get elected. He was born in Kansas and spent some part of his childhood on Kaw lands.

When Curtis entered politics, he was clearly a Kansas Republican above all else. He was a spokesman for agriculture and free enterprise, Prohibition, the gold standard, Americanism, and other values dear to the hearts of the non-Native Kansas population. He championed women's suffrage, and he lobbied hard to win federal programs for his state and for his Kaw people. He was a very effective compromiser, and as a congressman and a U.S. senator he became the dominant voice on committees dealing with Native American policy. He engineered the passage of the Curtis Act, which effectively destroyed "Indian Territory" and opened almost all of Oklahoma for new settlement. The Act extended the allotment provisions of the Dawes Act to Oklahoma. Curtis was an assimilationist, and he truly believed, as did many Natives of mixed blood, that the future of Native communities lay in adapting to the larger society. He adapted very well indeed, being picked as Herbert Hoover's running mate in the 1928 presidential election and serving as vice president of the United States from 1929 through 1933. He was defeated for reelection on the Hoover ticket in 1932 and died four years later.

Adaptation and irony were hallmarks of Curtis's career. He had actually been baptized in the Roman Catholic faith on a Potawatomi reservation in Kansas in 1863, but he became a lifelong Methodist—a much better fit in Kansas and American politics of the time. Ironically, this "baptized" Catholic became vice president in the 1928 election, when his ticket defeated Democratic candidate Al Smith, who was much maligned in the campaign for his Catholicism. Smith could not adapt politically. Curtis could, and in the process he achieved the highest political position ever held by a Native American in the U.S. government.

Ada E. Deer (1935–)

Ada E. Deer became assistant secretary for Indian affairs in the Department of the Interior in 1993. She had earned the appointment with a life-long devotion to justice for Native peoples. One of her priorities was the restoration of tribal status for her Menominees in Wisconsin. The Menominees were one of the largest tribes to suffer termination in the 1950s.

Deer was born in Keshena on the Menominee reservation in 1935. She was educated in public schools and received a bachelor's degree in social work from the University of Wisconsin in Madison, the first member of her peoples to receive a degree from that university. She then became the first Native American to earn a master's degree in social work from Columbia University. Deer subsequently served as a social worker in New York City and Milwaukee, as well as being a Peace Corps volunteer in Panama. In the 1970s, she returned to her Menominee home to help engineer the campaign for renewed federal recognition of her peoples. She formed a political action group called Determined Rights and Unity for Menominee Shareholders (DRUMS), and with the help of the Native American Rights Fund won congressional enactment of a restoration bill. President Nixon signed the restoration act on December 22, 1973. Ada E. Deer returned to Madison where she taught in the American Indian Studies program until 1993 when President Clinton selected her as head of the Bureau of Indian Affairs.

Dekanawidah (c. 14th century)

Various Iroquois tribes were engaged in constant combat with one another during the fourteenth and fifteenth centuries. The fighting destroyed opportunities for a productive existence. Dekanawidah came from an outside tribe, the Hurons. Born to fulfill a mission of peace in a foreign land, he became known as the peacemaker. It was in that capacity that he traveled to Mohawk (one of the Iroquois tribes) country to spread the word of peace. As he traveled, he conceptualized a plan of confederate government among all five Iroquois tribes—Mohawk, Onondaga, Oneida, Cayuga, and Seneca. However, the visionary Dekanawidah had a speech impairment, and his ability to use oral argument to convince the peoples of the need for confederation was limited. Fortunately for him, he met the very articulate Hiawatha, who was living among the Onondaga. (*See also* Hiawatha.)

George Erasmus (1948–)

George Erasmus was born on August 8, 1948, in the Northwest Territories. He became activated into political affairs as the result of a reaction to the "White Paper" of 1969. He led the Dene peoples in their opposition to the national assimilation policy, and he also was prominent in the Denes' attempts to stop construction of a petroleum pipeline in their northern homelands. In 1985, he became the leader of the Assembly of First Nations. He represented the assembly as its spokesman at the Canadian constitutional conferences from 1983 through 1987.

Peter Fontaine (1944–)

In 1997, Peter Fontaine was selected as the national chief of the Assembly of First Nations. He has also served as the president of the National Congress of American Indians. In his role as the leader of the Canadian First Nations, he built bridges with indigenous peoples throughout North America.

Fontaine, an Anishabe, was also the chief of the Sagkeeng peoples of Manitoba. As a Native leader, he was the first person to publicly expose serious abuses in the operations of the Residential Schools for Canadian Natives. He also began child and family services, as well as Canada's first on-reserve treatment center for alcohol abuse. Fontaine resigned his posts with Native associations to take an official seat as the chief commissioner of the Canada Indian Claims Commission.

Geronimo (1829–1909)

Geronimo was born in the late 1820s on Apache lands, which were first claimed by the Spanish, then the Mexican Nation, and later by the United States. The Apache, however, resisted all outsiders' claims on their homes. The Apache did not sign treaties in exchange for promises. They fought. As the nineteenth century unfolded, Geronimo became the leader of their fights.

Geronimo personally suffered the pains of war, as Mexican armies raided his village killing his mother, wife, and three children. Geronimo retaliated with more fighting. Soon he led raid after raid into Mexican territory to steal cattle and other goods.

The Apaches and the U.S. Army began to engage in conflicts in the 1860s and 1870s as the federal government desired peace along trade routes and routes for westward settlers. Several Apache groups were pushed onto reservations by force. Geronimo himself was apprehended in 1876 and confined to the San Carlos Reservation. From there he escaped with a contingent of about seventy-five men into the Mexican hills. From Mexico he launched hit-and-run attacks on American troops. The American armies sent more and more forces after him. As many as 5,000 soldiers were involved in a pursuit that led into Mexico. Finally, Geronimo was surrounded, and in 1886 he surrendered. The U.S. Army then placed the Apache leader and 500 other Apaches in chains and exiled them to a prison first in Florida and then in Alabama. Quanah Parker negotiated to allow Geronimo and his peoples to come to his Oklahoma reservation in 1894, where the leader died in 1909. Geronimo was never permitted to return to his Arizona homelands.

Tim Giago (1934–)

Tim Giago, one of the leading spokesmen for Native America, is the editor of *Indian Country Today,* the premier print news media outlet for Native peoples. He was born on the Pine Ridge Reservation in South Dakota in 1934. After a high school education at a Catholic mission school, he joined the Navy and was wounded during the Korean War. After the war, Giago returned to the United States to work several "odd jobs" mixed with a college education at the University of Nevada, Reno, and later Harvard University.

Giago began a journalism career in Rapid City in 1979. Two years later he launched his own newspaper, known as the *Lakota Times.* It later became *Indian Country Today,* and its editions are published in both Rapid City and Scottsdale, Arizona. Circulation now exceeds 50,000. Giago also writes syndicated columns for the Knight Ridder News Service. His articles have appeared in all the leading newspapers in the United States. He has received many journalism and human rights awards for his defense of the Native community and his rejection of the degradation of Native peoples in the symbols of the sports world. Giago has written several books on Native culture including *The Aboriginal Sin* and *Notes from Indian Country*.

Elijah Harper (1949–)

As a member of Manitoba's Parliament, Elijah Harper refused to agree to a call for unanimous consent and thereby singlehandedly caused the defeat of the Meech Lake Accords. The Accords guaranteed extra rights to Quebec but totally ignored the indigenous people of Canada.

An Ojibwa-Cree, Harper was born at the Red Sucker Lake Reserve in northern Manitoba in 1949. He completed high school in Winnipeg and then earned a degree in anthropology from the University of Manitoba. He was elected chief of his reserve, and in 1981, he won a seat in the provincial parliament. In 1993, he was elected to the House of Commons in Ottawa. In 1995, he helped organize the first Sacred Assembly of First Nations People in Hull, Quebec.

Hiawatha (c. 14th century)

Hiawatha, a member of the Onondaga tribe, had a vision that commanded him to help the Iroquois people achieve peace. Hiawatha became a spokesman for Dekanawidah, a member of the Hurons, who also had a vision for peace for the five Iroquois tribes but was unable to communicate his vision effectively. The two traveled among all the tribes, convincing forty-nine chiefs of the need to adopt the plan for a common government council among the five. The Iroquois League achieved peace, and working together, the five tribes—later joined by the Tuscaroras from North Carolina—made the Iroquois the most powerful Native American people in the Northeast. The Iroquois League also became a model of federal government closely examined by the Founding Fathers. The Iroquois League survived for over 300 years, finally breaking up as a result of divided alliances during the Revolutionary War.

Chief Joseph (1840–1904)

Chief Joseph, known to his people as Hin-mah-too-Yah-lat-kekt, was born about 1840. Joseph's father (Old Chief Joseph) was a leader among the Wallowas, a tribe of Nez Perce peoples. The younger Joseph spent a quiet childhood in northeastern Oregon. But an influx of gold-seekers changed his people in the 1860s. Some Nez Perce bands signed away their lands in treaties, but the Wallowas refused to do so. Nonetheless, U.S. government officials sought to force the Wallowas Nez Perce onto reservations away from their homes.

Joseph's father died in 1871, and the younger Joseph assumed leadership in May 1877 when the order to move was given by Army General O. O. Howard. In June, three tribal youth avenged a perceived wrong by murdering a settler. Soon settler-Native skirmishes erupted, ending only after twenty-one settlers were killed. The U.S. Army decided that a wholesale attack on Natives refusing to move was justified. Chief Joseph rallied his followers, and at the Battle of White Bird Canyon his forces defeated the Army, killing thirty-three U.S. soldiers while suffering no casualties. The Army regrouped and called for more troops and heavy weapons.

Chief Joseph and about 750 followers (155 were warriors, the rest elderly, women, and children) chose to run rather than surrender or die fighting a much larger force. They ultimately sought refuge in Canada among Sitting Bull's people. Sitting Bull had escaped to Canada after the Battle of Little Big Horn. For four months Joseph led his followers over a 1,500-mile trail of harsh terrain. He won many small skirmishes as he kept eluding the larger American army. However, within a day's travel of the Canadian border he and 400 followers surrendered. Many of the children and elderly were too weak to go on, and he would not leave them. Several hundred others were able to make the border and escape. The Nez Perce that surrendered were imprisoned and with Chief Joseph moved to Indian Territory (now Oklahoma). In 1884, they were permitted to move to Washington and the Colville Reservation. There Joseph died in 1904, never being allowed to return to his homelands in Oregon and Idaho. A Nez Perce reservation was later established in Idaho.

Philip Martin (1926–)

Philip Martin, tribal chief of the Mississippi Choctaw, is recognized as a premier Native American official in terms of promoting tribal self-sufficiency and economic development. Martin was born in Philadelphia, Mississippi, in 1926. The segregated education system in the South at the time left no provision for public education of Native peoples beyond basic grades. Therefore, Martin attended the Cherokee High School in North Carolina. Afterward, he served in the U.S. Air Force for ten years. The "outside" experience gave him ideas for helping his people. He returned to the Choctaw lands in the mid-1950s and began a career of public service. He was on the tribal council, housing authority, and community action council, prior to becoming chief in 1959. His tenure has seen the development of Chata Enterprises, Choctaw Electronics Company, the Silver Star Casino, as well as an industrial park that furnishes space to outside private companies, including Ford Motor Company and American Greeting Cards. Martin's efforts are considered a model for other Native American tribes, and he has been recognized countless times for his leadership.

Massasoit (1580–1661)

Massasoit, the leader of the Wampanoag, was born in 1580. He controlled the peoples who occupied the Massachusetts coastal lands at the time of the arrival of the Pilgrims (1620) and Puritans (1630). Massasoit was of vital importance in maintaining peace between his people and the new English settlers. He helped the Pilgrims build a food supply by instructing them in farming and hunting in the wilderness. As the English continually pushed their presence onto Native lands, tensions grew. However, through the leadership of Massasoit, peace continued until his death in 1661. In this task he was aided by Squanto. (*See also* Metacom; Squanto.)

Russell Means (1940–)

Russell Means was born in 1940 near Wounded Knee on the Pine Ridge Reservation. Early in his life he was active in many pursuits, including rodeo riding and a professional life as a public accountant. He became a leader in the AIM activities of the 1970s. Dennis Banks was later influential in protests calling for protection of Native American graves. His actions led to new federal legislation. Both Banks and Means have established themselves as credible actors, starring together in the 1992 film *The Last of the Mohicans.*

Ovide William Mercredi (1945–)

Ovide William Mercredi, a Cree political leader, has served as the leader of the Assembly of First Nations since 1991. He was born in Manitoba in 1945. He is well educated, having received a law degree from the University of Manitoba in 1977. Mercredi made his political mark by leading Canadian Native opposition to the Meech Lake Accord in 1990. As leader of the assembly, however, he was actively involved in designing the failed Charlottetown Accords of 1992.

Metacom (1639–1676)

Massasoit's son Metacom (known to the English as King Philip) was born in 1639 and upon the death of his father in 1661 took over as tribal leader of the Wampanoag. Metacom refused to accept the hostility of the expansionist Puritans, especially their religious leaders who considered the Natives to be inferior savages. In 1675, a general war (King Philip's War) broke out in New England. In 1676, Metacom was captured and executed. His head was severed and put on public display in an English village for the next twenty years. The war eliminated obstacles to the complete domination of New England by the new settlers.

Ely Samuel Parker (1828–1895)

Ely Samuel Parker became the first Native American to hold the position of commissioner of Indian affairs (head of the Bureau of Indian Affairs). He was born a Seneca in New York in 1828. His father was a chief of the Tonawanda Seneca, and his grandfather was Red Jacket, an ally of the British in the Revolutionary War and a diplomat for Native-U.S. relations afterward. As a young man, Parker helped author Lewis Morgan write his major work on the Iroquois League. Well educated, Parker received degrees in both law and engineering. In both cases professional advancement was blocked by prejudice against Natives. However, he did practice engineering, and while working on a building project in Galena, Illinois, he met Ulysses S. Grant, a resident of that town. They became friends, and during the Civil War, Grant helped Parker win an officer's position with an engineering unit. He also elevated Parker to a lieutenant general's post as his executive secretary. Parker was present at Lee's surrender at Appomattox and actually penned the documents of the occasion.

Parker remained in the military until Grant was elected president. In 1869, Grant gave him the post of Indian commissioner, and in this office he pushed for Native American rights and fair treatment in the West. He also sought to end corruption in the Bureau. In doing so, he incurred the wrath of several congressional leaders who instigated an investigation of fraud against Parker. The charges were dismissed as being contrived. However, the matter disillusioned Parker, and he left government service in 1871. He returned to an engineering practice in New York City, where he died in 1895.

Leonard Peltier (1944–)

Leonard Peltier presents the sad case of a person who was at the wrong place at the wrong time, appearing on the scene just when federal officials eagerly wanted a symbol of guilt for the violence that was occurring between Native protesters and FBI agents. Considerable doubt remains whether or not Peltier was the guilty culprit a jury found him to be. Born in Grand Forks, North Dakota, in 1944, Peltier was educated in the Native American school at Wahpeton. He joined AIM and became a leader in the BIA building takeover protest in 1972. In 1975, he was involved in a protest at Pine Ridge. A firefight with FBI agents resulted in the death of two agents, and several Native Americans were brought to trial for the deaths. Peltier was among those arrested, but he was tried separately from the others. While the other defendants were found innocent of charges, he was found guilty and given two life sentences. Following an escape from prison in 1989 and his recapture, he was given an additional seven-year sentence. His cause, and his claims of innocence, are presented in Peter Matthiessen's books, *In the Spirit of Crazy Horse* and *The Nations*, as well as in the documentary film, *Incident at Oglala*. Peltier's confinement remains the subject of numerous protests.

Pocahontas (1595–1617)

Born in 1595, Powhatan's daughter Pocahontas was kidnapped by English settlers in 1612 and held captive for two years. During this time she learned the English language and converted to

Christianity. She helped maintain peaceful relations between her people and the English. In 1614 she married the English settler John Rolfe. The two soon departed for England where she became a spokesperson for the Jamestown colony. Unfortunately, at age twenty-two, she succumbed to a disease for which she had no immunity.

Pontiac (1720–1769)

Pontiac was a chief of the Ottawas. Following the French and Indian War, he sought to prevent the English from occupying the lands around the Great Lakes and intruding upon Native territories. Pontiac was greatly influenced by "The Delaware Prophet," who received religious visions that instructed that Native Americans would receive salvation if they returned to their pre-Contact customs and drove the English off their lands. Using the fervor of this religious message, Pontiac organized a confederacy of many nations—Ottawa, Chippewa, Huron, Delaware, and Potawatomi—and struck out against several English posts in the Great Lakes area. All forts except those at Pittsburgh and Detroit were overrun. Pontiac hoped that the French would aid his effort. However, this hope became futile when they signed a peace treaty with the British in 1763, and Pontiac's alliance weakened with defections. The general war ended in 1764, but Pontiac maintained his resistance until 1766 when he agreed to a peace treaty with the British. He was murdered by a member of the Kaskaskia tribe at a trading post in Cahokia, Illinois, in 1769.

Pontiac is significant as one of the first leaders to bring together Native Americans from widely divergent tribes into an active alliance.

Poundmaker (c. 1842–1886)

Crowfoot's adoptive son, Poundmaker, was born in the early 1840s and was a Cree. Poundmaker did not accept Crowfoot's path of peace, although he did negotiate an 1876 Treaty (Number Six) for the Crees and other Native peoples in northern Saskatchewan. Even though he signed a treaty of peace, he joined with other Cree as an ally of Louis Riel Jr. in the second Metis uprising in Saskatchewan. For this action he was arrested and imprisoned. He became ill in captivity, and he was released only to die shortly afterward in 1886. (*See also* Crowfoot; Louis Riel Jr.).

Powhatan (c. 1550–1618)

The chief of the Powhatan people, known also as Wahun-sonacock, was born in Virginia during the mid-sixteenth century. He welcomed Captain John Smith as the Englishman established his settlement in Jamestown in 1607. Powhatan exchanged gifts with the king of England and as chief was instrumental in bringing harmony to relations between the two peoples. Powhatan's daughter Pocahontas was born in 1595. Powhatan died in 1618, and with the passing of these two agents of peace—Powhatan and John Smith—warfare erupted between the settlers and the Powhatan Confederacy. Hostilities continued through the 1620s until peace was resumed.

Louis Riel Jr. (1844–1885)

Louis Riel Jr. was born in 1844 in the Red River Metis Settlement in present-day Manitoba. His father was a Metis with Ojibwa heritage, and his mother was a French Canadian. Riel was well educated, having studied law in Montreal. In 1869, he led the resistance against an intrusion of immigrating Euro-Canadian settlers. He helped set up a provisional Metis government and served as its leader. However, in 1870 the national government in Ottawa imposed a new provincial government on the area. A conflict arose between Metis residents and the Canadian Army, with the latter being victorious. Riel himself was elected to the Canadian Parliament, but he did not take his seat, fearing an arrest if he went east. Instead he migrated to Montana where he became a school teacher. Most of his Metis followers left the Red River Settlement for areas further west in Canada.

In 1884, history began to repeat itself. Eastern migrants invaded the area of a Metis colony in what is now Saskatchewan, and the Metis called upon Riel for leadership. He returned to Canada and again formed a provisional government. He led armed Metis in a skirmish that resulted in the deaths of several Royal Canadian Mounted policemen. The central government in Ottawa reacted by sending in the army and again subduing the Metis. Riel was arrested, tried for treason, and on November 16, 1885, he was executed. For over a century he has been a martyr symbolizing the quests of both Metis and French Canadians for autonomy and self-sufficient community within the Greater Canadian Society. (*See also* Crowfoot; Poundmaker.)

John Ross (1790–1866)

John Ross was born in 1790. He served as the president of the Convention chosen to write a Cherokee Constitution in 1827. The next year he was elected chief of his people. He pushed them toward modernization with hopes that they would be accepted by the American Republic. Unfortunately, when gold was discovered in their Georgia homelands, greed took precedence over any notion of a rational policy toward Native Americans.

After the Cherokees were forcibly removed westward, Ross retained his leadership role. In the 1860s, he negotiated an alliance with the Confederate States of America. In the early stages of the Civil War, Cherokees fought beside the Confederates. Ross survived to 1866, long enough to see his peoples again punished, this time for being on the wrong side in the Civil War.

Sitting Bull (1831–1890)

Sitting Bull was one of two leading warriors of Sioux peoples in their resistance to the westward migrations of Americans and to broken treaty promises that they inflicted upon Native peoples. Sitting Bull came to prominence when he refused to acquiesce in yielding lands under the Fort Laramie Treaty of 1868. He rallied thousands of warriors from several tribes together to meet the invasion of the area by the U.S. Army. Troops under his command were responsible for the destruction of General George Armstrong Custer's army at the Battle of the Little Big Horn in 1876. However, Sitting Bull and hundreds of his followers soon fled to Canada. The U.S. Army burned all the fields near the Canadian border and forced the buffalo herds southward. Sitting Bull's people, cut off from food and starving, returned to a reservation at Standing Rock, North Dakota, where Sitting Bull surrendered in 1881. Later, Sitting Bull toured the country as part of Buffalo Bill Cody's Wild West show. He was mysteriously killed, presumably by tribal police in 1890.

Squanto (c.1590–1630)

Squanto, a Native American, was kidnapped by English sailors along the Atlantic Coast and taken to Europe. There he was able to escape and find passage back to America on another ship. During his time in captivity, Squanto learned the English language.

He helped Massasoit maintain peace between the Native peoples and the new English settlers. (*See also* Massasoit; Metacom.)

Tecumseh (1768–1813)

Two Shawnee brothers worked to bring the nations of the trans-Appalachian region together in resistance to the onslaught of non-Native settlements. The elder of the two, Tecumseh, was born near present-day Springfield, Ohio, in 1768. In his youth he traveled in the Midwestern region joining with the armies of many different tribes in fights against the invading settlers. In 1791, he fought beside Little Turtle as the Native Americans defeated a force of a thousand under the command of General Arthur Sinclair. Over 700 U.S. troops were lost in the biggest defeat ever of the U.S. Army on American soil. General Anthony Wayne regained the military initiative for the United States, but Tecumseh repudiated treaties forced on the Native peoples. He continued a campaign of resistance. After his younger brother Tenskwatawa attacked the U.S. Army at Prophetstown, a village on the Tippecanoe Creek in Indiana, and was forced to withdraw, Tecumseh broke relations with his brother. Tecumseh joined with the British Army during the War of 1812 and continued to fight. It was his hope that with a British defeat of the Americans, a Native American buffer land could be established separating the British and the Americans. It was not to be. He was killed in the Battle of Thames in 1813, and all remnants of his Native alliance ended. (*See also* Tenskwatawa.)

Tenskwatawa (1778–1837)

Tecumseh's younger brother, Tenskwatawa, was born in 1778. He wasted his youth in alcoholic dependence. However, in 1806 he experienced a vision in which the Great Spirit told him to lead the Native peoples back to their traditional ways and to avoid contact with Americans. By following this mandate of the Great Spirit, the Native Americans would be protected in battle, and they would regain their lands and achieve salvation. Tenskwatawa, who became known as "the Prophet," was the spiritual force behind Tecumseh, who as the elder brother organized the many tribes of the Midwest and South to fight the United States.

In 1811, however, at a time of Tecumseh's absence, the

younger brother urged his followers in Prophetstown, a village on the Tippecanoe Creek in Indiana, to attack the army. They were not protected by the Great Spirit. When William Henry Harrison's forces compelled them to withdraw from the area, he burned their village. At this point, Tecumseh broke relations with his brother. The discredited Tenskwatawa lived in Canadian exile for fifteen years, later returning to Native lands in Kansas where he died in 1837.

Jim Thorpe (1888–1953)

Jim Thorpe was known as the greatest athlete in the world. Born in 1888, he was of the Sac and Fox tribe. Thorpe attended the Carlisle Indian School in Pennsylvania where he was an All-American football player. In 1912, he won both the pentathlon and decathlon events at the Stockholm World Olympic games. He later played both professional baseball and football. He is a member of the college and pro football halls of fame. Jim Thorpe died at his California home in 1953.

Wovoka (c.1856–1932)

The Paiute religious leader Wovoka was born in the late 1850s near Walker Lake, Nevada. He was the son of a medicine man, and in his youth he also lived with a very religious non-Native man, David Wilson. Wilson encouraged Wovoka's spiritual development. In 1888, Wovoka became very ill from scarlet fever and drifted into a coma. As the fever broke, he came to consciousness just as a solar eclipse was ending. The coincidence of his miraculous revival and the return of the sun was considered to be an important sign. As Wovoka was revived, he related that he had had a vision and had met the Great Spirit. Wovoka was told that his people would again have all their lands, as the non-Natives would leave them. The animals—buffalo and deer and eagles—would also return in abundance. All the dead among the Paiutes would come to life in this new land. To achieve this heaven on earth, the people had to live in peace and wear special clothes as they engaged in a ritual called the Ghost Dance.

Wovoka's story spread quickly. Native Americans from throughout the West visited him and learned more about his vision. As the the Natives of the Plains learned the story, they saw active Ghost Dance participation as itself driving settlers out of their lands. In fear that the dance would lead the Natives to violence, the U.S. Army in the West forbade the Sioux from practicing the dance. Pine Ridge Sioux ignored the rulings, having been led to believe that the special shirts they were wearing would resist bullets from the Army. A confrontation over the Ghost Dance led to the massacre of over 300 Native Americans at Wounded Knee, South Dakota, in 1890.

Non-Native Contributors to Stronger Native Communities

The quest for stronger Native communities occurred concomitantly with the desire to strengthen all communities in America. The quest for Native America was a special one, however, as the case is not difficult to make that the weakness of Native communities has been a consequence of the deliberate actions of governments established by non-Natives after European Contact. The quest for self-sufficiency in Native communities will be a continuing one.

Since the moment of Contact in 1492, many and perhaps even most issues affecting Native peoples have found resolution in councils controlled by non-Natives. No member of the U.S. Supreme Court has been a Native American, no president has been a Native American (although one vice president was), and very few Native Americans have served in Congress (only two of the twentieth century's senators were Native Americans). A listing of biographies of personalities who have had "impact" on issues affecting Native Americans cannot neglect the inclusion of several non-Natives. The reader can readily find information about presidents and senators and judges in other places. Moreover, a good deal on presidential and judicial attitudes toward Native Americans is revealed in Chapters 7 and 8.

We will now recognize a few non-Native individuals who made significant "positive" contributions to greatly strengthening Native community over the past five centuries. One individual has been selected from each of the six centuries since Columbus. A selective group is presented as representatives of the twenty-first century. The first person recognized is Spanish and never lived in the Western Hemisphere. The others include one

Canadian and several Americans whose impact was formed on North American soil.

Francisco de Vitoria (c. 1483–1546)

Theologian, philosopher, and legal scholar, Francisco de Vitoria set forth doctrines establishing the fact for the European community that the Native Americans were free peoples, that they had human rights and could not be enslaved, that they held their lands as legal possessors, and that they must be respected as such. Self-defense provided the only justification for warfare against Native America, and land could move from Natives to the Spanish only through lawful purchase or conquest in a justified war. However, he did believe that international trade was the right of all nations and that Native Americans had to permit Europeans to enter their lands for purposes of trade. Vitoria also opposed compulsory conversion of Native Americans to Christianity.

Francisco de Vitoria was born in about 1483 in Alava, Spain, near Burgos. His intellectual career began at the University in Valladolid where he taught from 1523 to 1526. He then moved to the University of Salamanca where he held the professorship in philosophy until his death in 1546. In 1532, Vitoria began to lecture on the rights of Native Americans. His teachings took written form as the *Treatise De Indis et Iure Belli Relectiones* (Readings on Indians and the Law of War). His principles of international relations emphasized justice and morality. Some consider Vitoria to be the "Founder of International Law."

His notions were contrasted with those of Juan de Sepulveda who used Aristotelian thinking to support a notion that Native peoples were, as non-Christians, uncivilized and beyond the scope of enjoying human liberties. Sepulveda felt that it was the duty of the European Christians to subjugate and enslave Native Americans. Vitoria's views were endorsed by Father Bartolome de Las Casas and by governmental leaders in Spain. However, the viewpoint of Sepulveda often was carried by Spanish *conquistadors* and by the religious conquerors of Native lands as well. Nonetheless, Vitorian notions were followed in the formal treatments accorded the Natives by many other Europeans, including French, English, and Dutch. The legal principles he established constitute a measuring stick by which current Americans can assess and criticize their own national history.

Roger Williams (1603–1684)

Roger Williams was the conscience of the new settlers of Native lands in New England. He was born in England in 1603 and educated at Cambridge University. He became an ordained minister of the Anglican Church. However, he was a staunch individualist, and as such he criticized church doctrine and the church hierarchy to an extent that made it advisable for him to emigrate to the American colonies. In 1631 he sailed for Boston and settled in Salem where he began a ministry. However, he soon was in trouble again, for now he criticized Massachusetts officials for their mistreatment of Native Americans—especially for their unfair seizures of Native properties. Williams adhered to the principles set forth by Vitoria; thus, it was that he challenged any European claims to lands unless the lands were gained by fair purchases and treaty agreements with the Native peoples.

Williams also believed that individuals should have personal freedoms of religious beliefs, an idea that had no support in the government-controlled church of the colony. The expression of this notion resulted in his being banned from Massachusetts. He fled to the wilderness of Rhode Island where he started a new colony. As its leader, Williams adopted democratic policies requiring that new settlers must purchase lands from Native Americans, and also must give humane treatment to the Native peoples. He prevented land speculators from cheating members of the Narragansett tribe out of large tracts of lands. Williams also wrote a dictionary of Native languages and traveled widely among the peoples. Although he was recognized during most of his life as a true friend of Native American rights, he did take up arms against Metacom when the Narragansetts renounced their peace treaty and engaged settlers in "King Philip's War."

Benjamin Franklin (1706–1790)

Benjamin Franklin has often been recognized as "the universal man of the eighteenth century." He may also be called the first true American—that is, non-Native American. He was the premier diplomat of the early American Republic, he authored the first plan for national union (the Albany Plan of 1754), and he was a principal contributor to the writing of the Declaration of Independence, the Articles of Confederation, and the Constitution. In all of these accomplishments, Franklin looked to his interactions with Native Americans and to knowledge he gained from their political practices.

Franklin was born in Boston in 1706, and as a young man he was apprenticed to his older brother as a printer. Unable to accept a subservient role, he ran away to Philadelphia, where he developed his own printing trade, became wealthy, and experimented with science and politics. As a printer, he came to learn much about the Native peoples as he published several early treaties. In 1853, the colonial governor of Pennsylvania commissioned Franklin to negotiate a peaceful understanding with Native Americans in anticipation of the French and Indian War. His meeting in the town of Carlisle with members of the Six Iroquois Nations, the Delaware, Shawnee, and Miami gave him his first experience as a diplomat. The meetings also heightened his knowledge of the Iroquois system of federal government, which he used as a guide for his Albany plan to unite the American colonies. Although the plan was not then adopted, its notions of shared and balanced powers were incorporated into the Articles of Confederation and Constitution, both of which were greatly influenced by Franklin. Franklin also drew upon his Carlisle experience and the knowledge it brought him about Native life in his future interpretations of Native relationships. His knowledge of Native personal liberties and independence from authority became incorporated in the Declaration of Independence, written by Thomas Jefferson with counsel from Franklin. Franklin's respect for Native Nations is best demonstrated in his willingness to accept their processes of liberty and government for the new American nation.

Although Franklin himself was a land speculator, he was also personally sympathetic with the rights of Native peoples. Following a massacre of a defenseless Native community in Lancaster, Pennsylvania, led by the "Paxton Boys," a group of ruffians who terrorized their community, Franklin organized the Pennsylvania militia in Philadelphia to stop the spread of this terrorism. With moral indignation and at great political risk, he published his condemnation of the incidents as his *Narrative of the Late Massacres in Lancaster County.*

Helen Hunt Jackson (1830–1885)

Helen Marie Fisk was born on October 14, 1830, in Amherst, Massachusetts. Her father was a language professor at Amherst College, and Helen was exposed to a rigorous academic environment all during her youth. She was taught to question and challenge authority. She applied her talents in discussions in Boston and East Coast society during her youth and young adulthood, albeit in the role of a young woman, wife, and mother. Her first husband, Edward Bissell Hunt, died early in their marriage, and she also lost her two children. In 1875, she married William Sharples Jackson and moved to Colorado to escape the memories of her tragic losses. There she became acquainted with the "Indian Problem." However, the spark that made her a "firebrand" came on a visit home to Boston in 1879. There she heard Standing Bear, the chief of the Ponca tribe, speak on his national tour. Standing Bear was seeking national support and sympathy for the grievances afflicted upon his peoples.

Helen Jackson took up the cause of the Poncas, who had been subjected to several forced removals. She said she became "a woman with a hobby." In truth, she became obsessed, "a soul on fire." Her crusade was to alert the public, and her tool was political activity and the written word. She fed the reformers of the Women's National Indian Association and the Indian Rights Association with her two greatest books, *A Century of Dishonor* (1881) and *Ramona* (1884). The 1881 work represented the first time a non-Native intellectual had documented the mistreatment of Native America in such a scathing manner. She condemned both national policy and national policy makers. The book led to a congressional investigation that spurred on the call for reform. The second work was intended to be an in-depth look at the tragedy of a woman's life in the Mission tribes of California. Again it was an indictment. However, later Hollywood and the popular media twisted the story—which did include a romantic subplot—into a love story. Though instrumental in launching the reform movement of the 1880s, Jackson was unable to witness the unfortunate turn of the movement toward the allotment and assimilation policies of the Dawes Act. She died in 1885.

John Collier (1884–1968)

A man of vision, John Collier was able to turn policy making away from notions of assimilation and toward self-sufficiency and tribal identification for Native Americans. His neglect of the need for detailed implementation and constant political support resulted in many temporary setbacks, animosities from friends and opponents alike, and even the emergence of a decade of retrenchment with the Truman-Eisenhower Termination efforts. Whereas specific failures dramatically revealed Collier's imperfections, his devotion to a vision resulted in the modern acceptance of tribal autonomy in America.

John Collier was born into an Old South aristocratic family in Atlanta in 1884. His elite surroundings generated within him a sense of obligation to the less fortunate. He devoted his career to social work and community development. In 1920, he visited Taos, New Mexico, and from that time he was converted to the cause of helping Native America preserve its identification and lifestyles. He especially sought land rights for Pueblo tribes. In 1923, Collier helped found the American Indian Defense Association, and he served as its executive secretary until 1933. From that platform he became the leading critic of federal policy toward Native peoples. He began service as the commissioner of the Bureau of Indian Affairs in 1933 and held the post for twelve years—longer than anyone else in history. He soon found that serving with responsibilities was more difficult than serving as a critic. His accomplishments were many. He stopped the allotment policy of the Dawes Act; he protected Native arts and crafts; and he promoted Native governments. However, his accomplishments came with a price: His devotion to his personal vision blinded him from the political goals of others who did not place Native American affairs at the tops of their agendas. The time was the Depression, and other national concerns took precedence. His bills were amended in ways that reduced Native American political control over some tribal matters that he wished to bring about.

Collier's "plan" for tribal governments was imposed upon the various tribes; it was not a result of tribal deliberations. His concern for economic stability on reservations led him to neglect local desires. This was especially damaging for his reputation among the Navajo and Tonono O'odham tribes when he ordered a reduction in their livestock herds because grazing lands were being depleted. He overlooked the vital role sheepherding had in child development as well as craft employment for tribal women. His vision was pure, but his inattentiveness to local needs caused much anger. He left office in 1945 as President Truman was beginning to launch a drive for Termination. Fortunately, he lived long enough to witness the death of the Termination policy and the emergence of policies fostering tribal self-sufficiency as well as a self-supported drive for recognition among Native peoples. The details differed, but his vision was beginning to see fulfillment.

The Twenty-First Century:
Lawyers for Native Peoples

The community strength of Native Americans in the modern era has been greatly enhanced by the actions of judicial bodies. Court cases of special note are reviewed in the next chapter. Special notice is also given to attorneys, some of whom were themselves Native Americans, but most of those who have led the charge on behalf of Native communities as their advocates have not been Native Americans. This contemporary listing is necessarily very brief and selective. These are but representatives of a group of important people who have helped the Native cause.

Several Native as well as non-Native attorneys have given their skills through associations such as the Indian Rights Association, the Institute for the Development of Indian Law, or the Native American Rights Fund (NARF). Bruce Greene gained experience with NARF when it was established in California, and then he moved with the organization to Boulder, Colorado. Born in 1943, Greene attended the University of California, and graduated from Hastings College of Law. After working with NARF, he went into private practice specializing in Indian law. Among his notable judicial triumphs was a federal district court judgment requiring Wisconsin to allow casino gambling on reservations. The Lac du Flambeau case held that since the lottery law of the state was written in a manner that enabled the lottery organization to have casino-type games, the tribes could have the games. Greene also was instrumental in the decisions leading to casino gambling on tribal lands in Michigan.

Glenn M. Feldman came to his legal practice through political activity. Born in Chicago in 1947, he received his undergraduate education at the University of Illinois and his law degree at Georgetown. He remained in Washington and worked as staff counsel to both senators George McGovern and James Abourezk through the 1970s. He now practices in Phoenix, Arizona, and his clients have included many tribes in the Southwest. His renown derives from several cases, and one in particular: he was the attorney who presented the case for Native American casinos to the U.S. Supreme Court in *California v. Cabazon* in 1987.

George Vlassis also practices law in Phoenix. Born in Portsmouth, Ohio, in 1930, he graduated from the University of Indiana and then the University of Virginia Law School in 1957.

Following law school, he moved west and became an activist in Native political and legal advocacy. He ventured to Washington, D.C., in 1972 with the American Indian Movement's "Trail of Broken Treaties" March. There 500 Native protesters occupied the Bureau of Indian Affairs Building. Vlassis was the only non-Native inside the building with the group. He became the communications conduit with the outside and was instrumental in keeping the episode peaceful. Afterward Vlassis served as the general counsel to the Navajo peoples, and he represented tribal chairman Peter MacDonald in legal battles.

Michael Vaclav Stuhff is a Las Vegas attorney who has literally "worked in the trenches" with Native people. Born in 1947 and raised in Las Vegas, he attended the University of Nevada, Las Vegas, before receiving a law degree from the University of Utah in 1973. He then moved to Window Rock, Arizona, where he began a twelve-year career as an attorney for the Navajos. In that role he served specifically as an adviser to the tribal judiciary system, then as the head of the legal aid service for the tribe, and later as the director of paralegal training for the tribe on matters concerning joint land jurisdiction disputes with the Hopi. He returned to Las Vegas in 1985, where he has become a major advocate in matters concerning the enrollment and disenrollment of members of tribes. This has become a critical area of Indian law, especially with the advent of tribal distributions of funds to members as a result of enterprise activity, especially gambling enterprise.

Scott Crowell practices law in Kirkland near Seattle, Washington. His efforts have resulted in stronger Native communities throughout the Northwest. Crowell was born in 1958, and he received his bachelor's degree and legal education at Arizona State University in 1984. Shortly afterward he began working with an Arizona firm and became lead counsel in a case that resolved questions of state law enforcement jurisdiction on Indian lands. After moving to Washington, he became engrossed in Indian gambling law. His clients include reservations and tribal entities in Washington, Oregon, Idaho, Texas, and California. He has often testified in front of Congress and state lawmaking bodies, as well as the National Gambling Impact Study Commission.

Alain DuBuc is among Canada's leading national attorneys. Born in Montreal in 1948, he attended Carleton University and received his legal training at Osgood Hall, University of Toronto. He is now based in Ottawa, where he works with bands throughout the country on myriad questions of Native rights, including the rights to have casino gambling. He is a legal political negotiator as well and is credited with formulating the documents and directing the legal and political processes that resulted in creating the Territory of Nunavut, a seminal move in the quest for self-sufficiency and community for the indigenous peoples of Canada.

7

Legislation, Litigation, and Statistics

Legislative Viewpoints: Acts of Parliaments and Congress

The modern era has witnessed considerable sympathy and support for Native peoples, as expressed in legislation passed in the latter part of the twentieth century, as well as in proclamations at all levels of government.

The United Nations has joined the chorus in endorsing a high level of rights for indigenous peoples. In 1993, the U.N. Commission on Human Rights adopted a draft declaration on "Discrimination Against Indigenous Peoples." The document covered many items, yet its main thrust spoke not just to indigenous peoples but to all peoples. The statement "affirmed" that all "doctrines, policies and practices based" on "superiority of peoples" on the basis of "national origin, racial, religious, ethnic or cultural differences" were "racist, scientifically false, legally invalid, morally condemnable and socially unjust." Though not saying so in so many words, the "affirmation" could certainly be interpreted to mean that "superior" advantages such as monopoly rights to have casinos run by only persons of certain "origins" are also "legally invalid."

The declaration addressed many specific concerns regarding the rights of "indigenous families and communities" to have control and responsibility for the well-being of their children, to be

159

able to control their lands, and to have respect for their cultural practices.

The legislative councils of governments, American and Canadian, national and state or provincial, have expressed policy toward Native Americans since colonial times. In contrast to today, some of the early expressions of legislative members have been downright disgraceful, whereas others have been quite enlightened. In the former category are disrespectful comments sometimes expressed in public forums. For example, the public record includes the words of Minnesota congressman James Michael Cavanaugh, as explained below. General Philip Sheridan is commonly given "credit" for first uttering the cruel words "The Only Good Indian is . . ." Indeed, he made such a remark in 1869. The context of the occasion suggests that the remark was probably made in humorous jest. An Indian chief named Old Toch-a-way was introduced to the general, and Old Toch-a-way informed Sheridan, "Me good Indian," to which Sheridan responded, "The only good Indians I ever saw were dead." A similar remark, however, was uttered the previous year in the halls of the House of Representatives in Washington, D.C., by Congressman Cavanaugh, as he responded to another congressman who was speaking favorably about Native Americans. There is no question about the context of his remark. He was not being humorous; clearly, he did not like Indians:

> I will say frankly that, in my judgment, the entire Indian policy of the country is wrong from its very inception. In the first place, you offer a premium for rascality by paying a beggarly pittance to your Indian agents. The gentleman from Massachusetts may denounce the sentiment as atrocious, but I will say that I like an Indian better dead than living. I have never in my life seen a good Indian—and I have seen thousands—except when I have seen a dead Indian. I believe in the Indian policy pursued by New England in years long gone. I believe in the Indian policy which was taught by the great chieftain of Massachusetts, Miles Standish. I believe in the policy that exterminates the Indians, drives them outside the boundaries of civilization, because you can't civilize them . . . You have made your treaties with the Indians, but they have not been observed . . . The Indian will make a treaty in the Fall, and in the Spring he is again "upon the war-

path." The torch, the scalping knife, plunder, and desolation follow wherever the Indian goes. (*The Congressional Globe* May 28, 1868, p. 2638)

Very few of the Congress's actual policies carry Representative Cavanaugh's venom, but unfortunately many may have taken aim for the goals he seemed to be seeking.

The Quebec Act (1774)

One of the "obnoxious acts" of the British Parliament that precipitated the Revolutionary War, this Act expanded upon policy set forth in a Royal Proclamation of 1763 restricting Euro-American migrations across the Appalachian Mountains. The western lands were put under the direct control of the London government, and colonists could not purchase them directly from the Native Americans. In 1774, the area was placed under the governance of Quebec—a province that did not follow British principles of law. The costs of the lands were also raised sharply.

The Declaration of Independence (1776)

The Declaration of Independence was written by Thomas Jefferson and adopted by the Second Continental Congress. The document set forth the reasons the colonies were severing their political ties with England. The reasons included the king's policies that made it difficult to move to the western lands and also that the king had "excited domestic insurrection amongst us, and has endeavored to bring on the inhabitants of our frontiers, the merciless Indian Savages, whose known rule of warfare, is an undistinguishable destruction of all ages, sexes and conditions."

Articles of Confederation (1777 [Ratified 1781])

Article VI . . . No state shall engage in any war without the consent of the United States in Congress assembled, unless such state be actually invaded by enemies, or shall have received certain advice of a resolution being formed by some nation of Indians to invade such state, and the danger is so imminent as not to admit of a delay till the United States in Congress assembled can be consulted . . .

Article IX . . . the United States in Congress assembled shall also have the sole and exclusive right and power of . . . regulating the trade and managing all affairs with the Indians, not members of any state, provided that the legislative right of any state within its own limits be not infringed or violated . . .

The Northwest Ordinance (1787)

Article III . . . The utmost good faith shall always be observed toward the Indians; their lands and property shall never be taken from them without their consent; and in their property, rights, and liberty they never shall be invaded or disturbed unless in just and lawful wars authorized by Congress; but laws founded in justice and humanity shall from time to time, be made, for preventing wrongs being done to them, and for preserving peace and friendship with them.

The Constitution (1787 [Ratified 1789])

Article I, Section 8, The Congress shall have power . . . To regulate commerce with foreign nations, and among the several States, and with the Indian tribes . . .

Trade and Intercourse Acts

1. July 22, 1790 (1 US Stat 137). This was the first of a series of Acts regarding trade between Native Americans and non-Natives. The first Congress under the Constitution sought to establish peaceful relations with Native Americans by regulating persons conducting trade with the tribes. Traders were required to secure licenses and to follow rules in commercial activities with Native Americans. Licenses were limited to two years at a time. The Act also restricted purchases of Native lands by parties other than the federal government. Non-Natives who committed crimes against Natives or on Native lands were subject to the same penalties they would have received if they had committed the crimes in their own jurisdictions.
2. March 1, 1793 (1 US Stat 329). This Act prohibited whites from settling on Native lands. It also exempted Native Americans from state restrictions on trade.

3. May 19, 1796 (1 US Stat 743). The Act prohibited the movement of livestock across Native lands and required passports for travel into the lands. Also in 1796 (1 US Stat 452; April 18, 1796) Congress established government trading houses that had exclusive rights to sell to Natives on their lands. Sales were made without profits. The trading houses existed until 1822.
4. March 3, 1799. This Act made additional minor changes in previous Acts.
5. March 30, 1802 (2 US Stat 139). The first permanent Trade and Intercourse Act was passed. A major point of the Act involved the president's power to control liquor sales on Native lands.

Indian Removal Act, 4 US Stat 411, May 28, 1830

The president was authorized to trade lands belonging to the United States and west of the Mississippi for lands in the east where Native Americans resided. The president was empowered to compensate Native Americans for any improvements they had made on their eastern lands as well as for the costs of moving westward. The exchanges were to be "voluntary" ones. The United States was to guarantee that the new lands would forever belong to the Native Americans. Congress appropriated $500,000 to implement the Act.

Organization of Department of Indian Affairs, 4 US Stat 735, June 30, 1834

In 1824, the secretary of war without congressional approval set up a Bureau of Indian Affairs. This Act in 1834 formalized the organizational structure of the operations. The Act designated areas for appointments of superintendents, agents, and sub-agents for Indian affairs. The secretary of war was authorized to distribute treaty funds and goods to Natives, and employees of the Indian Affairs Bureau were prohibited from having a personal interest in any trading with the Native Americans. In 1849 (9 Stat. 395; March 3, 1849), the functions of the Indian Affairs Bureau were transferred from the War Department to the newly established Interior Department.

British North American Act, July 1, 1867

The British Parliament created the Canadian Confederation by bringing into one union the provinces of Nova Scotia, New Brunswick, Quebec, and Ontario. The Act, also known as the Constitution Act, provided a structure for the national government as well as a division of authority between the central national government and the provincial governments. Authority over the relationships between Native and non-Native peoples was given to the national government.

Treaty Making Process Ended, 16 US Stat 566, March 3, 1871

In 1867, Congress passed an Act repealing "all laws" allowing the president or others to make treaties with Native Americans (15 Stat 7; March 29, 1867). However, four months later the Act was repealed (15 Stat 18; July 20, 1867). Nevertheless, the seeds for change had been planted. The House of Representatives was concerned that it was being left out of the Native American policy process, as treaties were made by the president and approved by the Senate. In 1871, a rider (amendment) was added to an appropriation bill that provided that thereafter "no Indian nation . . . shall be . . . recognized as an independent nation . . . with whom the United States may contract by treaty." However, all previous treaties remained in force.

Indian Act, April 12, 1876

An Act of the Canadian Parliament ratified procedures for governing Native reserves as outlined in treaties. The Act sought assimilation of Natives into non-Native culture by providing individual shares of land for farming, and also the right to vote for those Natives choosing to give up Native status. The Act also prohibited the introduction of alcoholic beverages onto reserves.

Major Crimes Act, 25 US Stat 385, March 3, 1885

Congress determined that if Native Americans committed any of seven major crimes on reservation lands, the case would be taken to the courts of the United States. The crimes were murder, manslaughter, rape, assault with the intent to kill, burglary, larceny, and arson. The law was passed in reaction to the U.S. Supreme Court ruling in *Ex Parte Crow Dog* (1883). In 1976, amendments added several offenses to the list including: kidnapping, incest, "statutory" rape, assault with the intent to commit rape, and assault with a deadly weapon (90 US Stat 90; May 29, 1976).

General Allotment Act, 24 US Stat 388, February 8, 1887

Congress mandated surveys to be taken of Native lands. The president was authorized to divide the lands that could be farmed into parcels, which could be distributed to individual Native Americans and their families. The parcels would then be held as private lands, which after twenty-five years could be sold to non-Natives. In the meantime, the parcels could be leased. Excess lands, left over after each Native family was given its "share," were sold by the government with the proceeds going to members of the tribe. Between 1887 and 1934, over two-thirds of Native lands were allotted and lost to the tribes. This amounted to over 90 million acres. The Act did not apply to the tribes of the Indian Territory (Oklahoma). The purpose of the Act, also known as the Dawes Act, was to assimilate Natives into the land-owning farming population. Citizenship rights were given to Native Americans making the desired transition to self-sufficiency. The Act was modified with several amendments. In 1891, for instance, lands were permitted to be sold before twenty-five years elapsed (26 Stat 794; February 28, 1891).

Intoxication in Indian Country Act, 27 US Stat 260, July 23, 1892

Alcoholic beverages could not be transported to or be sold within "Indian Country." The law was repealed in 1953.

The Curtis Act, 30 US Stat 497, June 28, 1898

The provisions of the General Allotment Act of 1887 were extended to tribal lands in Indian Territory (Oklahoma). The Act abolished the tribal courts and the governments of the Five

Civilized Nations: Seminole, Creek, Chickasaw, Cherokees, and Choctaws.

Citizenship for World War Veterans, 41 US Stat 350, November 6, 1919

Over 12,000 Native Americans served in the United States armed services during World War I. Almost all of them served as volunteers. Those who received honorable discharges were granted full citizenship, "with all the privileges pertaining thereto . . ."

Indian Citizenship Act, 43 US Stat 253, June 2, 1924

The secretary of the interior was authorized to issue certifications of citizenship to all Native Americans born within the territorial limits of the United States. The granting of citizenship did not impair any other civil, political, or property rights of the Natives.

Johnson O'Malley Act, 48 US Stat 596, April 16, 1934

The federal government was permitted to make contracts with states to offer health, education, and welfare services to Native Americans. The secretary of the interior was also authorized to set standards for the delivery of those services. Two Acts passed in 1934, including the Johnson O'Malley Act, effectively repealed the General Allotment Act of 1887.

Indian Reorganization Act, 48 US Stat 984, June 18, 1934

This Act was the culmination of the recommendations of the Meriam Report of 1928. Its passage was under the guiding hand of Indian Affairs commissioner John Collier. The Act emphasized tribal revival, strong self-government, and economic self-sufficiency. Future allotments of lands were prohibited, and measures were taken to restore many lands lost under the allotment process. The Act also created a revolving fund of $10 million to be used for investments in tribal businesses. Tribes were empowered to adopt constitutions, which were to be ratified by majority vote of all adult members. If constitutions were not adopted, the tribes were exempt from provisions of the Act.

Indian Arts and Craft Board, 49 US Stat 891, August 27, 1935

This Act created a five-person board to encourage Native American economic development through arts and crafts industries. The board was empowered to conduct market research, create federal trademarks, and offer technical business assistance. The Act made it a federal offense to represent products as Native crafts if they were not authentic. The powers of the board were expanded in 1990 (Public Law 101-644, November 29, 1990).

Indian Claims Commission Act, 60 US Stat 1049, August 13, 1946

This Act was passed because Congress was being besieged with requests to settle claims for lands wrongfully taken from tribes. Congress set up a commission that met until 1978. Native American tribes having claims settled by the Commission could not raise the issues again. Claims could be settled only for financial compensation for the value of lands when they were wrongfully taken. The Commission could not order the return of the lands. For this reason, many tribes decided not to present claims to the Commission. The Act also provided funds for expert witnesses to be used by the tribes, and it allowed tribal attorneys to be paid on a contingency basis.

Termination Resolution, House Concurrent Resolution 108, 67 US Stat 132, August 1, 1953

It is declared to be the sense of Congress that, at the earliest time, all of the Indian tribes and the individual members thereof located within the state of California, Florida, New York, and Texas, and all the following names Indian tribes ... should be freed from federal supervision and control and from all disabilities and limitations specifically applicable to Indians. (For these tribes) officers of the Bureau of Indian Affairs . . . should be abolished . . . Whereas it is the policy of Congress as rapidly as possible, to make the Indians . . . subject to the same laws and entitled to the same privileges and responsibilities as are applicable to other citizens . . . to end their status as wards . . .

Public Law 280, 67 US Stat 588, August 15, 1953

This Act of Congress gave several states jurisdiction over offenses committed on Native lands. The states included California, Nebraska, Minnesota (except Red Lake Reservation), Oregon (except Warm Springs Reservation), and Wisconsin (except Menominee Reservation). Other states could request the jurisdiction later. States also acquired some civil jurisdiction over disputes upon Native lands. However, they were not given either regulatory or taxation authority over the Native lands. The Indian Civil Rights Act of 1968 allowed states to withdraw this authority and also required that tribes give approval before new states took over the authority.

The Indian Civil Rights Act of 1968, 87 US Stat 77, April 11, 1968 (Titles II–VIII of the 1968 Civil Rights Act)

The Bill of Rights and the Fourteenth Amendment offered protections against the actions of the federal and state governments. This Act filled a gap by giving individuals civil rights protections against tribal government actions—particularly actions by tribal judicial systems. Included in the protections were the free expression of religion, freedom of speech, the right to speedy trial, the right to confront witnesses, and the ability to seek habeas corpus remedies. Also, the Act prohibited illegal searches, excessive bail, cruel and unusual punishments, bills of attainder, ex post facto laws, and self-incrimination.

Alaska Native Claims Settlement Act, 85 US Stat 688, December 18, 1971

Congress found that "there is an immediate need for fair and just settlement of all claims by . . . Native groups of Alaska." The Act provided for the enrollment of Natives and their organization into twelve regional corporations. U.S. citizens with one-fourth or more Alaskan Native blood were qualified to be enrolled. Each of the corporations was divided into villages (200 in all), which were given grants of lands. Forty million acres were distributed to the villages. The lands were not placed into trust. The regional corporations were collectively given $962,500,000, which in turn was distributed to members as stock shares. The moneys came from the U.S. Treasury and from future revenues from Alaskan oil deposits. This amount was four times the total given all tribes in the thirty-two-year period of the Indian Claims Commission. In 1988, the Act was amended to increase individual control over their share of the settlement (101 Stat 1788, February 3, 1988).

Indian Financing Act, 88 US Stat 77, April 12, 1974

This Act extends the authority of the Indian Reorganization Act by increasing funding of a revolving loan fund for Native American business ventures, and also establishing a program for business grants. Such financial help is necessitated by the reluctance of banks to give loans to tribal businesses, which could not be collateralized with lands and buildings held in trust by the federal government.

Indian Self Determination and Education Assistance Act, 88 US Stat 2203, January 4, 1975

Tribal organizations were authorized to enter into contracts with federal agencies to directly administer educational and other service programs on reservations. Grants were authorized for tribes so that they could operate school and health programs. Funds could be given to public schools for the education of Native American children only if they demonstrated that they had "objectives that adequately addressed the educational needs" of the students. Also, the Native American parents had to be given a voice on school boards that accepted such grants. The program was enlarged with the Tribally Controlled Schools Act of 1988 (Public Law 102-385, April 28, 1988). Also in 1978 Congress passed an act to give grants to Native community colleges: Tribally Controlled Community College Assistance Act (Public Law 92-1325, October 17, 1978).

Indian Health Care Improvement Act, 90 US Stat 1400, September 30, 1976

This Act seeks to improve Native American health by encouraging Native Americans to seek education and training in the health professions. The Act also increases funding for Native health facilities and for water and sanitary waste facilities. In addition, the Act encourages the establishment of health services for urban Natives and authorizes a feasibility study for the creation of a Native American School of Medicine.

American Religious Freedom Act, 92 US Stat 469, August 11, 1978

This "Act" was really a joint resolution of both houses of Congress. The resolution proclaims a policy "to protect and preserve" the "inherent right (of Native Americans) to freedom to believe, express, and exercise the traditional religions . . . including but not limited to access to sites, use and possession of sacred objects, and the freedom to worship through ceremonials and traditions." The president was directed to inform all federal agencies of the resolution and require that they adjust any of their policies adverse to it.

Indian Child Welfare Act, 92 US Stat 3069, November 8, 1978

Many Native American children were being placed for adoption in homes of non-Natives. This practice was considered to be very destructive of Native cultures. The Act seeks the "best interests" of children by promoting the stability of Native family ties. Standards are set for adoptions, and preference is given first to adoptions within the child's extended family, then within the tribe, and next to Native foster homes.

Archaeological Resources Protection Act, 93 US Stat 721, October 31, 1979

This Act recognizes certain cultural and religious rights of Native Americans. Archaeological resources on public lands and Native lands are protected. Persons excavating sites on these lands must receive permits to do so, and they must account for their findings. Penalties are provided for violations of the Act.

The Indian Gaming Regulatory Act, 102 US Stat 2467, October 17, 1988

This Act provides a mechanism for authorizing and regulating gambling on Native American lands. A tribe may pass an ordinance and have a form of gambling if that form is permitted by a state for any purpose or by any organization. There are three classes of gambling under the Act. Class one games include traditional Native games with low-stakes prizes. These games are regulated exclusively by the tribes offering the games. Class two games include bingo, pull tabs, and nonbanked card games (ones contested among players only). These games are initially regulated by a National Indian Gaming Commission. Later, the tribes may be certified to self-regulate the games. Class three games include most casino games, race betting, and lotteries. These games are regulated in accordance with agreements negotiated by tribes and state governments. If states refuse to negotiate, the tribes may sue the states in federal court to force negotiations. The National Indian Gaming Commission approves operational agreements between tribes and non-Native management companies. The Commission has three members, two of whom must be Native Americans.

National Museum of the American Indian Act, 103 US Stat 1336, November 28, 1989

Congress established a "living memorial to Native Americans and their traditions . . . known as the National Museum of the American Indian" within the Smithsonian Institution. In addition to collecting and preserving Native American objects, the museum will provide for research and study programs. A facility has been constructed on the National Mall at Independence and Fourth Street, SW in the District of Columbia. The federal government paid two-thirds of the building cost, private donors one-third.

Native American Languages Act, 104 US Stat 1153, October 30, 1990

This Act recognizes traditional languages as integral parts of Native American cultures. The policy of the United States is to preserve the rights of Native Americans to use and develop languages. Use of the languages is encouraged in Native American educational programs both as an object for study and as a medium for study. The use of Native languages shall not be restricted in any public proceedings.

Native American Graves Protection and Repatriation Act, 104 US Stat 3048, November 16, 1990

This Act seeks to protect Native American gravesites and human remains. All Native American cultural items excavated on public lands are to be the property of the appropriate tribal organization. Trafficking in such human remains and cultural items becomes a federal offense. Also, all museums holding such objects or remains must make an inventory of them as well as the tribes from which the items came. Upon request, the items shall be returned to the tribes.

Indian Child Protection and Family Abuse Prevention Act, 104 US Stat 4544, November 28, 1990

This Act recognizes a growing problem of family violence. Reports of abuses of Native children are to be made to appropriate authorities. A central registry of cases has been established. The Act creates grants so that the tribes may set up counseling and treatment programs. Each office of the Bureau of Indian Affairs is authorized to set up an Indian Child Resource and Family Service Center.

American Indian Religious Freedom Act Amendments of 1994, 108 US Stat 3124, October 6, 1994

The amendments specifically recognize the legality of the use of peyote in traditional Native religions, as well as the use of eagle feathers. A Commission on the Religious Freedom of Native American Prisoners was established, and Native prisoners were given access to counselors and provided opportunities to engage in their traditional religious practices such as sweat lodge experiences.

From the Bench: Major U.S. and Canadian Supreme Court Cases

Johnson v. McIntosh, 21 U.S. (8 Wheaton) 543 (1823)

This is the first of three cases by the John Marshall–led Court. Two parties argued about ownership of lands in Illinois. Johnson purchased the lands directly from Native Americans before the Revolutionary War, while McIntosh held the lands under a federal government grant. Marshall reasoned that the Native Americans have sovereign rights on their lands, but the sovereignty is not complete. Rather, the Europeans by conquest or by discovery acquired a legal claim to the lands held by the Natives, while the Natives retained a right of occupancy. The right did not include a right to sell legal title. The English achieved title by discoveries, and these titles passed to the U.S. government after the Revolution. Johnson's title, claimed by direct purchase from Natives, was, therefore, not enforceable. McIntosh's title was valid.

Cherokee Nation v. Georgia, 30 U.S. (5 Peters) 1 (1831)

With the Treaty of Hopewell, hostilities between the United States and the Cherokee Nation were ended; the United States guaranteed protection to the Cherokees and gave them the exclusive right to occupy lands that were within the state of Georgia. In 1802, Georgia ceded certain western lands, and in exchange the federal government agreed to extinguish Cherokee land titles. The state of Georgia then placed the Cherokee lands under the authority of new county governments. The Cherokees sued in the U.S. Supreme Court to enjoin enforcement of local Georgia laws on their lands. Although Justice Marshall was sympathetic, he refused to order Georgia to "back off." Marshall ruled that the Court did not have jurisdiction to hear the case. It could only hear suits against a state if they were brought by another state or by a foreign nation.

Worcester v. Georgia, 31 U.S. (6 Peters) 515 (1831)

In 1829, the state of Georgia passed a law requiring a non-Native to have a permit in order to enter Cherokee lands. Worcester, a missionary, had not secured the required permit. He was convicted of violating the Georgia law and sentenced to four years in prison. His appeal came to the Supreme Court, and the Court held that the state of Georgia had no jurisdiction over Native American lands. The tribes were "distinct, independent, political communities," that maintained authority over their internal affairs, subject only to treaties and laws of the United States. The treaties and the Constitution did put the internal affairs of the Native Americans outside the reach of state governments. The state law was void. Worcester had to wait sometime for relief, as the state of Georgia refused to release him from custody, and the Court did not have powers to order U.S. officials to enforce his release. President Jackson was purported to have said: "John Marshall has made his decision; now let him enforce it" (reported in Horace Greeley, *American Conflict,* p. 106 [1864]). Some doubt he said the words. However, embarrassment over the case caused Jackson to ask the Georgia governor to pardon Worcester, which he did in 1833 (Getches, Wilkinson, and Williams, p. 149).

Ex Parte Crow Dog, 109 U.S. 556 (1883)

Crow Dog, a Sioux, murdered Spotted Tail, also a Sioux, on reservation lands in Dakota Territory. A tribal court required Crow Dog's family to make restitution to Spotted Tail's family.

The federal district attorney, not satisfied with the judgment, brought murder charges against Crow Dog in federal courts. After conviction and a sentence of death, Crow Dog appealed, claiming that the federal courts had no jurisdiction over the crime. Acts of Congress were somewhat contradictory. However, the Supreme Court held that the statutes needed to be very specific if the federal government was to assume jurisdiction over matters among Natives on Native lands. Otherwise, the government would be abridging Native sovereignty. The conviction was overturned.

United States v. Kagama, 118 U.S. 375 (1886)

Congress deemed the result in the Crow Dog case to be unacceptable. Accordingly, in 1885, the Major Crimes Act was passed. It gave federal courts jurisdiction in cases of murder and other indicated major crimes by Natives on Native lands. Here two Natives murdered another Native American on the Hoopa Valley Reservation in California. They challenged the jurisdiction of the federal courts in the case. The Supreme Court upheld their conviction and the constitutionality of the 1885 Act. Justice Miller wrote that the matter was "within the competency of Congress. These Indian tribes are the wards of the nation. They are communities dependent on the United States. Dependent largely for their daily food. Dependent for their political rights. They owe no allegiance to the states, and receive from them no protection . . ."

Talton v. Mayes, 163 U.S. 376 (1896)

This was a review of another murder case on reservation lands. Here a Cherokee was convicted in tribal courts. However, he was brought to trial as a result of actions by a five-person grand jury. The Bill of Rights (Fifth Amendment) required larger grand juries. The Court held that the Bill of Rights did not apply to tribal court procedures. "The powers of local self-government enjoyed by the Cherokee Nation existed prior to the constitution . . ." This principle—that the Bill of Rights did not apply to tribal procedures—was altered considerably with the passage of the Indian Civil Rights Act of 1968.

Lone Wolf v. Hitchcock, 187 U.S. 553 (1903)

The 1867 Treaty of Medicine Lodge stipulated that the lands of the Kiowa Comanche Reservation could not be reduced without a three-fourths approval vote of the adult males. However, under the Dawes Act, lands were allotted to individual tribal members, and excess lands were placed up for sale to outsiders. The tribe charged that the treaty had been violated. The Supreme Court disagreed. The justices held that Congress had "plenary authority over the tribal relations . . . from the beginning, and the power has always been deemed a political one, not subject to be controlled by the (courts)." Included in the power is "the power to abrogate the provisions of an Indian treaty."

Winters v. United States, 297 U.S. 564 (1908)

The Supreme Court established the doctrine of reserved water rights. The Fort Belknap Reservation of Montana had been established in 1884. Afterward settlers in the area claimed, by the law of prior appropriation, rights to waters otherwise available to the reservation. When the reservation later sought to begin agricultural operations, it did not have sufficient water. It sought rights to waters already claimed by the settlers. The Court held that when the reservation was set up the national government reserved sufficient waters for the Indians so that they could develop their lands to their best use at a future time. The practical effect of the case was that the states and their non-Natives and the Native Americans would negotiate agreements on the amounts of water each would have. In cases of disputes, the matters could go to either federal or state courts. However, the McCarran Act of 1952 indicated that the cases should first go to state courts so as to reduce the problems of dual litigation. State decisions could be appealed to the U.S. Supreme Court.

In Re Eskimo, 1939 Sup. Ct. Rp. 104 (1939)

The Canadian Supreme Court determined that references to "Indians" in the British North American Act of 1867 meant all Native peoples including the Inuits of Quebec Province. The national government, not the provinces, had jurisdiction over Inuit activities.

Williams v. Lee, 358 U.S. 217 (1959)

A non-Native general store operator (Lee) sold goods on credit to a Navajo (Williams). The store was on the Navajo reservation.

When Williams did not pay the debt, Lee sued in Arizona courts for payment. He won a judgment that was upheld in the Arizona Supreme Court. Williams appealed. The U.S. Supreme Court reversed the Arizona rulings, holding that Congress had "acted consistently upon the assumption that the states have no power to regulate the affairs of Indians on a reservation." Commerce on a reservation remains under the jurisdiction of the tribes and Congress, unless Congress specifically gives jurisdiction to another party. Justice Hugo Black indicated that "It is immaterial that (Lee) is not an Indian. He was on the reservation and the transaction with an Indian took place there."

Warren Trading Post v. Arizona Tax Commission, 380 U.S. 685 (1965)

Warren, a non-Native, had a store on the Navajo reservation in Arizona. The state levied its 2 percent sales tax on the gross income of the store. The Arizona Supreme Court upheld the levy, and Warren appealed. The Supreme Court recognized that numerous acts of Congress had established the dominant "sole power" role of the federal government in regulating trade with Native Americans. The Court held that the tax "would to a substantial extent frustrate the ensuring that no burden shall be imposed upon . . . trading . . . on reservations except as authorized by Acts of Congress . . ." The tax was nullified.

Calder v. Attorney General of British Columbia, 1973 Sup. Ct. Rp. 313 (1973)

The Canadian Supreme Court recognized that Native Canadians had original legal rights to their lands and that the rights could be secured from them by non-Natives only through legal processes—through treaties or proper land purchases. If the land was acquired through the treaty process, the provisions of the treaties would be subject to enforcement by the Canadian government. The ruling led the Canadian government to create an Office of Native Claims.

McClanahan v. Arizona State Tax Commission, 441 U.S. 164 (1973)

McClanahan is a Navajo. All her 1967 income was earned on the reservation. When Arizona withheld state income tax from her, she sued for a tax refund. The Arizona courts denied the refund, and she appealed. Justice Thurgood Marshall wrote for a unanimous Court in reversing Arizona and ordering the refund. Marshall analyzed treaties with the Navajos and found no provisions allowing state taxation. Instead, the treaties implied that the Navajos would be under federal protection. Arizona had decided not to seek Public Act 280 control over reservations and hence had no claim to levy taxes.

United States v. Mazurie, 419 U.S. 544 (1975)

In 1953, Congress passed a local option law for alcoholic beverages in "Indian Country." The Wind River, Wyoming, reservation permitted sales if distributors followed state licensing laws. Mazurie was given a state license to operate a tavern on fee lands (private lands) within the reservation boundaries. Later the Wind River tribes passed an ordinance requiring a tribal license to sell alcoholic beverages. Mazurie applied for a tribal license for the tavern. He was turned down following a public hearing. Mazurie closed the tavern but later reopened it and was charged with violating the tribal ordinance. Mazurie appealed. Lower federal courts overturned the tribal conviction; however, the Supreme Court reversed, and upheld the conviction. Justice Rehnquist defended the 1953 congressional delegation of power to the tribe as being consistent with tribal sovereignty to regulate tribal internal affairs.

Bryan v. Itasca County, 426 U.S. 373 (1976)

Bryan—a Chippewa—owned a mobile home on the Leech Lake Reservation in Minnesota. The local county government (non-Native) assessed a personal property tax against Bryan's home (which he personally owned). Bryan objected, but the Minnesota courts upheld the tax. Bryan appealed. Minnesota claimed that as a state covered by Public Act 280 it could tax the "private" property of tribal members. Public Act 280 gave states jurisdiction over criminal matters and matters of general civil law, an exception being taxation on tribal property. The Court held that taxation authority was not covered by the Act nor were matters of civil regulation. The justices reasoned that the "taxation exception" was not limiting, but that the power to tax would have required a very specific positive statement. The tax was nullified.

United States v. Washington, 520 F. 2d 676 (1974), 423 U.S. 1086 (1976)

This case is part of a series of cases (see *Puyallup* cases in Chapter 4) in several states regarding the off-reservation fishing and hunting rights of Native Americans. When Washington State tribes gave up lands in treaties in the 1850s, they were permitted to retain the right to fish in nonreservation areas. The Treaty of Medicine Creek was typical: "The right of taking fish, at all usual and accustomed grounds and stations, is further secured to said Indians, in common with all citizens of the territory . . ." The state sought to impose restrictions on Native fishing, and several tribes challenged the state in court. As a result, the federal district court held that the Native Americans had the right to have one-half of the catch taken in the state. The state was empowered to limit the overall catch for purposes of conservation. However, the state could not regulate the methods the Natives used in gaining their catch, even though they could apply the rules to non-Natives.

United States v. Wheeler, 435 U.S. 322 (1978)

Wheeler, a Navajo, pleaded guilty to disorderly conduct and contributing to the delinquency of a minor in tribal court. He was convicted. Later, federal charges were made against him for rape. The crime alleged was part of the incident for which he had been convicted. He was found guilty in federal court. Was this double jeopardy prohibited by the Fifth Amendment of the United States Constitution? The Supreme Court said it was not. Double jeopardy protections apply to actions by a single sovereign government. They do not apply to separate charges made by federal and state governments because of the same incident, as state and federal courts are under different sovereign entities. Similarly, the Court reasoned that tribal courts are under a different sovereignty than are federal courts. "The powers of Indian tribes are, in general, inherent powers of a limited sovereignty which has never been extinguished." Even though Congress may control tribal affairs, this does not mean tribal courts are under the same jurisdiction as federal courts.

Oliphant v. Squamish, 435 U.S. 191 (1978)

Non-Native David Oliphant was arrested on the reservation by Squamish tribal police for assaulting an officer and resisting arrest. The Squamish have a tribal Law and Order Code. Tribal juries do not include non-Natives. The Supreme Court ruled that tribal courts did not have jurisdiction over criminal charges against non-Natives. Justice Rehnquist analyzed several federal statutes and found that they consistently supported the notion that tribes did not have criminal jurisdiction over non-Natives. He reasoned that they lacked such power unless Congress specifically gave it to them in legislation. While some tribal courts are sophisticated and the Indian Civil Rights Act (1968) provides protections to defendants, the question of subjecting non-Natives to the court's jurisdiction is a political matter for Congress to determine.

Santa Clara Pueblo v. Martinez, 436 U.S. 439 (1978)

Mrs. Martinez is a member of the Santa Clara Pueblo. She married a Navajo. Her children were denied membership in the Pueblo, and denied tribal benefits, because their father was not from the Santa Clara Pueblo. On the other hand, the children of a Santa Clara Pueblo father and a non-Pueblo mother would be considered a member of the patriarchal Pueblo community. The Martinez children sue the Pueblo for membership on the basis of the Indian Civil Rights Act (1968), which guarantees equal protection of the law. The Pueblo's claims of sovereign immunity were disregarded by the Court on the grounds that the ICRA provided legal mechanisms for assuring rights. However, the Supreme Court reversed the lower courts and denied relief to the Martinez family. The Court maintained that the definition of tribal (Pueblo) membership was clearly a matter of tribal sovereignty that preceded the writing of the U.S. Constitution and the ICRA. The membership criteria could be altered only with very specific legislation from Congress.

Queen v. Dick, 1985 (2) Sup. Ct. Rp. 309 (1985)

A province's fishing and hunting laws were held not to apply to status Indians off their reservations, as these Native Canadians preserved rights to hunt and fish from a time prior to the establishment of their reserves.

Derrickson v. Derrickson, 1986 (1) Sup. Ct. Rp. 285 (1986)

The Canadian Supreme Court held that provincial laws relating to domestic matters such as the division of property at the time of a divorce do not apply to Native peoples.

California v. Cabazon, 480 U.S. 94 (1987)

The Cabazon band was operating bingo and poker games in ways that were not permitted by California gaming regulations. California allowed the games with certain restrictions as to hours and prize limits. These restrictions were not followed by the Cabazon band. The Court ruled that California—a Public Act 280 state—could not prohibit the Native gaming, as the gaming restrictions were "regulatory" and not "prohibitory." If they were "prohibitory," nobody would be allowed to have bingo and poker games in California. The case ruling meant, in essence, that a tribe could offer a game that was legal within a state, and they could operate the gaming totally unregulated by the state. The fear of unregulated Native American gaming enterprise and the possibilities of organized crime involvement led to the passage of the Indian Gaming Regulatory Act of 1988.

Lyng v. Northwest Indian Cemetery Protective Association, 485 U.S. 439 (1988)

The federal government sought to build a seventy-five-mile paved road through national forest lands outside of all reservations but near three reservations. Three tribes (the Association) protested that the road and its traffic would disturb their religious practices. They engaged in meditations at spiritual places within the forest. An initial environmental statement suggested that the road would violate the Natives' free exercise of their religion. The Forest Service took this into consideration but decided to build the road anyway. The tribes challenged the decision. A split Supreme Court ruled in favor of the Forest Service. Justice O'Connor wrote that the construction of the road in no way coerced the Native Americans or anyone else regarding religious practices, even though it would interfere with the practices. However, the government could not operate if it were required to satisfy every citizen's religious needs and desires.

Seminole Tribe of Florida v. Florida, 517 U.S. 1133 (1996)

The U.S. Supreme Court refused to review a lower court ruling, hence, letting the ruling stand. The ruling held that part of the Indian Gaming Regulatory Act, which allowed tribes to sue state governments to force negotiations to permit casino gambling, was unconstitutional. The courts ruled that state governments as sovereign entities could not be brought to federal courts as the Eleventh Amendment of the Constitution gave them immunity from most suits in federal courts.

The Queen v. Marshall, 3 Sup. Ct. Rp. (1999)

The Supreme Court of Canada ruled on September 17, 1999, that Donald Marshall, a Mi'kmaq of Nova Scotia, had rights to engage in fishing without a license, out of season, and with nets that violated legal provisions of the province of Nova Scotia. The Court overturned an earlier conviction of Marshall as the justices argued that treaties from the 1760s gave Marshall the right to fish without being subject to provincial regulations.

As a result of the case, thirty-four Native bands in eastern Quebec and the Maritime (Atlantic) provinces began to fish for lobster out of season. Non-Native fishermen began to destroy their lobster nets, and a chaotic situation ensued. On November 17, 1999, the Court revisited the issue. It said that its ruling would stand, but it made clarifying points to the effect that governmental regulations specifically pertaining to conservation could be enforced against Native people. The Court also decreed that the Marshall decision did not extend to logging rights.

Miami Nation v. Norton, 7th Cir. 255 F. 3d 342 (2001), Affirmed, certiorari review denied February 19, 2002 (docket 01-776)

The Supreme Court refused to review a lower federal court that held that the Miami Nation of Indiana did not have standing to be recognized as a federal tribe for purposes of federal benefits. The tribe no longer occupied lands in Indiana and did not have political structures in the state. The holding came even though the tribe was previously in the state of Indiana and its tribal status had never been terminated.

Bay Mills Community v. Michigan, 626 N.W. 2d 169 (2001), Affirmed, certiorari review denied January 14, 2002 (docket 01-1036)

The Supreme Court let stand a Michigan court decision that allowed the state to sell tribal lands for repayment of taxes owed by the tribe to the state government. The taxes were imposed when the lands were owned by the tribe but were not being held in trust for the tribe. The lands were later put into trust, yet the tax bill remained effective.

United States v. Lara, 8th Cir., 324 F. 3d 635, 8th Cir., Reversed, U.S. Supreme Court, April 19, 2004 (docket 03-1271)

If a tribal court puts a non-Native person on trial, and an innocent verdict is rendered, that person may not be tried again in a non-Native federal court for the same crime. This is the case even if the trial in tribal court was in error because the court lacked jurisdiction to hear the case. It was held that the defendant had the double jeopardy protections of the Bill of Rights because the tribal court and the federal courts received their authority from the same sovereign, the U.S. government.

FIGURE 1
Federal Indian Reservations, 2005

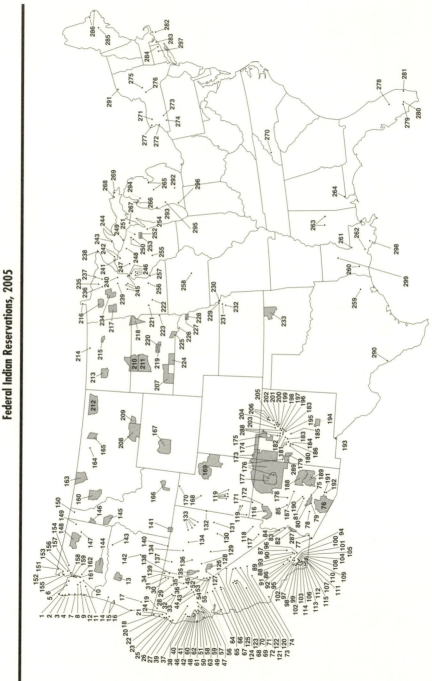

LEGEND

1. Makah
2. Ozene
3. Quileute
4. Hoh
5. Lower Elwha
6. Jamestown Klallam
7. Quinault
8. Skokomish
9. Squaxin
10. Nisqually
11. Chehalis
12. Shoalwater Bay
13. Warm Springs
14. Grand Ronde
15. Siletz
16. Coos, Lower Umpqua, and Siuslaw
17. Cow Creek of Umpqua
18. Smith River Rancheria
19. Karok
20. Resighini Rancheria
21. Yurok
22. Big Lagoon Rancheria
23. Trinidad Rancheria
24. Hoopa Valley

25. Blue Lake Rancheria
26. Table Bluff Rancheria
27. Rohnerville Rancheria
28. Big Bend Rancheria
29. Lookout Rancheria
30. Alturas Rancheria
31. XI Rancheria
32. Roaring Creek Rancheria
33. Montgomery Creek Rancheria
34. Likely Rancheria
35. Susanville Rancheria
36. Greenville Rancheria
37. Round Valley
38. Laytonville Rancheria
39. Grindstone Creek Rancheria
40. Sherwood Valley Rancheria
41. Redwood Valley Rancheria

42. Coyote Valley Rancheria
43. Enterprise Rancheria
44. Berry Creek Rancheria
45. Reno Sparks
46. Upper Lake Rancheria
47. Colusa Rancheria
48. Robinson Rancheria
49. Cortina Rancheria
50. Sulphur Bank Rancheria
51. Big Valley Rancheria
52. Carson Colony
53. Dresslerville Colony
54. Woodfords Indian Community
55. Washoe
56. Shingle Springs Rancheria
57. Rumsey Rancheria
58. Middletown Rancheria
59. Dry Creek Rancheria

60. Pinoleville Rancheria
61. Hopland Rancheria
62. Manchester Rancheria
63. Stewarts Point Rancheria
64. Jackson Rancheria
65. Sheep Ranch Rancheria
66. Chicken Ranch Rancheria
67. Tolumne Rancheria
68. Northfork Rancheria
69. Big Sandy Rancheria
70. Table Mountain Rancheria
71. Cold Springs Rancheria
72. Santa Rosa Rancheria
73. Tule River
74. Santa Ynes
75. Gila River
76. Tohono O'odham
77. Cocopah
78. Gila Bend

79. Maricopa
80. Gila River
81. Salt River
82. Colorado River
83. Chemehuevi
84. Fort Mojave
85. Yavapai
86. San Manuel
87. Twentynine Palms
88. Morongo
89. Agua Caliente
90. Cabazon
91. Saboba
92. Ramona
93. Augustine
94. Santa Rosa
95. Cahuilla
96. Torres-Martinez
97. Pechanga
98. Pala
99. Pauma
100. Los Coyotes
101. La Jollai
102. Rincon
103. San Pasqual
104. Mesa Grande
105. Santa Ysabel
106. Inaja-Cosmit
107. Capitan Grande

108. Cuyapaipe
109. Manzanita
110. Campo
111. La Posta
112. Sycuan
113. Jamul
114. Barona Rancheria
115. Viejas
116. Hualapai
117. Las Vegas Colony
118. Moapa River
119. Paiute
120. Lone Pine Rancheria
121. Fort Independence
122. Big Pine Rancheria
123. Bishop Rancheria
124. Benton Paiute
125. Bridgeport Rancheria
126. Walker River
127. Yerington
128. Fallon Colony and Rancheria
129. Yomba
130. Duckwater
131. Ely Colony
132. Goshute
133. Te-Moak

134. Winnemucca Colony
135. Pyramid Lake
136. Lovelock Colony
137. Summit Lake
138. Cedarville Rancheria
139. Fort Bidwell
140. Fort McDermitt
141. Duck Valley
142. Burns Paiute Colony
143. Umatilla
144. Yakima
145. Nez Perce
146. Couer D'Alene
147. Spokane
148. Colville
149. Kalispel
150. Kootenai
151. Noosack
152. Lummi
153. Upper Skagit
154. Sauk Suiattle
155. Swinomish
156. Stillaguamish
157. Tulalip
158. Port Gamble
159. Port Madison

160. Flathead
161. Puyallup
162. Muckleshoot
163. Blackfeet
164. Rocky Boys
165. Fort Belknap
166. Fort Hall
167. Wind River
168. Skull Valley
169. Unitah and Ouray
170. Northwestern Shoshoni
171. Kaibab
172. Havasuapi
173. Ute Mountain
174. Southern Ute
175. Jicarilla
176. Navajo (3)
177. Hopi
178. Camp Verde
179. Ramah Navajo
180. Acoma
181. Laguna (3)
182. Zai (2)
183. Santa Ana
184. Canoncito
185. Isleta
186. Alamo Navajo

187. Payson
     Community
188. Fort Apache
189. San Carlos
190. Fort McDowell
191. Pascua Yaqui
192. San Xavier
193. Ysleta Del Sur
194. Mescalero
195. Sandia
196. San Felipe
197. Santo Domingo
198. Cochiti
199. San Ildefonso
200. Tesuque
201. Nambe
202. Pojoaque
203. Santa Clara
204. San Juan
205. Picuris
206. Taos (2)
207. Pine Ridge
208. Crow
209. Northern
     Cheyenne
210. Standing Rock
211. Cheyenne River
212. Fort Peck
213. Fort Berthold
214. Turtle Mountain
215. Devils Lake
216. Red Lake (2)
217. White Earth
218. Lake Traverse
219. Lower Brule
220. Crow Creek
221. Upper Sioux
222. Lower Sioux
223. Flandreau
224. Rosebud
225. Yankton
226. Santee Sioux
227. Winnebago
228. Omaha
229. Sac and Fox
230. Iowa
231. Kickapoo
232. Potawatomi
233. Osage
234. Leech Lake
235. Bois Forte
236. Deer Creek
237. Vermillion Lake
238. Grand Portage
239. Sandy Lake
240. Fond Du Lac
241. Red Cliff
242. Bad River (2)
243. Ontonagon
244. L'Anse
245. Mille Lacs
246. St. Croix
247. Lac Courte Oreilles
248. Lac Du Flambeau
249. Lac Vieux Desert
250. Sokaogon
     Chippewa (2)
251. Forest County
     Potawatomi
252. Menominee
253. Stockbridge
254. Oneida
255. Ho-Chunk
256. Shakopee
257. Prune Island
258. Sac and Fox
     Settlement
259. Alabama-
     Coushatta
260. Coushatta
261. Tunica-Biloxi
262. Chitimacha
263. Mississippi
     Choctaw
264. Poarch Creek
265. Isabella (2)
266. Grand Traverse
267. Hannahville
268. Bay Mills
269. Sault Saint Marie
270. Cherokee
271. Tonawanda
272. Cattaraugus
273. Oil Springs
274. Allegany
275. Oneida
276. Onondaga
277. Tuscarora
278. Brighton
279. Big Cypress
280. Miccosukee
281. Hollywood
282. Wamponoog
283. Narragansett
284. Mashantucket
     Pequot
285. Penobscot
286. Passamaquoddy
     (2)
287. Fort Yuma
288. Jemez
289. Zuni
290. Texas Kickapoo
291. St. Regis
292. Huron Potawatomi
293. Little River Ottawa
294. Little Traverse Bay
295. Match-e-be-nash-
     she-wish
296. Pokagon
297. Mohegan
298. Houma
299. Jena

NOTE: Several reservations have been added to the federal system since this map was created in 1992.

Adapted from: Indian Lands Map, 1992. Compiled by the *Handbook of North American Indians* (Smithsonian Institute) in cooperation with the Bureau of Indian Affairs, prepared by the U.S. Geological Survey.

TABLE 1
Tribal Lands in the United States (Acres)

Year	Tribal Lands	Allotted Lands	Total
1871	111,761,558	10,231,725	121,993,283
1881	139,006,794	16,625,518	155,632,312
1887	119,375,930	17,018,965	136,394,895
1890	86,540,824	17,773,525	104,314,349
1900	52,455,827	25,409,546	77,865,373
1911	40,263,442	32,272,420	72,535,862
1920	35,501,661	37,158,655	72,660,316
1929	32,014,945	39,129,268	71,144,213
1933	29,481,685	40,106,736	69,588,421
1933	29,481,685	17,829,414	47,311,099
1939	35,402,440	17,594,376	52,996,816
1945	37,288,768	17,357,540	54,646,308
1953	42,785,935	14,674,763	57,460,698
1962	38,814,074	11,763,160	50,577,234
1974	40,772,934	10,244,481	51,017,415
1979	41,803,230	10,058,445	51,861,675
1983	42,385,031	10,226,180	52,611,211

Sources: Stuart, Paul. *Nations within a Nation: Historical Statistics of American Indians*. New York: Greenwood Press, 1987; and also *Annual Reports of Indian Lands*, Bureau of Indian Affairs.

TABLE 2
Native Lands by State (1983 Acreage)

State	Tribal Lands	Allotted Lands	Total
Alaska	89,759	705,445	792,204
Arizona	19,556,806	252,407	19,809,213
California	501,388	67,839	569,227
Colorado	783,903	3,043	786,946
Florida	79,495	—	79,495
Idaho	462,395	330,104	792,499
Iowa	4,164	—	4,164
Kansas	7,355	22,298	29,653
Louisiana	416	—	416
Maine	221,633	—	221,633
Michigan	12,230	9,266	21,496
Minnesota	714,118	51,259	765,377
Mississippi	17,635	19	17,654
Missouri	—	374	374
Montana	2,256,358	2,966,353	5,222,711
Nebraska	23,389	41,146	64,535
Nevada	1,141,501	78,567	1,220,068
New Mexico	6,499,030	674,701	7,173,731
North Carolina	56,461	—	56,461
North Dakota	210,116	632,166	842,282
Oklahoma	87,635	1,111,766	1,199,401
Oregon	622,297	136,851	759,148
South Dakota	2,636,292	2,456,043	5,092,335
Utah	2,249,726	33,423	2,283,149
Washington	2,027,475	477,644	2,505,119
Wisconsin	333,615	81,141	414,756
Wyoming	1,792,841	94,325	1,887,166
TOTAL	42,385,031	10,226,180	52,611,211

Source: *Annual Reports of Native Lands,* Bureau of Indian Affairs.

TABLE 3
The Largest Reservation Lands (1993 Acreage)

Reservation	Tribal	Allotted	Government	Total
Navajo, AZ, UT, NM	14,616,998	711,540	253,801	15,582,339
Papago, AZ	2,773,850	320	380	2,774,550
San Carlos, AZ	1,826,541	–	–	1,826,541
Wind River, WY	1,792,891	94,325	1,296	1,888,462
Ft. Apache, AZ	1,664,972	–	–	1,664,972
Hopi, AZ	1,560,993	220	–	1,561,213
Cheyenne River, SD	952,785	442,944	176	1,395,905
Yakima, WA	899,869	229,593	23	1,129,485
Pine Ridge, SD	695,613	1,089,344	1,231	1,786,188
Red Lake, MN	564,452	–	–	564,452

Source: Stuart, Paul. *Nations within a Nation: Historical Statistics of American Indians.* New York: Greenwood Press, 1987, p. 33.

TABLE 4
Native Populations, United States

Year	United States (except Alaska)	Alaska (Natives)	Total
1890	248,253	25,354	273,607
1900	237,196	29,536	266,732
1910	265,683	25,331	291,014
1920	244,437	26,558	270,995
1930	332,397	29,983	362,380
1940	333,969	32,458	366,427
1950	343,410	33,863	377,273
1960	509,147	42,489	551,636
1970	776,454	50,819	827,273
1980	1,356,297	64,103	1,420,400
1990	1,959,234	85,698	2,044,932
2000	2,377,913	98,043	2,475,956

Sources: 2000 U.S. Census; and Stuart, Paul. *Nations within a Nation: Historical Statistics of American Indians.* New York: Greenwood Press, 1987, pp. 53–56.

TABLE 5
Native Population by State

State	1890	1910	1930	1950	1970	1990	2000
Alaska	25,354	25,331	29,983	33,863	50,819	85,698	98,043
Alabama	1,143	909	465	928	2,443	16,506	22,430
Arizona	29,981	29,201	45,726	65,781	95,812	203,527	255,879
Arkansas	250	460	408	533	2,014	12,773	17,808
California	16,624	16,371	19,212	19,947	91,018	242,164	333,346
Colorado	1,092	1,482	1,395	1,567	8,836	27,776	44,241
Connecticut	228	152	162	333	2,222	6,654	9,639
Delaware	4	5	5	–	656	2,019	2,731
District of Columbia	25	68	40	330	956	1,466	1,713
Florida	171	74	587	1,011	6,677	36,335	53,541
Georgia	68	95	43	333	2,347	13,348	21,737
Hawaii	–	–	–	–	1,126	5,099	3,535
Idaho	4,223	3,488	3,638	3,800	6,687	13,780	17,645
Illinois	98	188	469	1,443	11,413	21,836	31,006
Indiana	343	279	285	438	3,887	12,720	15,815
Iowa	457	471	660	1,084	2,992	7,349	8,989
Kansas	1,682	2,444	2,454	2,381	8,672	21,965	24,936
Kentucky	71	234	22	234	1,531	5,769	8,616
Louisiana	628	780	1,536	409	5,294	18,541	25,477
Maine	559	892	1,012	1,522	2,195	5,998	7,098
Maryland	44	55	50	314	4,239	12,972	15,423
Massachusetts	428	688	674	1,201	4,475	12,241	15,015
Michigan	5,625	7,519	7,080	7,000	16,854	55,638	58,479
Minnesota	10,096	9,053	11,077	12,533	23,128	49,909	54,967
Mississippi	2,036	1,253	1,458	2,502	4,113	8,525	11,652

continues

TABLE 5 *cont.*

State	1890	1910	1930	1950	1970	1990	2000
Missouri	128	313	578	547	5,405	18,835	25,076
Montana	11,206	10,745	14,798	16,606	27,130	47,679	56,068
Nebraska	6,431	3,502	3,256	3,954	6,624	12,410	14,896
Nevada	5,156	5,240	4,871	5,025	7,933	19,637	26,420
New Hampshire	16	34	64	74	361	2,134	2,964
New Jersey	84	168	213	621	4,706	14,970	19,492
New Mexico	15,044	20,573	28,941	41,901	72,788	134,355	173,483
New York	6,044	6,046	6,973	10,640	28,355	62,651	82,461
North Carolina	1,516	7,851	16,579	3,742	44,406	80,155	99,551
North Dakota	8,174	6,486	8,387	10,766	14,369	25,917	31,329
Ohio	206	127	435	1,146	6,654	20,358	24,486
Oklahoma	64,456	74,825	92,725	53,769	98,468	252,420	273,230
Oregon	4,971	5,090	4,776	5,820	13,510	38,496	45,211
Pennsylvania	1,081	1,503	523	1,141	5,533	14,733	18,348
Rhode Island	180	284	318	385	1,390	4,071	5,121
South Carolina	173	331	959	554	2,241	8,246	13,718
South Dakota	19,854	19,137	21,833	23,344	32,365	50,575	62,283
Tennessee	146	216	171	339	2,276	10,039	15,152
Texas	708	702	1,001	2,736	17,957	65,877	118,362
Utah	3,456	3,123	2,869	4,201	11,273	24,283	29,684
Vermont	34	26	36	30	229	1,696	2,420
Virginia	349	539	799	1,056	4,853	15,282	21,172
Washington	11,181	10,997	11,253	13,816	33,386	81,483	93,301
West Virginia	9	36	18	160	751	2,458	3,606
Wisconsin	9,930	10,142	11,548	12,196	18,924	39,387	47,228
Wyoming	1,844	1,486	1,845	3,237	4,980	9,479	11,133
TOTAL	273,607	291,014	362,380	377,237	827,237	2,044,932	2,475,956

Source: 2000 U.S. Census.

TABLE 6
Family Incomes in the United States (1990)

	All Persons	Percent	Native Americans (Including Alaska)
Less than $5,000	2,582,206	11	49,114
$5,000 to $9,999	3,636,361	13	60,426
$10,000 to $14,999	4,676,092	12	54,908
$15,000 to $24,999	10,658,345	20	94,195
$25,000 to $34,999	10,729,951	15	71,009
$35,000 to $49,999	13,270,930	15	68,493
$50,000 to $74,999	11,857,079	10	46,094
$80,000 to $99,999	4,115,468	3	12,370
$100,000 or more	3,522,996	2	7,359
TOTAL	65,049,428	100	463,968
Median (dollars)	35,225	5	21,750
Mean (dollars)	43,803	6	28,028

Source: 1990 U.S. Census.

TABLE 7
Ten Largest Bands in Canada (1990)

	Population
1. Six Nations of the Grand River, Ontario	16,011
2. Kahnawake, Quebec	7,176
3. Bloo, Alberta	7,167
4. Mohawk of Akwesasue, Quebec	7,036
5. Saddle Lake, Alberta	5,765
6. Wikwemikong, Ontario	4,825
7. Lac La Range, Saskatchewan	4,737
8. Peguis, Manitoba	4,620
9. Peter Ballantyue, Saskatchewan	4,263
10. For Alexander, Manitoba	4,096

Source: 1990, Report, Department of Indian and Northern Affairs. "Native Peoples," in *The Canadian Global Almanac 1992: A Book of Facts* (Toronto: Global Press, 1992), pp. 564–567.

TABLE 8
Native Population of Canada (1986)

	Total Native Population[1]	Indigenous	On Reserve	No. of Bands	Metis	Inuit
Atlantic Provinces[2]	34,440 (4.8%)	27,570	12,968	31	3,455	4,650
Quebec	80,940 (11.4%)	68,585	33,802	39	11,435	7,360
Ontario	167,375 (23.5%)	150,715	58,702	126	18,265	2,956
Manitoba	85,235 (12.0%)	55,960	46,708	60	33,285	700
Saskatchewan	77,650 (10.9%)	55,215	39,336	70	25,695	190
Alberta	103,930 (14.6%)	68,965	37,873	42	40,125	1,125
British Columbia	126,625 (17.8%)	112,790	44,064	196	15,295	1,035
Yukon	4,995 (0.7%)	4,775	345	16	220	85
Northwest Territory	30,530 (4.3%)	9,380	194	21	3,825	18,360
TOTAL	711,725 (100%)	548,945	(273,992)	601	151,605	36,460

Source: 1986 Census of Canada.
[1]Figures not identical to total as some people are double counted.
[2]Newfoundland, Prince Edward Island, Nova Scotia, New Brunswick.

TABLE 9
Twenty-Five Largest Tribal Casinos

Casino	Casino Area	Employees	Tables	Machines	1990 Population	1990 Cap Income	1990 Poverty %	2000 Population	2000 Cap Income	2000 Poverty %
1. Mashantucket (CT)	284,236	10,687	312	4,585	50	10,271	0.0	590	27,261	3.1
2. Mille Lacs (MN)	270,000	2,334	87	2,875	354	2,189	84.0	2,325	15,880	13.2
3. Saginaw Chippewa (MI)	205,000	2,500	80	3,600	735	5,083	39.8	2,351	18,862	6.8
4. Mohegan (CT)	150,000	5,600	180	3,000	240	12,297	46.2	1,131	17,643	0.0
5. Ft. McDowell (AZ)	150,000	1,400	0	475	568	5,610	23.7	829	19,293	14.0
6. Hollywood (FL)	120,500	1,033	66	885	560	6,522	40.5	852	16,268	15.8
7. Viejas (CA)	120,000	1,600	73	1,132	229	5,588	26.0	188	22,269	10.8
8. Barona (CA)	115,000	1,100	32	1,000	351	6,916	25.0	237	32,313	15.1
9. Hochunk (WI)	112,000	2,025	91	2,634	526	4,376	41.6	4,050	11,125	18.6
10. St. Ste Marie (MI)	97,507	2,183	96	2,284	501	4,104	47.6	889	46,399	26.0
11. Oneida (WI)	95,908	1,520	80	2,500	2,450	7,109	27.5	1,063	25,689	4.0
12. St. Croix (WI)	95,000	1,112	44	1,270	436	4,294	44.6	1,294	10,798	23.8
13. Cabazon (CA)	94,000	550	10	800	37	4,454	50.0	800	7,734	19.5
14. San Manuel (CA)	92,000	1,400	50	1,000	38	3,437	81.8	80	8,849	62.0
15. Shakopee (MN)	90,000	4,000	120	2,500	182	27,119	5.8	403	146,000	0.0
16. White Earth (MN)	90,000	1,000	32	850	2,798	4,917	46.4	6,311	12,786	15.9

continues

TABLE 9 cont.

Casino	Casino Area	Employees	Tables	Machines	1990 Population	1990 Cap Income	1990 Poverty %	2000 Population	2000 Cap Income	2000 Poverty %
17. Choctaw (MS)	90,000	2,000	96	2,800	4,056	4,440	38.8	7,892	7,530	35.0
18. Fond du Lac (WI)	85,000	945	44	1,339	1,083	5,457	40.2	1,597	15,551	11.4
19. Prairie Island (MN)	80,000	1,400	60	1,500	26	3,609	71.4	226	26,955	6.1
20. Pojoaque (NM)	80,000	1,180	30	1,487	2,000	9,520	0.0	209	17,348	11.2
21. Morongo (CA)	80,000	800	49	1,627	526	6,438	30.1	740	17,413	14.7
22. Chukchansi (CA)	80,000	750	35	830	35	6,736	18.2	7	146,000	0.0
23. 29 Palms (CA)	72,000	300	21	600	0	0	0.0	0	0	0.0
24. Coushatta (LA)	71,000	2,100	60	2,010	42	4,588	61.5	586	18,828	0.0
25. Sycuan (CA)	70,000	1,100	72	444	0	0	0.0	52	58,012	0.0
	Total 2,889,151	Total 50,619	Total 1,820	Total 44,027	Total 17,823	Median 5,083	Median 39.8	Total 29,025	Median 17,413	Median 11.4
	Average 115,566	Average 2,024.76	Average 72.8	Average 1,761.08	Average 712.92			Average 1,161		

Sources: Thompson, William N. Gambling in America: An Encyclopedia of History, Issues, and Society. Santa Barbara and Denver: ABC-CLIO, 2001, pp. 258–259; U.S. Census Data 1990 (factfinder.census.gov); "Census 2000 Data for 539 Tribes" (factfinder.census.gov); and Casino Executive Magazine, June 1997.

TABLE 10
Twenty-Five Largest Tribes in Population

Tribes	Casino Area	Employees	Tables	Machines	1990 Population	1990 Cap Income	1990 Poverty %	2000 Population	2000 Cap Income	2000 Poverty %
1. Navajo (AZ-NM)	0	0	0	0	143,507	3,735	55.4	181,269	7,269	40.10
2. Pine Ridge (SD)	30,000	129	8	113	11,006	3,115	60.5	15,542	6,143	46.32
3. Ft. Apache (AZ)	5,300	700	5	299	9,902	3,805	49.9	12,383	6,358	42.21
4. Gila River (AZ)	68,000	1,200	40	771	9,101	3,176	62.8	11,287	6,133	46.92
5. Tohono O'odam (AZ)	48,000	750	28	500	8,490	3,113	62.8	10,734	6,998	40.46
6. Rosebud (SD)	0	0	0	0	7,998	3,739	57.6	10,369	7,279	45.90
7. Zuni (NM)	0	0	0	0	7,094	3,904	47.4	7,749	6,976	43.02
8. San Carlos (AZ)	65,000	350	10	500	7,060	3,173	59.8	9,385	5,200	48.15
9. Blackfeet (MT)	0	0	0	0	7,031	4,718	45.7	10,115	9,751	30.00
10. Hopi (AZ)	0	0	0	0	7,002	4,566	47.7	6,836	8,531	36.45
11. Turtle Mt. (ND)	22,800	323	10	0	6,730	4,681	51.9	8,244	9,017	35.08
12. Coquille (OR)	14,300	350	13	334	6,236	8,301	24.2	7,598	12,185	20.64
13. Yakima (WA)	0	0	0	0	6,198	4,927	42.5	31,731	10,618	24.40
14. Osage (OK)	0	0	0	0	6,100	7,236	26.5	44,437	16,656	10.31
15. Ft. Peck (MT)	0	0	0	0	5,822	4,778	41.8	10,320	10,691	30.06
16. Wind RV (WY)	0	0	0	0	5,717	4,340	47.8	23,237	14,661	15.94

continues

TABLE 10 cont.

Tribes	Casino Area	Employees	Tables	Machines	1990 Population	1990 Cap Income	1990 Poverty %	2000 Population	2000 Cap Income	2000 Poverty %
17. E. Cherokee (NC)	25,000	180	0	874	5,287	6,382	30.0	7,538	12,581	19.72
18. Flathead (MT)	0	0	0	0	5,182	6,428	31.8	26,203	14,503	15.78
19. Cheyenne RV (SD)	0	0	0	0	5,092	4,077	57.2	8,475	8,710	34.50
20. Standing Rock (ND)	42,000	400	12	470	4,872	3,421	54.9	8,241	8,192	33.10
21. Colorado River (AZ)	20,000	240	4	321	4,736	5,959	39.3	9,197	12,621	17.05
22. Crow (MT)	20,000	70	0	100	4,706	4,243	45.5	6,878	94,440	26.58
23. Choctaw (MS)	90,000	2,000	96	2,800	4,056	9,400	38.8	5,309	7,530	35.00
24. Colville (WA)	16,000	450	26	811	3,779	7,561	31.9	7,598	12,185	20.64
25. N. Cheyenne (MT)	5,000	50	0	46	3,564	4,479	46.4	4,471	7,736	39.32
	Total 471,400	Total 7,192	Total 252	Total 7,939	Total 296,268	Median 4,479	Median 47.4	Total 485,146	Median 8,710	Median 34.5
	Average 18,856	Average 287.68	Average 10.08	Average 317.56	Average 11,850.72			Average 19,405.84		

Sources: Thompson, William N. *Gambling in America: An Encyclopedia of History, Issues, and Society.* Santa Barbara and Denver: ABC-CLIO, 2001, pp. 258–259; U.S. Census, 1990, 2000; and *Casino Executive Magazine,* June 1997.

8

Points of View

The Words of Native Americans

Dekanawidah (Founder of the Iroquois League, circa 1300–1550)

I name the tree the Tree of the Great Long Leaves. Under the shade of this tree of the Great Peace we spread the soft white feather down of the glove thistle as seats for you. There shall you sit and watch the council fire of the confederacy of the Five Nations. Roots have spread out from the Tree, and the name of these roots is the Great White Roots of Peace. If any man or any nation shall show a desire to obey the laws of the Great Peace, they shall trace the roots to their source, and they shall be welcomed to take shelter beneath the Tree of the Long Leaves. The smoke of the confederate council fire shall pierce the sky so that all nations may discover the central council fire of the Great Peace.

Armstrong, Virginia. (1971). *I Have Spoken*. Chicago: Swallow Press, p. 10.

Canassatego

Canassatego spoke for the Iroquois at the Treaty of Lancaster, signed July 4, 1744. He replied to an offer of the Virginia Legislature to the Six Nations, inviting them to send six youths to be educated at the Williamsburg College of William and Mary.

We know you highly esteem the kind of Learning taught in these Colleges, and the maintenance of our young Men, while with you, would be very expensive to you. We are convinced, therefore, that you mean to do us Good by your Proposal; and we thank you heartily. But you who are so wise must know that different Nations have different Conceptions of things; and you will not therefore take it amiss, if our Ideas of this kind of Education happens not to be the same with yours. We have had some experience of it. Several of our young People were formerly brought up in the colleges of the Northern Provinces; they were instructed in all your Sciences; but, when they came back to us, they were bad Runners, ignorant of every means of living in the Woods, unable to bear either Cold or Hunger, knew neither how to build a Cabin, take a deer or kill an enemy, spoke our language imperfectly, were therefore neither fit for Hunters, Warriors, nor Counselors; they were totally good for nothing. We are however not the less obliged for your kind Offer, tho' we decline accepting it; and to show our grateful Sense of it, if the Gentlemen of Virginia shall send us a Dozen of their Sons, we will take great care of their Education, instruct them in all we know, and make Men of them.

Armstrong, Virginia. (1971). *I Have Spoken*. Chicago: Swallow Press, p. 16.

Tecumseh

This message was sent to President Madison in 1810.

These lands are ours. No one has the right to remove us, because we were the first owners. The Great Spirit above has appointed this place for us, on which to light our fires, and here we will remain. As to boundaries, the Great Spirit knows no boundaries, nor will his red children acknowledge any.

Champagne, Duane. (1994). *Chronology of Native North American History*. Detroit: Gale Research, p. 504.

Crazy Horse

We had buffalo for food, and their hides for clothing and our tepees. We preferred hunting to a life of idleness on the reservations, where we were driven against our will. At times we did not get enough to eat, and we were not allowed to leave the reservation to hunt.

We preferred our own way of living. We were no expense to the government then. All we wanted was peace and to be left alone. Soldiers were sent out in the winter, who destroyed our villages. Then "Long Hair" (Custer) came in the same way. They say we massacred him, but he would have done the same to us had we not defended ourselves and fought to the last. Our first impulse was to escape with our squaws and papooses, but we were so hemmed in that we had to fight.

Armstrong, Virginia. (1971). *I Have Spoken.* Chicago: Swallow Press, p. 116.

Crowfoot (Blackfoot Chief)

Crowfoot, speaking of the benefits of Treaty Provisions, which permitted Royal Canadian Mounted Police to guard reserves:
If the (Royal Canadian Mounted Police) hadn't come to the country, where would we all be now? Bad men and bad whisky was killing us so fast that very few, indeed, of us would have been left today. The police have protected us as the feathers of a bird protects it from the frosts of winter.

Armstrong, Virginia. (1971). *I Have Spoken.* Chicago: Swallow Press, p. 117.

Chief Joseph (Nez Perce leader)

This speech was made October 5, 1877, on the occasion of the Nez Perce surrender:
I am tired of fighting. Our chiefs are killed. Looking Glass is dead. Toohoolhoolzate (Too-hool-hool-suit) is dead. The old men are dead. It is the young men who say yes and no. He who led the young men is dead. It is cold and we have no blankets. The little children are freezing to death. My people, some of them, have run away to the hills and have no blankets, no food; no one knows where they are—perhaps freezing to death. I want to have time to look for my children and see how many I can find. Maybe I shall find them among the dead. Hear me, my chiefs. I am tired; my heart is sick and sad. From where the sun now stands I will fight no more forever.

Armstrong, Virginia. (1971). *I Have Spoken.* Chicago: Swallow Press, p. 115.

The Holy Man Wovoka

These words were spoken to his followers:

My people, before the white man came you were happy. You had many buffalo to eat and tall grass for your ponies—you could come and go like the wind. When it grew cold you could journey to the valleys of the south, where healing springs are; and when it grew warm, you could return to the mountains of the north. The white man came. He dug up the bones of our mother, the earth. He tore her bosom with steel. He built big trails and put iron horses on them. He fought you and beat you, and put you in barren places where a horned toad would die. He said you must stay there; you must not go hunt in the mountains.

Armstrong, Virginia. (1971). *I Have Spoken*. Chicago: Swallow Press, p. 129.

Clyde Warrior, President, National Indian Youth Council

We are not free. We do not make our choices. Our choices are made for us; we are the poor. For those of us who live on reservations these choices and decisions are made by federal administrators, bureaucrats, and their "yes men," euphemistically called tribal governments. Those of us who live in non-reservation areas have our lives controlled by local white power elites. We have many rulers. They are called social workers, "cops," school teachers, churches, etc., and now OEO employees. They call us into meetings to tell us what is good for us and how they've programmed us, or they come into our homes to instruct us and their manners are not always what one would call polite by Indian standards or perhaps by any standards. We are rarely accorded respect as fellow human beings. Our children come home from school to us with shame in their hearts and a sneer on their lips for their home and parents. We are the "poverty problem" and that is true; and perhaps it is also true that our lack of reasonable choices, our lack of freedoms, our poverty of spirit is not unconnected with our material poverty.

Testimony to President's National Advisory Commission on Rural Poverty, February 2, 1967.

American Indian Task Force

We, the first Americans, come to the congress of the United States that you give us the chance to try to solve what you call the Indian problem. You have had two hundred years and you have not succeeded by your standards. It is clear that you have not succeeded in ours.

We asked the Vice President of the United States to set into motion a process which would insure that our people could secure redress of grievances and could shape the government programs that affect and control their lives . . . we, ask the restoration of what you claimed at the founding of your nation—the inalienable right to pursue happiness. We cannot fare worse than the experts and the bureaucrats. We do not lack for knowledge—and we are not ashamed to hire experts and technicians. But our people do not lack for leaders, for sensitivity, for talent and ability. We ask for the right to pursue our dream—and we ask for you to respect that dream. That is the American way. We claim our birthright.

Press Statement, November 12, 1969.

Indians of All Tribes

Dear Brothers and Sisters . . . On November 20, 1969, 78 Indian people, under the name "Indians of all Tribes," moved onto Alcatraz Island, a former Federal Prison. We began cleaning up the Island and are still in the process of organizing, setting up classes and trying to instill the old Indian ways into our young.

We moved onto Alcatraz Island because we feel that Indian people need a Cultural Center of their own. For several decades, Indian people have not had enough control of training their own people. And without a cultural center of their own, we are afraid that the old Indian ways may be lost. We believe that the only way to keep them alive is for Indian people to do it themselves . . . We realize that their [sic] are more problems in Indian communities besides having our culture taken away. We have water problems, land problems, "social" problems, job opportunity problems, and many others . . . We realize too that we are not getting anywhere fast by working along as individual tribes. If we can gather together as brothers and come to a common agreement, we feel that we can be much more effective, doing things for ourselves, instead of having someone else doing it, telling us what is good for us.

So we must start somewhere. We feel that if we are going to succeed, we must hold on to the old ways. *This is the first and most important reason we went to Alcatraz Island.*

Alcatraz Island, December 16, 1969.

Frank Tenorio, Governor, San Felipe Pueblo

There has been a lot said about the sacredness of our land which is our body; and the values of our culture which is our soul; but water is the blood of our tribes, and if its life-giving flow is stopped, or it is polluted, all else will die and the many thousands of years of communal existence will come to an end.

Indian Water Policy in a Changing Environment, 1982.

Vine Deloria

Although the practical fact appears to be that Indians have forsaken their traditional special status for that of a needy minority, untangling the network of federal laws and protections that have been woven around Indians in the past two centuries will not be easy to accomplish. Extensive federal responsibilities attach to Indian properties, and loosening this iron grip without having Indian lands placed in jeopardy will be a major undertaking. Consequently, smaller policy considerations will undoubtedly occupy the attention of Indians and their friends and allies for several generations to come. Instead of broad national policies that speak of directions for programs and services, however, we may discover that constructing small models for stabilization of specific communities or functions [is] more suitable.

Deloria, Vine. (1985). *American Indian Policy in the Twentieth Century.* Norman: University of Oklahoma Press, pp. 255–256.

Albert Hale, President, Navajo Nation

[T]ribal sovereignty preceded the U.S. Constitution by hundreds of years. The federal government did not create tribal governments; it recognized them as sovereign entities and assumed the exclusive role of dealing with Indian nations.

Entering into treaties is an exercise of Indian nations' sovereign authority and is a recognition of that authority by the U.S. In these treaties, there are provisions which expressly mandate services to be provided to Indian nations and Indian people by the federal government. Contracts have the force of law and are enforceable according to the terms of the contract . . . However, the Contract with America agenda and the reinvention of the federal government have consistently failed to recognize that there are "first" contracts with America. These first contracts with America are treaties between the federal government and Indian nations. These treaties must be honored and the obligations specified must be fulfilled before any other contract is executed.

The words and promises found in Indian treaties are the words and promises of the American people to Indian nations and Indian people. After all, if we cannot hold sacred our words and our promises, then nothing is sacred anymore.

Indian Country Today, August 10, 1995, p. A-2.

Sam Deloria

[I]f we think of sovereignty as a strictly political and governmental concept, people get transfixed with that because they think in terms of absolutes. They mourn the fact that our sovereignty is not unlimited, as if it ever was. Let me tell you right now, there's no sovereignty on this earth that is unlimited. The United States at its most powerful does not have unlimited sovereignty . . . it has political and economic reality that limits its sovereignty . . . Our sovereignty is limited! Of course it is, everybody's is limited.

Even for Superman. Somebody always had a little rock of Kryptonite to whip out and Superman was toast.

. . .

In the name of tribal sovereignty, a few people are getting very rich [from gaming]. And the people who actually have a society to govern and a territory to govern it on are not getting much benefit out of it.

Deloria, Sam. (2002). "Commentary on Nation Building: The Future of Indian Nations." *Arizona State Law Journal* 34, pp. 55–61.

Tim Giago, Editor

Since Indian gaming became legal on many Indian reservations, I have been a strong supporter. I have always believed the good would far outweigh the bad. Of course, since there were no precedents to follow in Indian country, who could have predicted with any accuracy the good things and the bad that would become a part of the future of Indian gaming?

I have written on more than one occasion that tribal leaders should heed the advice of the wise, old leaders like Wendell Chino of the Mescalero Apache in New Mexico and Roger Jourdain of the Red Lake Band of Chippewa in Minnesota. Both these leaders at the very beginning cautioned the Indian nations to proceed with care. They warned them not to jump on the first management wagon that came along.

All of a sudden, out of the wood work, every conceivable type of management organization imaginable started to perch on the tribal fences offering their services. Newly formed management companies that didn't know an Indian from a gopher suddenly became "Indian experts" when it came to casinos. I named them the "casino vultures" and in several speeches to tribal leaders I repeated the words of Mr. Chino and Mr. Jourdain: "Proceed with caution."

In the seven years gaming has been legal in Indian country several managers of these non-Indian consulting firms have made enough money to retire. Some took the tribes for as much as 70 percent of their earnings. Other tribes have spent thousands of dollars trying to break contracts that gave the management companies everything but tribal membership. In many parts of the country the only people making money on some tribal casinos are the lawyers representing them and the casino management companies. I wish I could say this was a rare occurrence, but it was not.

Indian Country Today, August 10, 1995.

Sarah Winnemucca

I would place all the Indians of Nevada on ships in our harbor, take them to New York and land them as immigrants, that they might be received with open arms . . . and thus placed beyond the necessity of reservation help.

From Canfield, GaeWhimey. (1983). *Sarah Winnemucca of the Northern Paiutes.* Norman: University of Oklahoma Press.

The Words of U.S. Presidents

George Washington (1789–1797)

[T]he provisions heretofore made with a view to the protection of the Indians from the violence of the lawless part of our frontier inhabitants are insufficient. It is demonstrated that these violations can now be perpetuated with impunity, and it can need no argument to prove that unless the murdering of Indians can be restrained by bringing the murderers to condign punishment, all the exertions of the government to prevent destructive retaliations by the Indians will prove fruitless and all our present agreeable prospects illusory . . . To enforce upon the Indians the observance of justice it is indispensable that there shall be competent means of rendering justice to them.

Seventh Message to Congress, December 8, 1795.

John Adams (1797–1801)

In connection with this unpleasant state of things on our western frontier it is proper for me to mention the attempts of foreign agents to alienate the affections of the Indian nations and to excite them to actual hostilities against the United States. Great activity has been exerted by those persons who have insinuated themselves among the Indian tribes residing within the territory of the United States to influence them to transfer their affections and force to a foreign nation, to form them into a confederacy, and prepare them for war against the United States. Although measures have been taken to counteract these infractions of our rights, to prevent Indian hostilities, and to preserve entire their attachment to the United States, it is my duty to observe that to give a better effect to these measures and to obviate the consequences of a repetition of such practices a law providing adequate punishment for such offenses may be necessary.

First Annual Message to Congress, November 22, 1797.

Thomas Jefferson (1801–1809)

My friends and children, we are descended from the old nations which live beyond the great water, but we and our forefathers have been so long here that we seem like you to have grown out of this land. We consider ourselves no longer of the old nations . . . but as united in one family with our red brethren here . . . My friends and children, I have now an important advice to give you. I have already told you that you and all the red men are my children, and I wish you to live in peace and friendship with one another as brethren of the same family ought to do. How much better is it for neighbors to help than to hurt one another; how much happier must it make them . . . My children I have given this advice to all your red brethren on this side of the Mississippi; they are following it, they are increasing in their numbers, [and] are learning to clothe and provide for their families as we do.

Address to the People of the Mandan Nation of the Plains on their visit to Washington, D.C., December 30, 1806.

James Madison (1809–1817)

A distinguishing feature in the operations . . . is the use made by the enemy (the British) of the merciless savages under their influence. Whilst the benevolent policy of the United States invariably recommended peace and promoted civilization among that wretched portion of the human race, and was making exertions to dissuade them from taking either side in the war, the enemy has not scrupled to call to his aid their ruthless ferocity, armed with the horrors of those instruments of carnage and torture which are known to spare neither age nor sex . . . Nor can it be pretended that they are not answerable for the atrocities perpetrated, since the savages are employed with a knowledge, and even with menaces, that their fury could not be controlled.

Fourth Annual Message to Congress, November 4, 1812.

James Monroe (1817–1825)

The care of the Indian tribes within our limits has long been an essential part of our system, but, unfortunately, it has not been executed in a manner to accomplish all the objects intended by it. We have treated them as independent nations, without their having any substantial pretensions to that rank. The distinction has flattered their pride, retarded their improvement, and in many instances paved the way to their destruction. The progress of our settlements westward, supported as they are by a dense population, has constantly driven them back, with almost the total sacrifice of the lands which they have been compelled to abandon. They have claims on the magnanimity and, I may add, the justice of this nation which we must all feel. We should become their real benefactors; we should perform the office of their Great Father, the endearing title which they emphatically give to the chief magistrate of our Union. Their sovereignty over vast territories should cease, in lieu of which the right of soil should be secured to each individual and his posterity in competent portions; and for the territory thus ceded by each tribe some reasonable equivalent should be granted, to be vested in permanent funds for the support of civil government over them and for the education of their children, for their instructions in the arts of husbandry, and to provide sustenance for them until they could provide it for themselves.

Podell, Janet, and Steven Anzovia. (1988). *Speeches of the American Presidents.* New York: H. H. Wilson, p. 68.

John Quincy Adams (1825–1829)

We have been far more successful in the acquisition of their lands than in imparting to them the principles or inspiring them with the spirit of civilization. But in appropriating to ourselves their hunting grounds we have brought upon ourselves the obligation of providing them with subsistence; and when we have had the rare good fortune of teaching them the arts of civilization and the doctrines of Christianity we have unexpectedly found them forming in the midst of ourselves communities claiming to be independent of ours and rivals of sovereignty within the territories and members of our Union. This state of things requires that a remedy should be provided—a remedy which, while it shall do justice to those unfortunate children of nature, may secure to the members of our confederation the rights of sovereignty and soil.

Fourth Annual Message to Congress, December 2, 1828.

Andrew Jackson (1829–1837)

The consequences of a speedy removal will be important to the United States, to individual states, and to the Indians themselves. The pecuniary advantages which it promises to the government are the least of its recommendations. It puts an end to all possible danger of collision between the authorities of the general and state governments on account of the Indians. It will place a dense and civilized population in large tracts of country now occupied by a few savage hunters. By opening the whole territory between Tennessee on the north and Louisiana on the south to the settlement of whites it will incalculably strengthen the southwestern frontier and render the adjacent states strong enough to repel future invasions without remote aid. It will relieve the whole state of Mississippi and the western part of Alabama of Indian occupancy, and enable those states to advance rapidly in population, wealth, and power. It will separate the Indians from immediate contact with settlements of whites; free them from the power of the states; enable them to pursue happiness in their own way and under their own institutions; will retard the progress of decay, which is lessening their numbers, and perhaps cause them gradually, under the protection of the government and through the influence of good counsels, to cast off their savage habits and become an interesting, civilized, and Christian community. These consequences, some of them so certain and the rest so probably, make the complete execution of the plan sanctioned by Congress and object of much solicitude. Toward the aborigines of the country, no one can indulge a more friendly feeling than myself, or would go further in attempting to reclaim them from their wandering habits and make them a happy, prosperous people.

Second Annual Message to Congress, December 6, 1830.

Martin Van Buren (1837–1841)

It affords me sincere pleasure to be able to appraise [sic] you of the entire removal of the Cherokee Nation of Indians to their new homes west of the Mississippi. The measures authorized by Congress at its last session with a view to the long-standing controversy with them, have had the happiest effects. By an agreement concluded with them by the commanding general in that country, who has performed the duties assigned to him on the occasion with commendable energy and humanity, their removal has been principally under the conduct of their own chiefs, and they have emigrated without any apparent reluctance . . . [This government's] dealings with the Indian tribes have been just and friendly throughout; its efforts for their civilization constant, and directed by the best feelings of humanity.

Second Annual Message to Congress, December 3, 1838.

William Henry Harrison (1841)

William Henry Harrison served as president for only thirty days; he mentioned Native Americans on only one public occasion while in the highest office—his inauguration. While his mention was very brief, he is one of a very few presidents to have recognized the nation's inaugural peoples in an inaugural address.

In our intercourse with our aboriginal neighbors the same liberality and justice which marked the course prescribed to me by two of my illustrious predecessors (Jefferson and Madison) when acting under their direction in the discharge of the duties of superintendent and commissioner shall be strictly observed. I can conceive of no more sublime spectacle, none more likely to propitiate an impartial and common Creator, than a rigid adherence to the principles of justice on the part of a powerful nation in its transactions with a weaker and uncivilized people whom circumstances have placed at its disposal.

Inaugural Address, March 4, 1841.

John Tyler (1841–1845)

I have authorized the colonel in command [of Florida] . . . to declare that hostilities against the Indian have ceased, and that they will not be renewed unless provoked and rendered indispensable by new outrages on their part . . . He is instructed to open communications with those yet remaining, and endeavor by all peaceable means to persuade them to consult their true interests by joining their brethren at the West; and direction has been given for establishing a cordon or line of protection for the inhabitants by the necessary number of troops. But to render this system of protection effectual it is essential that settlements of our citizens should be made within the line so established, and that they should be armed, so as to repel any attack. In order to afford inducements to such settlements, I submit the propriety of allowing a reasonable quantity of land to the head of each family that shall permanently occupy it . . . and to permit the issue of rations for the subsistence of the settlers for one year, and . . . to authorize the loan of muskets . . . By such means it is hoped that a hardy population will soon occupy the rich soil of the frontiers of Florida.

Special Message to Congress, May 10, 1842.

James Polk (1845–1849)

New Mexico is a frontier province, and has never been of any considerable value to Mexico . . . There is another consideration which induced the belief that the Mexican government might even desire to place this province under the protection of the government of the United States. Numerous bands of fierce and warlike savages wander over it and upon its borders. Mexico has been and must continue to be too feeble to restrain them from committing depredations, robberies, and murders, not only upon the inhabitants of New Mexico itself, but upon those of other northern states of Mexico. It would be a blessing to all these northern states to have their citizens protected against them by the power of the United States. At this moment many Mexicans, principally females and children, are in captivity among them. If New Mexico were held and governed by the United States, we could effectually prevent these tribes from committing such outrages, and compel them to release these captives and restore them to their families and friends. In proposing to acquire New Mexico and the Californias, it was known that but an inconsiderable portion of the Mexican people would be transferred with them, the country embraced within these provinces being chiefly an uninhabited region.

Third Annual Message to Congress, December 7, 1847.

Zachary Taylor (1849–1850)

President Taylor's tenure in office was the third shortest among the chief executives, only sixteen months. Before dying in office, he rarely mentioned Native American matters. On one occasion he talked of creating Indian agencies for Salt Lake and Santa Fe. On another occasion he wrote to the Senate asking for ratification of a treaty which broke an earlier treaty:

I transmit herewith, to be laid before the Senate for its constitutional action thereon, a treaty concluded with the half-breeds of the Dacotah or Sioux Indians for lands reserved for them in the treaty of July 15, 1830, with the Sioux and other Indians.

Letter to the President of the Senate, January 14, 1850.

Millard Fillmore (1850–1853)

The annexation of Texas and the acquisition of California and New Mexico have given increased importance to our Indian relations . . . Texas and New Mexico are surrounded by powerful tribes of Indians who are a source of constant terror and annoyance to the inhabitants . . . The great roads leading into the country are infested with them, whereby traveling is rendered extremely dangerous and immigration is almost entirely arrested. The Mexican frontier, which by the eleventh article of the treaty of Guadalupe Hidalgo we are bound to protect against the Indians within our own borders, is exposed to these excursions equally with our own . . . We are bound to protect the territory of Mexico against the incursions of the savage tribes within our borders "with equal diligence and energy" as if the same were made within our territory or against our citizens . . . Orders have been given to the officers commanding on that frontier to consider the Mexican territory and its inhabitants as equally with our own entitled to their protection.

Second Annual Message to Congress, December 2, 1851.

Franklin Pierce (1853–1857)

In the Territories of Washington and Oregon numerous bands of Indians are in arms and are waging a war of extermination against the white inhabitants . . . On the Western plains, . . . [tribes] have maintained hostile intentions and been guilty of outrages which, if not designed to provoke a conflict, serve to show that the apprehension of it is insufficient wholly to restrain their vicious propensities . . . The hostile Indians have not been removed from the State of Florida, and the withdrawal of troops there from, leaving that object unaccomplished, would be most injurious to the inhabitants and a breach of the positive engagement of the General Government. To refuse supplies to the Army . . . is to compel the complete cessation of all its operations and its practical disbandment, and thus to invite hordes of predatory savages from the Western plains and the Rocky Mountains to spread devastation along a frontier of more than 4000 miles in extent and to deliver up the sparse population of a vast tract of country to rapine and murder.

Special Annual Message to Congress, August 21, 1856.

James Buchanan (1857–1861)

Our system for the disposal of public lands, originating with the fathers of the Republic, has been improved as experience pointed the way, and gradually adapted to the growth and settlement of our Western States and Territories. It has worked well in practice . . . What a boundless prospect this presents to our country of future prosperity and power! We have heretofore disposed of 363,862,464 acres of the public land. Whilst the public lands, as a source of revenue, are of great importance, their importance is far greater as furnishing homes for a hardy and independent race of honest and industrious citizens who desire to subdue and cultivate the soil . . . The extension of our limits has brought within our jurisdiction many additional and populous tribes of Indians, a large proportion of which are wild, untractable, and difficult to control. Predatory and warlike in their disposition and habits, it is impossible altogether to restrain them from committing aggressions on each other, as well as upon frontier citizens and those emigrating to our distant States and Territories. Hence expensive military expeditions are frequently necessary to overawe and chastise the more lawless and hostile.

First Annual Message to Congress, December 8, 1857.

Abraham Lincoln (1861–1865)

In compliance with your resolution . . . requesting . . . all information touching the late Indian barbarities in the State of Minnesota, and also the evidence . . . upon which some of the principal actors or headmen were tried and condemned to death, I have the honor to state (the following) . . . Anxious to not act with so much clemency as to encourage another outbreak on the one hand, nor with so much severity as to be real cruelty on the other, I caused a careful examination of the records of the trials to be made, in view of first ordering the execution of such as had been proved guilty of violating females. Contrary to expectations only two of this class were found. I then directed . . . a classification of all who were proven to have participated in massacres, as distinguished from participation in battles. This class numbered forty, and included the two convicted of female violation. (One was recommended for commutation) . . . I have ordered the other thirty-nine to be executed on Friday the 19th instant.

Letter to the Senate, December 11, 1862.

Andrew Johnson (1865–1869)

Instigated by real or imaginary grievances, the Indians occasionally committed acts of barbarous violence upon emigrants and our frontier settlements . . . It is of vital importance that our distant Territories should be exempt from Indian outbreaks, and that the construction of the Pacific Railroad, an object of national importance, should not be interrupted by hostile tribes. These objects, as well as the material interests and the moral and intellectual improvement of the Indians, can be most effectually secured by concentrating them upon portions of country set apart for their exclusive use and located at points remote from our highways and encroaching white settlements.

Third Annual Message to Congress, December 3, 1867.

Ulysses S. Grant (1869–1877)

A policy has been adopted toward the Indian tribes inhabiting a large portion of the territory of the United States which has been humane and has substantially ended Indian hostilities in the whole land except in a portion of Nebraska, and Dakota, Wyoming, and Montana Territories—The Black Hills region and approaches thereto. Hostilities there have grown out of the avarice of the white man, who has violated our treaty stipulations in his search for gold. The question might be asked why the government has not enforced obedience to the terms of the treaty prohibiting the occupation of the Black Hills region by whites. The answer is simple. The first immigrants to the Black Hills were removed by troops, but rumors of rich discoveries of gold took into that region increased numbers. Gold has actually been found in paying quantity, and an effort to remove the miners would only result in the desertion of the bulk of the troops that might be sent there to remove them. All difficulty in this matter has, however, been removed—subject to the approval of Congress—by a treaty ceding the Black Hills and approaches to settlements by citizens.

Eighth Annual Message to Congress, December 5, 1876.

Rutherford Birchard Hayes (1877–1881)

They were the aboriginal occupants of the land we now possess. They have been driven from place to place. The purchase money paid to them in some cases for what they called their own has still left them poor. In many instances, when they had settled down upon land assigned to them by compact and begun to support themselves by their own labor, they were rudely jostled off and thrust into the wilderness again. Many, if not most, of our Indian wars have had their origin in broken promises and acts of injustice on our part, and the advance of the Indians in civilization has been slow because the treatment they received did not permit it to be faster and more general . . . I see no reason why Indians who can give satisfactory proof of having by their own labor supported their families for a number of years, and who are willing to detach themselves from their tribal relations, should not be admitted to the benefit of the homestead act and the privileges of citizenship, and I recommend the passage of a law to that effect.

First Annual Message to Congress, December 3, 1877.

James Garfield (1881)

James Garfield held the presidency for only six months. In that time he made no public speeches referring to Native Americans. However, he did actively participate in congressional debates over Native American policy while he was in the United States House of Representatives for eight terms.

His personal diary contains two references to Native Americans while he was in the White House. A committee of five Presbyterians asked for the appointment of a secretary of the interior who favored missionary work among the Native Americans (March 18, 1881). He later recorded these words:

Questions of Indian Policy so far as the relation of appointment of agents on recommendation of churches is concerned, quite fully discussed. I concluded to ask general cooperation of the churches, but not to let them control appointments. It brings sectarian strife into the government. (April 14, 1981)

Brown, Harry James, and Frederick D. Williams, eds. (1981). *The Diary of James A. Garfield IV, 1878–1881.* East Lansing: Michigan State University Press, pp. 575–576.

Chester Arthur (1881–1885)

Prominent among the matters which challenge the attention of Congress at its present session is the management of Indian affairs. While this question has been a cause of trouble and embarrassment from the infancy of government, it is but recently that any effort has been made for its solution at once serious, determined, consistent, and promising success. It has been easier to resort to convenient makeshifts for tiding over temporary difficulties than to grapple with the permanent problem, and accordingly the easier course has almost invariably been pursued . . . We have to deal with the appalling fact that though thousands of lives have been sacrificed and hundreds of millions of dollars expended in the attempt to solve the Indian problem, it has until within the past few years seemed scarcely nearer a solution than it was half a century ago. But the Government has of late been cautiously but steadily feeling its way to the adoption of a policy which has already produced gratifying results . . .

[I recommend] the enactment of a general law permitting the allotment in severalty, to such Indians, at least, as desire it, of a reasonable quantity of land secured to them by patent . . . In return for such considerate action on the part of the Government, there is reason to believe that the Indians in large numbers would be persuaded to sever their tribal relations and to engage at once in agricultural pursuits . . . A resort to the allotment system would have a direct and powerful influence in dissolving the tribal bond, which is so prominent a feature of savage life, and which tends so strongly to perpetuate it.

First Annual Message to Congress, December 6, 1881.

Grover Cleveland (1885–1889; 1893–1897)

The condition of our Indian population continues to improve . . . [T]he transforming change which shall substitute for barbarism enlightenment and civilizing education is in favorable progress . . . These conditions testify to the value of the higher tone of consideration and humanity which has governed the later methods of dealing with them, and commend its continued observance. Allotments . . . have been made on some reservations until all those entitled to land thereon have had their shares assigned . . . No measure of general effect has ever been entered on from which more may be fairly hoped if it shall be discretely administered. It proffers opportunity and inducement to that independence of spirit and life which the Indian peculiarly needs, while at the same time the inalienability of title affords security against the risks his inexperience of affairs or weakness of character may expose him in dealing with others. Whenever begun upon any reservation it should be made complete, so that all are brought to the same condition, and as soon as possible community in lands should cease by opening such as remain unalloted to settlement. Contact with the ways of industrious and successful farmers will perhaps add a healthy emulation which will both instruct and stimulate.

Fourth Annual Message to Congress, December 3, 1888.

Benjamin Harrison (1889–1893)

The report of the Secretary of the Interior exhibits with great fullness and clearness the vast work of that Department and the satisfactory results attained . . . The several acts of Congress looking to the reduction of the larger Indian reservations, to the more rapid settlement of Indians upon individual allotments, and the restoration to the public domains of lands in excess of their needs have been largely carried into effect . . . Agreements have been concluded since March 4, 1889, involving the cession to the United States of about 14,726,000 acres of land.

Second Annual Message to Congress, December 1, 1890.

William McKinley (1897–1901)

The present bill proposes to open to miners and prospectors, and to the operation of the mining laws, a substantial portion of this (Navajo) reservation, including a part of the lands covered by the recent order . . . The Indians could not understand how lands given to them in January as necessary for their use should be taken away without previous notice in May of the same year. While the Indians are the wards of the Government, and must submit to that which is deemed for their best interests by the sovereign guardian, they should, nevertheless, be dealt with in a manner calculated to give them confidence in the Government and to assist them in passing through the inevitable transition to a state of civilization and full citizenship.

Veto Message (H.B. 4001) to the House of Representatives, May 3, 1900.

Theodore Roosevelt (1901–1909)

In dealing with the Indians our aim should be their ultimate absorption into the body of our people. But in many cases this absorption must and should be very slow ... The large Indian schools situated remote from any Indian reservation do a special and peculiar work of great importance. But, excellent though these are, an immense amount of additional work must be done on the reservations themselves among the old, and above all among the young Indians. The first and most important step toward absorption of the Indian is to teach him to earn his living ... Every effort should be made to develop the Indian along the lines of natural aptitude, and to encourage the existing native industries peculiar to certain tribes, such as various kinds of basket weaving, canoe building, smith work, and blanket work. Above all, the Indian boys and girls should be given confident command of colloquial English, and should ordinarily be prepared for a vigorous struggle with the conditions under which their people live, rather than for immediate absorption into some more highly developed community.

Second Annual Speech to Congress, December 2, 1902.

William Howard Taft (1909–1913)

In spite of everything which has been said in criticism of the policy of our Government toward the Indians, the amount of wealth which is now held by it for these wards per capita shows that the Government has been generous; but the management of so large an estate, with the great variety of circumstances that surround each tribe and each case, calls for the exercise of the highest business discretion, and the machinery provided in the Indian Bureau for the discharge of this function is entirely inadequate.

Annual Message to Congress, December 19, 1912.

Woodrow Wilson (1913–1921)

The twenty-seventh president, who "kept the nation out of war," and who fought "the war to end all wars" (12,000 Native Americans served in World War I), established his mark as one of the greatest presidents with his international concern for a League of Nations, sovereignty and open agreements, and honest borders among different peoples. Alas, his concern was for the people in the Balkans and South America. He was oblivious to the existence of "Nations Within." In his eight years in office, he made only one public utterance regarding Native America. President Wilson made a "brand-new speech into a talking machine recorder." It was reproduced to be played to Native Americans "through the phonograph." "It was addressed to the Indian wards of the Government, whom the President called 'my brothers' and 'my children.'" Wilson's speech was not even original, as it quoted Thomas Jefferson:

I rejoice to foresee the day when the red men become truly one people with us enjoying all the rights and privileges we do and living in peace and plenty.

New York Times, May 25, 1913, p. 3.

Warren G. Harding (1921–1923)

I doubt if anywhere an aboriginal people has been so fast assimilated to civilization, industry, intelligence and education, as have the Alaska Indians. Doubtless this is because they have had the full advantage of the more enlightened policy adopted by the government toward the Indians in recent times; but it is also due to the fact that the Alaskan Indians are a fine, peace-loving, hard-working people. They are going to be a great asset to the country and a most useful element in its citizenship.

Last Speeches of Warren G. Harding, President of the United States, delivered during the course of his tour to Alaska, June 20 to August 2, 1923.

Calvin Coolidge (1923–1929)

It was with satisfaction that I approved . . . the Indian Citizenship act, of June 2, 1924. This made all native-born American Indians citizens of the United States. It symbolized the consummation of what for many years had been the purpose of the Federal Government—to merge the Indians into the general citizenry and body politic of the nation . . . I realize that much of the progress that has been made by the Indians is due to the sacrifices of the early missionaries and that the missionaries of today are important factors contributing much to their education and moral advancement, making it more possible for the Government to carry out the policy of making them all self-supporting citizens. More than 10,000 Indian young men served in the army and 2000 in the navy during the World War . . . [T]hey proved to be courageous and rendered distinguished service . . . Those of us who were present on the occasion of the burial of the Unknown Soldier in the National Cemetery across the river from Washington will not soon forget the closing act of the ceremony. A group of old Indian warriors, some of whom were Sioux, arranged themselves around the tomb, while one, acting for the whole Indian people, laid upon the bier his war bonnet. This was not an idle gesture. It symbolized the outstanding fact that the red men and their neighbors had been brought together as one people and that never again would there be hostility between the two races. As one of those old warriors said: "Who knows but that this Unknown Soldier was an Indian boy?"

Speech to ten thousand Sioux at Pine Ridge, South Dakota, August 17, 1927. *New York Times*, August 18, 1927, p. 12.

Herbert Hoover (1929–1933)

We have 338,000 Indians. The broad problem is to better train the Indian youth to take care of themselves and their property. It is the only course by which we can ultimately discharge this problem from the nation, and blend them as a self-supporting people into the nation as a whole.

Myers, William Starr, and Walter H. Newton. (1936). *The Hoover Administration*. New York: Scribner's, p. 442.

Franklin D. Roosevelt (1933–1945)

We can and should, without further delay, extend to the Indian the fundamental rights of political liberty and local self-government and the opportunities of education and economic assistance that they require in order to attain a wholesome American life. This is but the obligation of honor of a powerful Nation toward a people living among us and dependent upon our protection. Certainly the continuance of autocratic rule, by a Federal Department, over the lives of more than two hundred thousand citizens of this Nation is incompatible with American ideals of liberty. It is also destructive of the character and self-respect of a great race.

Statement endorsing Indian Reorganization Act, April 28, 1934.

Harry S. Truman (1945–1953)

In the history of our country the women have always been a help in its settlement, in civilizing it, and in keeping it a republic. If you remember, in Puritan times, in Virginia, when the first settlers came in, the women manned the forts just as the men did. In the late 1840's and early 1850's, my grandmothers were first settlers in western Missouri, and they had trouble with Indians at that time. My grandfathers were in the trading business across the plains, and my red-haired grandmother, on one occasion, routed a whole band of Indians by herself and two great big shepherd dogs, and they didn't come back and bother her anymore.

Speech to members of the Defense Advisory Committee on Women in the Services, November 5, 1951.

Dwight D. Eisenhower (1953–1961)

Although I have grave doubts as to the wisdom of certain provisions contained in (Public Act 280), I have today signed it because its basic purpose represents still another step in granting complete political equality to all Indians in our nation . . . The Indian tribes regard this as a long step forward in removing them from the status of "second class" citizens. Indeed in the five states where state jurisdiction will soon be paramount, the Indians have enthusiastically endorsed this bill . . . My objection . . . arises because of the inclusion of Sections [which] permit other states to impose on Indian tribes within their borders, criminal and civil jurisdiction of the state, removing the Indians from Federal jurisdiction and, in some instances, effective self-government. The failure to include in these provisions a requirement of full consultation in order to ascertain the wishes and desires of the Indians and of final Federal approval, was unfortunate.

Statement Upon Signing of Public Act 280, August 15, 1953.

John F. Kennedy (1961–1963)

I fully appreciate the reasons underlying the Seneca Nation of Indians objections to the construction of Kinzua Dam on the Allegheny River. Involved are very deep sentiments over the loss of a portion of the lands which have been owned by the Seneca Nation for centuries . . . I have now had an opportunity to review the subject and have concluded that it is not possible to halt the construction of Kinzua Dam currently under way. Impounding of the funds appropriated by the Congress after long and exhaustive Congressional review, and after resolution by our judicial process of the legal right of the Federal Government to acquire the property necessary to the construction of the reservoir, would not be proper . . . I have directed the departments and agencies of the Federal Government to take every action within their authority to assist the Seneca Nation and its members who must be relocated in adjusting to the new situation.

Letter to the President of the Seneca Nation, August 11, 1961.

Lyndon B. Johnson (1963–1969)

The greatest hope for Indian progress lies in the emergence of Indian leadership and initiative in solving Indian problems. Indians must have a voice in making the plans and decisions in programs which are important to their daily life . . . [W]e must pledge to respect fully the dignity and uniqueness of the Indian citizen. That means partnership—not paternalism. We must affirm the right of the first Americans to remain Indians while exercising their rights as Americans. We must affirm their freedom to choice and self-determination.

1968–1969 Public Papers, I:335.

Richard Nixon (1969–1974)

The first Americans—the Indians—are the most deprived and most isolated minority group in our nation. On virtually every scale of measurement—employment, income, education, health—the condition of the Indian people ranks at the bottom. This condition is the heritage of centuries of injustice. From the time of their first contact with European settlers, the American Indians have been oppressed and brutalized, deprived of their ancestral lands and denied the opportunity to control their own destiny. Even the Federal programs which are intended to meet their needs have frequently proven to be ineffective and demeaning . . . This then must be the goal of any new national policy toward the Indian people: to strengthen the Indian's sense of autonomy without threatening his sense of community. We must assure the Indian that he can assume control of his own life without being separated involuntarily from the tribal group. And we must make it clear that Indians can become independent of Federal control without being cut off from Federal concern and Federal support . . . The Indians of America need Federal assistance—this much has long been clear. What has not always been clear, however, is that the Federal government needs Indian energies and Indian leadership if its assistance is to be effective in improving the conditions of Indian life.

Special Message on Indian Affairs, July 8, 1970.

Gerald R. Ford (1974–1977)

No domestic matter has given me greater pride than my administration's record of turning about the discrimination and neglect that all Indians faced for so many years. In January of 1975, I signed the Indian Self-Determination Act, a Magna Charta for Indian people. Today, we recognize Indian tribal governments, including those in Oklahoma, as vital government organizations in their own right . . . In a few minutes, I will sign a Presidential proclamation declaring October 10 to 16 as Native American Awareness Week. The administration's support for Indian programs is not just rhetoric. We back up our words with action . . . There are one million American Indian citizens, and some may say this is a very small minority. I count American Indian people, however, not in numbers but in the honored place that they hold in our multicultural society and in the future of our Nation. The 215 million of us are keenly concerned with the one million. The welfare and the progress of Native Americans is high on the agenda of the American conscience.

Remarks made in Lawton, Oklahoma, upon signing the Proclamation for the Observance of Native American Awareness Week, October 8, 1976.

Jimmy Carter (1977–1981)

The Federal Government has a special responsibility to Native Americans, and I intend to continue to exercise this responsibility fairly and sensitively. My Administration will continue to seek negotiated settlements to difficult conflicts over land, water, and other resources and will ensure that the trust relationship and self-determination principles continue to guide Indian policy. There are difficult conflicts which occasionally divide Indian and non-Indian citizens of this country. We will seek to exercise leadership to resolve these problems equitably and compassionately.

State of the Union Address, January 23, 1979.

Ronald Reagan (1981–1989)

Let me tell you just a little something about the American Indian in our land. We have provided millions of acres of land for what are called preservations, or reservations, I should say. They, from the beginning, announced that they wanted to maintain their way of life, as they had always lived there in the desert and the plains and so forth. And we set up these reservations so they could, and have a Bureau of Indian Affairs to help take care of them. At the same time, we provide education for them—schools on the reservations. And they're free also to leave the reservations and be American citizens among the rest of us, and many do. Some still prefer, however, that early way of life. And we've done everything we can to meet their demands as to how they want to live. Maybe we made a mistake. Maybe we should not have humored them in that wanting to stay in that kind of primitive lifestyle. Maybe we should have said, "No, come join us; be citizens along with the rest of us." As I say, many have; many have been very successful. . . . And you'd be surprised; some of them became very wealthy because some of those reservations were overlaying great pools of oil, and you can get very rich pumping oil. And so, I don't know what their complaint might be.

Statement made in a question and answer session with students and faculty at Moscow State University, May 31, 1988.

George H. W. Bush (1989–1993)

I take pride in acknowledging and reaffirming the existence and durability of our unique government-to-government relationship . . . The concept of forced termination and excessive dependency on the Federal Government must now be relegated, once and for all, to the history books. Today we move forward toward a permanent relationship of understanding and trust, a relationship in which the tribes of the nation sit in positions of dependent sovereignty along with the other governments that compose the family that is America.

Statement for National Flag Day, June 14, 1991.

William J. Clinton (1993–2001)

The United States Government has a unique legal relationship with Native American tribal governments as set forth in the Constitution of the United States, treaties, statutes, and court decisions. [The Government's] activities should be implemented in a knowledgeable, sensitive manner respectful of tribal sovereignty. . . . I am outlining principles that executive departments and agencies . . . are to follow in their interactions with Native American tribal governments. The purpose of these principles is to clarify our responsibility to ensure that the Federal Government operates within a government-to-government relationship with federally recognized Native American tribes. I am strongly committed to building a more effective day-to-day working relationship reflecting respect for the rights of self-government due to the sovereign tribal governments.

Address to leaders of Native American Nations, April 29, 1994.

George W. Bush (2001–)

Long before others came to the land called America, the story of this land was yours, alone. Indians on this continent had their own languages and customs, just as you have today. They had jurisdiction over their lands and territories, just as you have today. And these sovereign tribal nations had their own systems of self governance, just as you have today. The National Museum of the American Indian affirms that this young country is home to an ancient, noble and enduring native culture. And all Americans are proud of that culture. Like many Indian dwellings, the new museum faces east, toward the rising sun. And as we celebrate this new museum and we look to the future, we can say that the sun is rising on Indian country.

September 23, 2004, in commemoration of the opening of the Museum of the American Indian.

The Words of Leading Prime Ministers of Canada

John A. MacDonald (1867–1873)

There is, I think . . . nothing to be feared from [Louis] Riel. In his answer to the invitation sent to him, which was a temperate and unobjectionable paper, he spoke of some claims he had against the government. I presume these refer to his land claims which he forfeited on conviction and banishment. I think we shall deal liberally with him and make him a good subject again.

MacDonald letter to Henry Lansdowne, August 5, 1984.

Quoted in Creighton, Donald. (1965). *John A. MacDonald.* Toronto: Macmillan, p. 288.

John G. Diefenbaker (1957–1963)

Indian lore and Indian history . . . have always fascinated me. Over the years, I think that the Indians have understood my feelings for them, and they have shown their reaction by making me a chief of five or six tribes in Saskatchewan and Alberta. I felt it most unjust that they were treated as less than full citizens of Canada, that they did not have the vote. I promised that if I ever had the power to do so, they would be given that right. This I carried out when I was Prime Minister.

Diefenbaker, John G. (1975). *One Canada.* Toronto: Macmillan of Canada, p. 29.

Pierre Elliott Trudeau
(1968–1979; 1980–1984)

[On the White Paper] . . . I'm sure that we were naive in some of the statements we made in the paper. We had perhaps the prejudices of small "l" liberals, and white men at that, who thought that equality meant the same law for everybody, and that's why as a result of this we said, "Well, let's abolish the Indian Act and make Indians citizens of Canada like everyone else. And let's let Indians dispose of their lands just like every other Canadian." But we have learnt in the process that we were a bit too theoretical, we were a bit too abstract, we were not . . . perhaps pragmatic enough or understanding enough.

Meeting with the Indian Association of Alberta and National Indian Brotherhood, Ottawa, June 4, 1970.

9

Directory of Organizations

Federal Government Organizations

United States

A move to consolidate (or nationalize) political and social relations between Native Americans and Euro-Americans began during the period of English colonization. The English government in London negotiated treaties with Native peoples and brought together the activities of Native affairs into two offices of the colonial regime—one for the Northern colonies and another for the Southern colonies. After independence, the new United States government maintained the same pattern, but added an office for the Middle States. The first commissioners for the three offices were James Wilson, Benjamin Franklin, and Patrick Henry. The Articles of Confederation (1781–1789) gave power over commerce with the Native Americans to the central congress. The congress appointed the commissioners. Under the Constitution (ratified 1789), Congress first placed responsibility for relationships with Native peoples in the hands of the secretary of war. In 1806, the position of superintendent of Indian trade was created in the Office of Indian Trade under the secretary.

In 1822, the office was abolished, and two years later an Office of Indian Affairs was created by the secretary. In 1832, Congress formally recognized the office by passing legislation authorizing its activities. Congress created the Department of the Interior in 1849, and the Office of Indian Affairs was transferred to the new department. The office was renamed the Bureau of Indian Affairs (BIA) in 1947. In 1977, the head of the BIA was designated as an assistant secretary of the interior for Indian affairs. Most of the duties of the federal government pertaining to Native Americans are performed by agencies of the BIA in the Department of the Interior. Some duties are performed by agencies in other departments and offices. These and the agencies within the Department of the Interior are listed here.

The White House
Special Assistant to the President for Intergovernmental Affairs
1600 Pennsylvania Avenue NW
Washington, DC 20500

Office subdivisions:
Indian Affairs
Indian Education
Indian Health Services

U.S. Department of Agriculture
Native American Programs
USDA Office of Outreach
1400 Independence Avenue SW, Ste. 4039
Washington, DC 20250

U.S. Department of Commerce
Office of Native American Affairs
1410 Constitution Avenue NW
Washington, DC 20230

U.S. Department of Energy
Indian Energy Resource Development
1000 Independence Avenue SW
Washington, DC 20585

U.S. Department of Health and Human Services
Indian Health Services
The Reyes Building
801 Thompson Avenue SW, Ste. 400
Rockville, MD 20852

U.S. Department of the Interior
Bureau of Indian Affairs

1849 C Street NW, MS 4140-M1B
Washington, DC 20240-0001

Office subdivisions:
Office of Indian Education Programs
Office of Indian Water Rights
Office of Tribal Services
Office of Trust Responsibilities
Office of Economic Development
Office of Indian Gaming Management
Office of Alcohol and Substance Abuse Prevention
Indian Arts and Crafts Board
Division of Law Enforcement
National Indian Gaming Commission

Canada

The British North American Act of 1867 gave "dominion" status to the Canadian federal nation. The Act provided that responsibilities for Native Americans and their lands would rest with the central (Ottawa) government of the new nation. From 1867 until 1873, an Office of Indian Affairs was placed within the Department of the Secretary of State. In 1873, a Department of Interior was created and within it was placed the Indian Branch, which was headed by a superintendent general. In 1880, the branch was elevated to status of Department of Indian Affairs, however, it remained within the Ministry of the Interior. In the twentieth century the department was given jurisdiction over northern affairs and gained independence; it now has a full cabinet-level ministry.

Ministry of Indian and Northern Affairs
Les Terrasses de la Chaudiere
Ottawa, ON KIA OK1
(819) 997-9885

Subdivisions:
Claims and Northern Affairs Program
Intergovernmental Affairs
Land, Revenue, and Trust Sector
Policy and Consultation

Regional Offices: Alberta, British Columbia, Manitoba,
Atlantic, North West Territories, Ontario, Quebec,
Saskatchewan, and Yukon
Regional Offices/Northern Affairs

U.S. State Government Organizations

Alabama Indian Affairs Commission
770 South McDonough
Montgomery, AL 36130
(334) 242-2831

Alaska Office of the Governor
P.O. Box A
Juneau, AK 99811
(907) 465-3500
Mike Irwin, Special Staff Assistant

Arizona Commission on Indian Affairs
1400 W. Washington, Ste. 300
Phoenix, AZ 85007
(602) 542-3123
http://www.indianaffairs.state.az.us

California Native American Heritage Commission
915 Capitol Mall, Room 288
Sacramento, CA 95814
(916) 322-7791

Colorado Commission of Indian Affairs
State Capital Building
200 E. Colfax, Room 130
Denver, CO 80203
(303) 866-3027

Connecticut Indian Affairs Council
Department of Environmental Protection
165 Capitol Avenue, Room 24
Hartford, CT 06106
(203) 566-5191

Delaware Human Relations Division
820 N. French, 4th Floor
Wilmington, DE 19801
(302) 571-3716

Florida Governor's Council on Indian Affairs, Inc.
1341 Cross Creek Circle
Tallahassee, FL 32301
(850) 488-0730
http://www.fgcia.com

State Council on Hawaiian Heritage
P.O. Box 3022
Honolulu, HI 96807
(808) 586-0335
Director: Keahi Allen

Office of Hawaiian Affairs
5562 Kalanianaole Highway
Honolulu, HI 96821
(808) 377-5391

American Indian Center
1630 W. Wilson Avenue
Chicago, IL 60640
(312) 275-5871

Iowa Governor's Liaison
1405 Truman Place, State Capitol
Ames, IA 50010
(515) 232-5320

Native American Affairs Office
1430 S.W. Topeka Blvd.
Topeka, KS 66612
(785) 368-7319
http://www.hr.state.ks.us/konaa/html/index.html

Kentucky Native American Heritage Commission
1788 Laurel Lake Road

London, KY 40741
(606) 864-7895

Governor's Commission on Indian Affairs
P.O. Box 44072
Baton Rouge, LA 70804
(504) 342-9796

Maine Indian Affairs Commission
State House Station, #38
Augusta, ME 04333
(207) 287-5800
Fax: (207) 287-5900

Maine Indian Tribal State Commission
P.O. Box 87
Hallowell, ME 04347
(207) 626-0069

Maryland Commission on Indian Affairs
100 Community Place
Crownsville, MD 21032
(410) 514-7616
http://www.dhcd.state.md.us/mcia

Massachusetts Commission on Indian Affairs
One Congress Street, 10th Floor
Boston, MA 02114
(619) 727-6394

Michigan Commission on Indian Affairs
Dept. of Management and Budget
Box 30026
611 W. Ottawa Street, 3rd Floor
Lansing, MI 48909
(517) 373-0654

Minnesota Indian Affairs Council
3801 Bemidji Avenue
Bemidji, MN 56601
(218) 755-3825
http://www.indians.state.mn.us

Governor's Office of Indian Affairs
State Coordinator of Indian Affairs
1218 E. Sixth Avenue
Helena, MT 59620
(406) 444-3702

Nebraska State Commission on Indian Affairs
Box 94981, State Capitol, 6th Floor East
Lincoln, NE 68509
(402) 471-3475
http://www.indianaffairs.state.ne.us

Nevada Indian Commission
3100 Mill Street, Ste. 206
Reno, NV 89502
(702) 789-0347

New Mexico Office on Indian Affairs
228 East Palace Avenue, 3rd Floor
Santa Fe, NM 87501
(505) 827-6440
Fax: (505) 827-6445
http://www.state.nm.us/oia

New York State Department of Indian Affairs
125 Main Street, Room 475
Buffalo, NY 14203

North Carolina Commission on Indian Affairs
1317 Mail Service Center
Raleigh, NC 27699
(919) 733-5998
http://http://www.doa.state.nc.us/doa/cia/indian.htm

North Dakota Indian Affairs Commission
600 E. Blvd., 1st Floor, Judicial Wing
Bismark, ND 58505
(701) 224-2428

North American Indian Cultural Centers
1062 Triplett Blvd.

Akron, OH 44306
(216) 724-1280

Oklahoma Indian Affairs Commission
4545 N. Lincoln Blvd., Ste. 282
Oklahoma City, OK 73105
(405) 521-3828
http://www.oiac.state.ok.us

Oregon Commission on Indian Services
454 State Capitol
Salem, OR 97310
(503) 986-1067

South Carolina Council on Native Americans
P.O. Box 219221
Columbia, SC 29221

South Dakota Indian Affairs Office
Public Safety Building
118 W. Capitol, Room 300
Pierre, SD 57501
(605) 773-3415
http://www.state.sd.us/oia.html

Tennessee Commission on Indian Affairs
112 Cynthia Lane, Apt. C
Knoxville, TN 37922
Chairperson: John Martin

Tennessee Commission of Indian Affairs
401 Church St., Land C Towers, 10th Floor
Nashville, TN 37243
(615) 532-0745
Executive Director: Luvenia H. Butler

Texas Indian Commission
P.O. Box 2960
Austin, TX 78768-2960
(512) 458-1203
Executive Director: Raymond D. Apodaca

Utah Division of Indian Affairs
324 S. State Street, Ste. 103
Salt Lake City, UT 84111
(801) 538-8808
Fax: (801) 538-8888
http://www.dced.utah.gov/indian

**The Governor's Advisory Commission on
  Native American Affairs**
Pavillion Office Building
109 State Street
Montpelier, VT 05609
(802) 828-3333
Contact: Jeff Benay

Virginia Council on Indians
22258 Cool Water Drive
Ruther Glen, VA 22546
(804) 448-3707
Director: Gary Flowers

Governor's Office of Indian Affairs
531 15th Avenue SE
P.O. Box 40909
Olympia, WA 98504
(206) 753-2411
http://www.goia.wa.gov

Wisconsin Governor's Indian Desk
P.O. Box 7863
Madison, WI 53701

Governor's Indian Commission
U.S. West Building, Room 259B
6101 Yellowstone
Cheyenne, WY 82002
(307) 777-6779
Commissioner: Gary Maier

Private Organizations

Allied Indian and Metis Society
2716 Clark
Vancouver, BC V5N 3H6
(604) 874-9610

American Indian Anti-Defamation Council
215 W. Fifth Avenue
Denver, CO 80204
(303) 871-0463

The Council monitors public media and advises representatives of the media on concerns of Native America.

American Indian Heritage Foundation
6051 Arlington Blvd.
Falls Church, VA 22044
(703) 237-7500
President: Princess Pale Moon
Executive Director: Wil Rose

The purpose of the Foundation, which began operations in 1973, is to inform non-Natives about Native culture and heritage. It sponsors pow wows and craft festivals as well as an annual National Children's Thanksgiving Concert. The Foundation publishes *Pathfinder*, a periodic newsletter.

American Indian Law Center
P.O. Box 4456, Station A
1117 Stanford NE
Albuquerque, NM 87196
Executive Director: Philip S. Deloria
(505) 277-5462
http://lawschool.unm.edu/AILC

Staffed by attorneys, the Center offers several services in the area of research and training in the area of the law. It conducts programs for tribal judges and prosecutors, and it provides scholarships for law students. Founded in 1967, the Center publishes the *American Indian Law Newsletter*, as well as various law manuals.

American Indian Movement
2940 16th Street, Ste. 104
San Francisco, CA 94103
Founding Chairman: Dennis Banks

The AIM was founded in 1986 to assist relocated urban Native Americans in adjusting to new life environments. Their interests quickly extended to national concerns for all Native peoples as they sponsored several protests and demonstrations of Native solidarity.

Americans for Indian Opportunity
681 Juniper Hill Road
Bernalillo, NM 87004
(505) 867-0278
President: LaDonna Harris
http://www.aio.org

The organization was founded in 1970 with the goal of promoting coalitions of Native peoples and others working to enhance cultural, social, political, and economic self-sufficiency among tribes. They publish an occasional report called *Red Alert.*

Arrow Incorporated (Americans for the Restoration and Righting of Old Wrongs)
1000 Connecticut Avenue NW, Ste. 1206
Washington, DC 20036
President: R. L. Bennett
Executive Director: Tom Colosimo

Arrow Incorporated is concerned primarily with matters of health and justice for Native peoples. The organization conducts training programs for health givers as well as tribal court and law enforcement personnel. Founded in 1949, the organization publishes training manuals and an annual report.

Assembly of First Nations
55 Murray Street
Ottawa, ON KIN 7B7
(613) 241-6789
National Chief: Ovide Mercredi

Founded as the National Indian Brotherhood of Canada in 1968, this organization has taken the lead in advocating constitutional revision and sovereign rights for the First Nations of Canada.

Association of American Indian Affairs
966 Hungeford Drive, Ste. 12B
Rockville, MD 20850
(240) 314-7155
http://www.indian-affairs.org

This 50,000-member organization was founded in 1922 to advocate policies that will benefit Native Americans. The Association sponsors many scholarships and has published many books as well as a quarterly newsletter entitled *Indian Affairs*.

Canadian Alliance in Solidarity with the Native People
P.O. Box 574, St. P
Toronto, ON M5S 2T1
(416) 972-1573

The Alliance was founded in 1960 to promote the interests of Native peoples in the areas of child welfare, prison reform, the environment, spirituality, and self-determination.

Canadian Council for Native Business
405 St. George Street, 2nd Floor
Toronto, ON M5R 2N5
(416) 961-8663

This organization seeks to promote the interests of Native American–owned businesses in Canada.

Council of Energy Resource Tribes (CERT)
695 S. Colorado Blvd., Ste. 10
Denver, CO 80246
(303) 282-7576
Executive Director: A. David Lester
http://www.certredearth.com

CERT consists of fifty-seven tribes that own energy resources. They have acted together since 1975 to seek ways to protect the resources through environmental controls and prudent management, and to enhance tribal revenues through appropriate and fair leasing procedures.

Indian Rights Association
1601 Market Street
Philadelphia, PA 19103
(215) 665-4523
Executive Director: Janney Montgomery

This is one of the pioneer organizations promoting rights for Native Americans. The Association began in 1882. It lobbies for programs to aid tribes, and it provides speakers who generate awareness of Native American culture and life. The Association publishes *Indian Truth*, a bimonthly newsletter.

Institute for the Development of Indian Law
Oklahoma City University—College of Law
2501 N. Blackwelder
Oklahoma City, OK 73106
(405) 521-5188
Executive Director: Kirke Kickingbird

The Institute conducts legal research on Native American issues and provides training programs for persons involved in Native law. The Institute publishes the quarterly *American Indian Journal*. The Institute started operations in 1971.

Metis National Council
350 Sparks Street, Ste. 201
Ottawa, ON K1R 7S8
(800) 928-6330
http://www.metisnation.ca
Executive Director: Ron Rivard

This is the leading advocacy group for the Metis peoples. The organization seeks official recognition of Metis from the federal government of Canada.

National Congress of American Indians
900 Pennsylvania Avenue SE
Washington, DC 20003
(202) 546-9404
President: Gaiashkibos
Executive Director: JoAnne Chase
http://www.ncai.org

This organization was founded in 1944 to foster cooperation among tribal governments and to promote policies beneficial to Native America. The Congress is a leading Native organization consisting of over 2,000 representatives from 155 tribes. It publishes a quarterly newsletter called *Sentinel,* and also the *NCAI News.*

National Indian Gaming Association
224 Second Street SE
Washington, DC 20003
(202) 546-7711
Chairperson: Rick Hill
Executive Director: Tim Wapato
http://www.indiangaming.org

The Association promotes Native American gaming operations through lobbying and training programs. It publishes the monthly *Indian Gaming Magazine.*

National Indian Policy Center
1301 Connecticut Avenue NW, Ste. 200
Washington, DC 20036
(202) 466-7767
Director: Ronald Trospe

The Center was created by a congressional mandate in 1990. Under the direction of a council consisting of tribal leaders and policy experts, it conducts research projects for Native Americans. It publishes research reports, policy papers, and bibliographies.

National Indian Youth Council
318 Elm Street SE
Albuquerque, NM 87102
President: Norman Ration
Executive Director: Kenneth Tsosie

The NIYC began in 1961 as a civil rights organization. The Council has also been active in campaigns to protect tribal financial resources and the environment. It publishes a monthly paper entitled *American Before Columbus,* and also periodical surveys of Native American attitudes on policy issues.

National Tribal Chairman's Association
Washington, DC 20006

(202) 293-0031
Executive Director: Raymond Field

The organization of tribal leaders in the United States promotes solidarity in political relations with federal and state governments. It publishes lists of chairmen and newsletters.

Native American Rights Fund
1506 Broadway
Boulder, CO 80302
(303) 447-8760
http://www.narf.org

The Native American Rights Fund (NARF) began operations in 1971. The organization conducts legal research and assists in litigation designed to protect tribal resources and human rights for Native Americans. The NARF publishes the quarterly *NARF Legal Review,* the monthly *Indian Law Support Center Reporter,* as well as a monthly newsletter.

Native Council of Canada
384 Bank Street, 2nd Floor
Ottawa, ON K2P 1Y4
(613) 238-3511
President: Dan Smith
Executive Director: Ron George

This is an organization of tribal and band leaders from throughout Canada.

Native Women's Association of Canada
1292 Wellington Street
Ottawa, ON K1Y 3A9
(613) 722-3033
http://www.nwac-hq.org

The Association was founded in 1974 in order to protect the human rights of Native women. It has published a booklet entitled *An Aboriginal Charter of Rights and Freedoms.*

Original Women's Network—Resource Center for Aboriginal Women
181 Higgins Avenue, 3rd Floor
Winnipeg, MB R38 3G1

(204) 942-2711
Executive Director: Kathy Mallett

Founded in 1985, the Center seeks to raise an awareness of issues concerning Native women. It maintains a radio station and also conducts training programs for women interested in business. The Center publishes the *Aboriginal Women's Community Bulletin* and the *Aboriginal Women's Resource Directory*.

United Native Americans
2434 Faria Avenue
Pinole, CA 94564
(415) 758-8160
Director: Lehman L. Brightman

This organization promotes the general welfare of Native peoples with legal aid, counseling, and scholarship programs. It publishes the monthly magazine *Warpath*.

10

Print and Nonprint Resources

Print Resources

Literally tens of thousands of books have been written about Native Americans and Native American policy issues. It has been no easy task to select a reasonably small number of these for inclusion in the following annotated bibliography. Quite frankly, the author has not read all the books: nor would there be enough time in a lifetime to read all the books. Therefore, some very arbitrary decisions had to be made in making the selections.

At the same time, some of the decisions followed quite explicit, identifiable criteria. First, it was decided to feature books dealing with political subjects and to exclude books dealing exclusively with cultural issues. Second, it was decided to include books covering Native Americans and their tribes generally rather than books focusing solely upon a single tribe. The list contains, with one exception, nonfiction works. The novel *Ramona* by Helen Hunt Jackson is included because it played a major role in policy development. Another bias was made in favor of books published in recent decades and reviewed in major journals of Native American affairs (e.g., *American Indian Quarterly, American Indian Law Review, American Indian Culture and Research Journal*).

The first group of print materials in this chapter includes selected governmental reports, the second group reference works, the third books appearing in series, and the fourth single-volume books. A fifth section provides selective references to journals and periodicals.

Quite unlike the section on films, the print sources—notably the single-volume books and journals—do not reflect a history of works that denigrate Native peoples, or that stereotype them in an inappropriate way. Quite to the contrary, a decided bias in the printed sources is to project an image of history that shows discrimination and unjustified wrongs done to Native peoples. This is done to the extent that objectivity is often—but not always—lost regarding episodes of interaction between Native peoples and others.

The author believes that the print resources collectively leave an impression that today's Native American scholars and writers—that is, individuals writing about Native Americans—may be quite unwilling to examine the full picture, or both sides of issues dealing with Native America. For instance, they seem unwilling to view the negative sides of the issue of gambling on tribal lands, instead concentrating only on positive (and perhaps selective) cases of the impacts of gambling on the tribes and on society as a whole. The writers collectively seek to portray an idea that all Native Americans are somehow "good" and that for the most part they have been "victims" in the larger scale of things. While this is a politically correct viewpoint, it lacks a genuineness that should be afforded any assessment of the conditions of the Native American community today. In a sense, the literature puts forth a stereotype that suggests that Native Americans are really unlike other groups of people—that they are all above criticism because of their genetic heritage. On the other hand, writers and publishers may suggest that the literature has the effect of balancing stereotypes of another nature that have been found in many films about Native peoples.

Government Reports

American Indian Policy Review Commission. *Final Report.* Washington, DC: U.S. Government Printing Office, 1977, v. 1, 624 pp; v. 2, 923 pp.

The Commission was created by Congress in 1975 to evaluate federal policy toward Native America. It was composed of five Native Americans and six members of Congress. Their report offered the conclusion that Native tribes were "sovereign political bodies" with law-making authority, law enforcement authority, and the authority to define their own membership. The role of the U.S. government as a trustee for the Native tribes was to assure their protection and to foster their economic development.

Brophy, William A., and Sophie D. Aberle. *The Indian: America's Unfinished Business: Report of the Commission on the Rights, Liberties, and Responsibilities of the American Indian.* Norman: University of Oklahoma Press, 1966. 236 pp.

The Commission was created in 1957 during the height of the "Termination era." The report called for extensive study before other tribes would experience an end of their trustee status. Policy makers were cautioned to make sure Native Americans had sufficient education and economic resources to stand fully independent before having their reservations taken from them.

Commission on the Organization of the Executive Branch of the Government (The Hoover Commission). *Report.* Washington, DC: U.S. Government Printing Office, 1949.

A commission was authorized by Congress in 1947 to make the federal government more efficient. It was led by former president Herbert Hoover. Its recommendations on Native American programs paved the way for the Termination policies of the Truman and Eisenhower administrations. It recommended that young Native Americans leave the reservations, and that tribal property by converted to private corporate property held by Native peoples and be taxed like other fee property. The Commission suggested that social programs for Natives be transferred to state governments and that the BIA be moved to a new department with social security and education programs.

Commission on the Rights, Liberties, and Responsibilities of the American Indian. *A Summary Report on Indian Affairs.* Washington, DC: Fund for the Republic, 1961.

This Commission did not entirely reject the policy of assimilation, but it did reject Termination as a method to achieve the goal. Rather, the Commission suggested that Native Americans should run their own affairs and that the best way to achieve this end would be to recognize the value of Native cultures and the viability of Native organizations. "The Bureau's aim should be to let Indians conduct their own affairs as soon as possible without supervision."

Department of Indian Affairs and Northern Development. *Statement of the Government of Canada on Indian Policy in 1969.* Ottawa: The Queen's Printer, 1969.

This "White Paper" provides the position taken by Canadian Prime Minister Pierre Trudeau and Minister of Indian Affairs Jean Chrétien toward Native peoples of their land in 1969. The policy called for "termination" of special Native status. It was firmly rejected by Native peoples and the non-Native public alike, and the government then turned toward policies linked to notions of self-determination.

Ewen, Alexander, ed. *Voices of Indigenous Peoples.* Santa Fe, NM: Clear Light Publ., 1994. 174 pp.

This volume presents twenty statements made by leaders of indigenous peoples to the United Nations during the International Year of the World's Indigenous Peoples (1993). Secretary General Boutros Boutros-Ghali provides an introduction, while an appendix includes a Statement of the Indigenous Nations Peoples and Organization, and the UN Draft Declaration of Indigenous Peoples' Rights.

Institute for Government Research, Studies in Administration. *The Problem of Indian Administration.* Baltimore, MD: Johns Hopkins University Press, 1928. 872 pp.

This is the official report of the Meriam Commission, which studied all aspects of Native life—social, economic, health, and welfare. The report was very critical of government programs for Native America. Its publication was influential in the Roosevelt administration's efforts to end policies of allotment and assimilation.

The Royal Commission on Aboriginal Peoples (RCAP). *Reports.* Ottawa: Canadian Government, 1996 et al.

This Canadian governmental commission issued several reports after its inception in 1994. The *Final Report* was published in 1996. Other report titles included: *Public Policy and Aboriginal Peoples, 1965–1992* (1994); *Looking Forward, Looking Back* (1996); *People to People, Nation to Nation* (1996); *Perspectives and Realities* (1996); and *Bridging the Cultural Divide: A Report on Aboriginal Peoples and Criminal Justice in Canada* (1996).

United States Commission on Civil Rights. *Indian Tribes: A Continuing Quest for Survival.* Washington, DC: U.S. Government Printing Office, 1981. 192 pp.

This report presents findings from research and hearings conducted from 1977 through 1979. The report focuses on issues of major concern, including criminal law enforcement on reservations, Native fishing rights, and land claims. The report concludes that there are few effective mechanisms for dealing with problems in a comprehensive manner to protect Native rights. Continuing unresolved conflicts between Native communities and others are only made worse by the lack of a system for conflict resolution.

United States Department of Commerce, Bureau of the Census. *We the First Americans.* Washington, DC: U.S. Government Printing Office, 1993. 17 pp.

This report is part of a series from the Racial Statistics Branch of the Census Bureau. It provides a variety of demographic data on Native peoples.

Reference Works

American Indian Lawyer Training Program. *Indian Tribes as Sovereign Governments: A Sourcebook on Federal-Tribal History, Law and Policy.* Oakland, CA: AILTP, 1988. 156 pp.

This concise, well-written, general survey of intergovernmental relations involving Native American issues reviews treaties, statutes, and case law in the context of tribal sovereignty. It is written for Native Americans and those working with Natives on governmental programs.

Bataille, Gretchen, with Laurie Lisa. *Native American Women.* New York and London: Garland Publishing, 1993. 331 pp.

This is a collection of biographical sketches on over 100 leading Native American women. Each concise sketch is followed by a list of references.

Bataille, Gretchen, and Kathleen M. Sands. *American Indian Women: A Guide to Research.* New York and London: Garland Publishing, 1991. 423 pp.

This annotated list of 1,573 sources covers several subjects: reference works, cultural history, politics and law, health, education and employment, the arts, literature, films, and biography.

Champagne, Duane. *Native America: Portrait of the Peoples.* Detroit: Visible Ink Press, 1994. 786 pp.

This is an abridged version of *The Native North American Almanac* (1994). With a foreword by Dennis Banks, it offers chapters on the development of Native American activism, and on the history and cultures of tribes in each major region of North America. Separate chapters treat Native religion, health, arts, literature, and the media—films, the stage, as well as print media. Biographical sketches appear throughout the book.

Champagne, Duane, ed. *Chronology of Native North American History: From Pre-Columbian Times to the Present.* Detroit: Gale Research, 1994. 574 pp.

This very useful work describes the events, the people, and the history of Native America. Initial chapters paint a broad overview of this history and a descriptive account of different tribes. Concluding chapters present excerpts from historical documents, and court cases, as well as a comprehensive bibliography. In between there are over 500 pages treating dates and events in chronological order. The comprehensive information examines tribes of both the United States and Canada.

Cohen, Felix S. *Handbook of Federal Indian Law.* Washington, DC: U.S. Government Printing Office, 1942. 662 pp.; Charlottesville, VA: The Michie Company, rev. ed., 1982. 912 pp.

The *Handbook* was written under the sponsorship of Bureau of Indian Affairs Commissioner John Collier. It represents the culmination of his desires to codify federal law on Native America. The essence of statutory, administrative, and case law is contained, along with extensive text providing historical context. The *Handbook* is considered the definitive work on the subject.

Davis, Mary, ed. *Native America in the Twentieth Century: An Encyclopedia.* New York: Garland Publishing, 1994. 787 pp.

This encyclopedia contains articles by leading historians, anthropologists, and other experts on Native America. Subjects address economics, health, education, politics, law, and languages of Native peoples. Reference lists follow each entry. Much of the work contains a Native perspective with authors including Deloria, Kickingbird, Fixico, and Harris.

Dockstader, Frederick J. *Great North American Indians: Profiles in Life and Leadership.* New York: Van Nostrand Reinhold Co., 1977. 386 pp.

This is a collection of biographies of Native Americans from before the European Contact until 1977. Each is concise, offering information on birth and death dates and places, families, and major events that established the figure's place in history. Many photographs and drawings are included.

Eagle/Walking Turtle. *Indian America: A Traveler's Companion.* Santa Fe, NM: John Muir Publications, 1989, 1991. 434 pp.

This is more than a traveler's guidebook. It is a listing of most Native American reservations with historical profiles. The well-illustrated book tells the origin of tribal names, and describes reservation locations, public ceremonies, and arts and crafts available at the reservation. An appendix includes a bibliography and a listing of dates of events.

Gattuso, John, ed. *Insight Guides: Native America.* Boston: Houghton Mifflin, 1993. 389 pp.

This volume is part of a series of guides that cover the globe. It offers the reader "a cultural journey, a passage of discovery" into Native American history and life. A team of several dozen present essays on Native art, pow wows, spiritual life, social problems, as well as history. Specific essays also address individual tribes and reservations. The book is well illustrated with hundreds of beautiful color photographs and a collection of maps.

Hilger, Michael. *The American Indian in Film.* Metuchen, NJ: Scarecrow Press, 1986. 196 pp.

Hilger presents the reader with a directory and short reviews of 830 films from 1903 through 1984. Introductory and concluding essays suggest that viewers must realize that the films are fiction and that they should look for their value in scenery and camera work, role creation, editing, music, and acting.

Hirschfelder, Arlene, and Martha Kreipe de Montano. *The Native American Almanac: A Portrait of Native America Today.* New York: Prentice Hall General Reference, 1993. 341 pp.

This short but comprehensive volume presents information about all aspects of Native American life. A concise history chapter is followed by demographic data, Supreme Court decisions, and treaties. One chapter is devoted to the structure of the BIA and another to tribal governments. Attention is also given to Native religion, sports, and the arts. The appendix lists all tribes, Native landmarks, and a chronology of Native American events.

Hirschfelder, Arlene, and Paulette Milon. *Encyclopedia of Native American Religion.* New York: Facts on File, 1992. 367 pp.

This encyclopedia includes over 1200 entries describing Native religious institutions, ceremonies, sacred lands and objects, historical events, and prominent religious leaders. There is an extensive bibliography.

Hoxie, Frederick E., and Harvey Markowitz. *Native Americans: An Annotated Bibliography.* Pasadena, CA: Salem Press, 1991. 325 pp.

Over 3,000 entries, mostly books, are included in this bibliography. It is organized into sections on general studies, periods of history, cultural and geographical areas, and contemporary issues—family, economics, resources, religion, health, law, art, and literature.

Klein, Barry T., ed. *Reference Encyclopedia of the American Indian.* 7th ed. West Nyack, NY: Todd Publications, 1995. 883 pp.

This encyclopedia offers a massive amount of information in a single volume. It presents many lists: all tribes and reservations, schools, private and governmental organizations, museums and monuments, books and films, casinos, and biographies. However, it does not contain any explanatory textual materials.

Kvasnicka, Robert M., and Herman J. Viola, eds. *The Commissioners of Indian Affairs, 1824–1977.* Lincoln: University of Nebraska Press, 1979. 384 pp.

The contributors have prepared short biographies of 43 individuals who led the Bureau of Indian Affairs over a 153-year period. Each essay includes descriptions of the Bureau's activities and the nature of Native American issues at the time the individual served in the Bureau.

Leitch, Barbara A. *A Concise Dictionary of Indian Tribes of North America.* Algonac, MI: Reference Publications, 1979. 646 pp.

This dictionary includes intelligible and concise entries for each current as well as historical tribe in North America. Each tribal sketch includes information about history, geography, and population, as well as social customs, language, and religions. Dozens of photographs accompany the text.

Patterson, Lotsee, and Mary Ellen Snodgrass. *Indian Terms of the Americas.* Englewood, CO: Libraries Unlimited, 1994. 275 pp.

The authors have prepared a descriptive dictionary with over 500 terms, including Native names for objects, activities, significant places, people, and events.

Prucha, Francis Paul. *Documents of United States Indian Policy.* 2d ed. Lincoln: University of Nebraska Press, 1990. 338 pp.

This is the essential aid for researchers and students of public policy and Native Americans. It is the best single-volume source for laws, treaties, executive proclamations, and court cases on issues concerning Native Americans.

Spaeth, Nicholas, et al., eds. *American Indian Law Desk Book: Conference of Western Attorneys General.* Niwot: University Press of Colorado, 1993. 466 pp.

This is a book about law written by lawyers for government. It presents a comprehensive analysis of legislation and case law on contemporary issues such as hunting and fishing rights, water rights, child welfare, Indian civil rights, and gambling. The passage of such a short period of time, however, makes the coverage in the latter area dated.

Vecsey, Christopher, ed. *Handbook of American Indian Religious Freedoms.* New York: Crossroads Publishing Co., 1991. 180 pp.

A collection of essays by leading writers including Sharon O'Brien, Walter EchoHawk, and Omar Stewart. Topics include use of peyote in religious rites, burial rights, sacred sites, and the history of national legislation.

Waldman, Carl. *Encyclopedia of Native American Tribes.* New York: Facts on File, 1988. 293 pp.

This encyclopedia offers a comprehensive discussion of more than 150 Native American tribes, covering both the United States and Canada. Listings provide information on tribal locations, histories, social and political structures, religion, and economic life. The book includes many color illustrations as well as maps, bibliography, and glossary.

Waldman, Carl, with Molly Braun. *Atlas of the North American Indian.* New York: Facts on File, 1985. 276 pp.

The atlas includes over 100 maps drawn by Molly Braun to show historical, military, and cultural aspects of Native American life. Waldman adds extensive text. He also offers an extensive chronology, bibliography, and listings of tribal lands in the United States and Canada.

Washburn, Wilcomb E., ed. *The American Indian and the United States: A Documentary History.* New York: Random House, 1973. 4 vols., 3119 pp.

These volumes offer an extensive collection of historical documents: reports of commissioners, debates in Congress, statutes, court decisions, and treaties.

Weatherford, Elizabeth, and Emelia Seubert. *Native Americans on Film and Video.* New York: Museum of the American Indian, 1981. 152 pp.

This resource guide presents descriptive critiques of 125 documentary films and videos produced by and about Native Americans. The films were entered into the Native American Film Festival.

Wildenthal, Bryan H. *Native American Sovereignty on Trial.* Santa Barbara, CA: ABC-CLIO, 2003. 357 pp.

The author places the development of Native American–non-Native government relationships within the context of legal cases and laws that address matters of tribal autonomy and jurisdiction over their own affairs. Resource materials include biographies of key people, tables of laws and cases, and a chronology of events.

Series; Multivolume Sets

Chelsea House. *Indians of North America.* New York: Chelsea House Publishers, 1980s–present.

This series offers interesting, well-written, readable books on over fifty Native tribes of North America. In addition, there are books entitled: *Federal Indian Policy, Literature of the American Indian, The Archaeology of North America,* and *Women in American Society.*

Editors of Chelsea House. *North American Indians of Achievement.* New York and Philadelphia: Chelsea House Publishers, Inc., 1987–present.

The series includes over twenty-five books devoted to great chiefs and leaders of the past (e.g., King Philip, Pontiac, Osceola, Sitting Bull), as well as more contemporary Native achievers (e.g., Jim Thorpe, Will Rogers, Wilma Mankiller). They are written in a style designed for young readers. The series is edited by W. David Baird, who offers introductory essays on the qualities of Native leadership.

Sturtevant, William C., general ed. *Handbook of North American Indians.* 20 vols. Washington, DC: Smithsonian Institution, 1972–1988.

Titles in this series include: *Indians in Contemporary Society, Environment, Origins, and Population, History of Indian-White Relations, Technology and Visual Arts, Languages, Biographical Dictionary,* as well as volumes devoted to geographic regions of the continent. This extensive collection is technical and detailed. It was written by many authors, including leading experts on Native America.

The Editors of Time-Life. *The American Indians.* Alexandria, VA: Time-Life Books, 1992–1994.

This is a series of ten volumes covering Native American history and culture from pre-Contact times to the present day. Separate volumes include the titles: *The First Americans, The European Challenge, The Spirit World, Cycles of Life, Realm of the Iroquois, The People of the Desert, The Way of the Warrior, The Buffalo Hunters, The Woman's Way,* and *The Mighty Chieftains.*

The Editors of Time-Life. *The Old West.* Alexandria, VA: Time-Life Books, 1973–1974.

The series includes two works by Benjamin Capps: *The Indians* (1973) and *The Great Chiefs* (1975). Both books are well illustrated with comprehensive text materials. Each offers a bibliography.

General Interest Books

Adams, David Wallace. *Education for Extinction: American Indians and the Boarding School Experience, 1875–1928.* Lawrence: University Press of Kansas, 1995. 396 pp.

Adams traces the effects of the assimilation politics of the pre-Dawes and Dawes era by looking at the policies of forcing Native children to attend government schools. Although the policy may have been generated by people with positive motives, the effects were often but not always negative ones. Nonetheless, the title of the work is on-target for revealing the contents.

Ambler, Marjane. *Breaking the Iron Bonds: Indian Control of Energy Development.* Lawrence: University Press of Kansas, 1990. 270 pp.

The proper development of energy resources can help Native Americans break their "Iron Bonds" to dependency. The author looks at the history of mineral leasing on Native lands and policies of the BIA, which have resulted in strengthening rather than weakening the bonds.

Bachman, Ronet. *Death and Violence on the Reservation.* New York: Auburn House, 1992. 167 pp.

It is the lot of minorities to be ignored. Accomplishments are overlooked, and so too are problems. The neglect robs people of pride, but it also makes society oblivious of the need to correct abuses. Bachman discusses several dysfunctional aspects of Native life—homicide, family violence, and suicide. Native Americans are compared with other groups. Statistics are analyzed, as are social causes and policy implications.

Barreiro, Jose, ed. *Indian Roots of Democracy.* Ithaca, NY: Akwekon Press, Cornell University, 1992. 209 pp.

Barreiro's collection of essays examines the contributions of Native political structures and processes to the development of federalism and democracy in the United States. Most of the essays concentrate on aspects of the Iroquois Confederation.

Benedict, Jeff. *Without Reservation: The Making of America's Most Powerful Indian Tribe and Foxwoods, the World's Largest Casino.* New York: HarperCollins, 2001. 404 pp.

This book "exposes" a fraud. Benedict offers evidence that the forces behind the creation of a new tribe—based upon a historical tribe—were non-Natives out to find casino wealth beyond their wildest dreams. They engaged in political maneuvers that violated the letter of the law, but won the support of politicians who were seeking their own rewards. The book leaves impressions that the gambling world and the cultural world of genuine Native peoples may not be all that compatible.

Brandon, William. *The American Heritage Book of Indians.* Edited by Alvin M. Josephy. New York: American Heritage Publishing Co., 1961. 424 pp.

This book offers a well-illustrated panorama of Native American history and cultures from before Contact to the mid-twentieth century. An introduction by President John F. Kennedy emphasizes the diversity of Native peoples and their customs as well as the contributions Native Americans have given to the newcomers on the continent.

Brown, Dee. *Bury My Heart at Wounded Knee.* New York: Holt, Rinehart and Winston, 1970. 487 pp.

Brown presents a detailed account of the American Westward movement written from the perspective of retreating Native Americans. The book is based on analysis of many primary documents—treaties and speeches. It paints an unpleasant picture of U.S. policy during its "conquest" of the West.

Canby, William. *American Indian Law in a Nutshell.* 4th ed. St. Paul, MN: Thomson-West Publishing Co., 2004. 496 pp.

United States Court of Appeals Judge Canby has prepared a readable guide to the very complicated topic of Native American law. The updated book provides a historical background to legal issues as well as introductory materials on tribal governments, sovereignty, and treaties. Other chapters examine questions of jurisdiction, taxation, land claims, hunting, fishing, mineral, and water rights.

Cardinal, Harold. *The Unjust Society: The Tragedy of Canada's Indians.* Edmonton, AB: M.G. Hurtig, 1969. 171 pp.

Cardinal is a member of a Canadian Cree Nation. He writes in reaction to the Trudeau government's White Paper calling for "termination" of special status for Native Nations. Cardinal rejects the policy of assimilation, advancing the notion that Native peoples can be at peace with themselves only under conditions of self-determination. He reviews Canadian-Native peoples' relationships through history, showing that the White Paper was a continuation of a long-term degradation of the Natives.

Champagne, Duane. *American Indian Societies: Strategies and Conditions of Political and Cultural Survival.* Cambridge, MA: Cultural Survival, 1990. 160 pp.

Champagne seeks to identify societal factors that can explain why some Native peoples are able to embrace change and economic development while others fail to grasp new "opportunities." He focuses on internal role divisions as well as on the factor of solidarity among peoples.

Collier, John. *Indians of the Americas.* New York: New American Library, 1947. 326 pp.

This is a history of Native America with a strong section on New Deal policies instituted by the author while he was the commissioner of the Bureau of Indian Affairs. A chapter of special interest addresses Native peoples of Central and South American venues. Collier concludes that "the group" has been the controlling factor in Native American life and that the factor contains the future elements of triumph for individual Native peoples.

Cornell, Stephen, and Joseph P. Kalt, eds. *What Can Tribes Do? Strategies and Institutions in American Indian Economic Development.* Los Angeles: American Indian Studies Center, UCLA, 1992. 336 pp.

These essays discuss the barriers to economic development faced by Native tribes. The solutions offered to overcome barriers include enhancement of sovereignty, creation of institutions to facilitate development, and selection of appropriate strategies. Casino revenues will help but only if a development plan is in place.

Cox, Bruce Alden, ed. *Native People, Native Lands: Canadian Indians, Inuit, and Metis.* Ottawa: Carleton University Press, 1988. 298 pp.

This is a collection of articles about the Native peoples of Canada. Most are written by non-Native anthropologists. The articles are arranged by geographic regions covered. A bibliography on Canadian Native studies is included.

Crow Dog, Mary, with Richard Erdoes. *Lakota Woman.* New York: Grove Weidenfeld, 1990. 263 pp.

Mary Crow Dog tells her own story—her own "two lives." In her first life she had to cope with dysfunctional surroundings: alcoholism, poverty, and the racism of a missionary school. Her rebellion led her on a path toward self-denial and self-condemnation. Her involvement with the American Indian Movement and her participation in events such as the occupation of BIA headquarters in 1972 led her toward self-respect in her "second" life, but it also made her aware of internal prejudices within AIM against Native women.

Debo, Angie. *And Still the Waters Run: The Betrayal of the Five Civilized Tribes.* Princeton, NJ: Princeton University Press, 1940. 417 pp.

A leading scholar of Native American life presents a methodical documentation of deprivations of Native peoples. Specific attention is given to events from 1900 to 1940, with an emphasis on the Five Civilized Tribes of Oklahoma. Debo concludes that the United States erred by degrading thousands of individual Native peoples.

Debo, Angie. *A History of the Indians of the United States.* Norman: University of Oklahoma Press, 1970. 386 pp.

Angie Debo grew up in Oklahoma asking questions about how her people came to the state and what happened to the people before them. Her interest grew into a career as a historian. Her history of Native America focuses on Oklahoma as illustrative of the cruelty of policies inflicted on Native peoples. She makes a plea for a new policy of hope, a policy of protecting Native lands, economic development, education, and cultural preservation. She urges that Native peoples involve themselves in making all policy affecting Native America.

Deloria, Vine, Jr., ed. *American Indian Policy in the Twentieth Century.* Norman: University of Oklahoma Press, 1985. 265 pp.

This volume presents eleven original essays on contemporary policy issues facing Native America. These include an essay on human rights by Sharon O'Brien, a study of voting by Daniel McCool, and a discussion of water rights by May Wallace. John Petoskey investigates the First Amendment rights of Native peoples. Other essays look at economics, tribal governments, and policy-making processes.

Deloria, Vine, Jr. *Custer Died for Your Sins: An Indian Manifesto.* New York: Macmillan, 1969. 279 pp.

The author uses "brutal wit" to tell about America's "disastrous" policies toward Native peoples—especially the policy of Termination. He examines laws, treaties, government agencies, and even the role of missionaries and anthropologists in the implementation of past wrongs, as he calls for a redefinition of "Indian Affairs" building around concepts of community development and a "neo-tribalism."

Deloria, Vine, Jr. *God Is Red: A Native View of Religion.* 2d ed. Golden, CO: Fulcrum Publishing, 1994. (1st ed., 1973). 313 pp.

Deloria contrasts Native religion with a very narrow view (essentially Fundamentalist) of Christianity. Accordingly, the value of his work is in his positive portrayal of the Native religious perspectives on time and space, particularly the notions of repeating cycles of life and the value of specific places in the cultures of Native people, notions that make Native Americans more responsive to environmental concerns. His view on Christianity is extremely shallow.

Deloria, Vine, Jr., with Kirke Kickingbird. *Behind the Trail of Broken Treaties: An Indian Declaration of Independence.* Austin: University of Texas Press, 1974. 296 pp.

Deloria takes a page from the "Twenty Points" declaration of protest in 1972 and elaborates upon why the federal government should institute a new round of treaty-writing with Native Americans. Two leading chapters review the legal and historical nature of the treaty process.

Deloria, Vine, Jr., and Clifford Lytle. *American Indians, American Justice.* Austin: University of Texas Press, 1983. 262 pp.

This volume highlights the mechanisms of justice within tribal governments. It explains the roles of tribal attorneys and assesses the civil and criminal justice systems.

Deloria, Vine, Jr., and Clifford Lytle. *The Nations Within: The Past and Future of Native American Sovereignty.* New York: Pantheon, 1984. 293 pp.

The authors explore John Collier's effort to bring reform to Native American policy, and they urge new policies that will enable Natives to control their own destiny. The key element in the new policies is a renewed sense of sovereignty based on government-to-government relationships established through treaties.

Dickason, Olive Patrick. *Canada's First Nations: A History of Founding Peoples from Earliest Times.* Norman: University of Oklahoma Press, 1992. 590 pp.

Dickason presents a comprehensive history of Canada's Native peoples. The book emphasizes the pre–European Contact era, as well as the active roles Natives—including Inuit and Metis peoples—played in the development of Canada after Contact. It is well written and documented. Its focus is more on events of past generations than on the current era.

Dorris, Michael. *The Broken Cord.* New York: Harper and Row, 1989. 300 pp.

The author adopted a Native child who was later diagnosed as having Fetal Alcohol Syndrome. This experience led Dorris to travel the country studying alcoholism in Native America and to sound a warning bell for pregnant women everywhere.

Eisler, Kim Isaac. *Revenge of the Pequots.* New York: Simon and Schuster, 2001. 267 pp.

Eisler presents the account of how the "nearly" nonexistent Pequot tribe of Connecticut rose to win status as a federally recognized tribe and then built the largest casino in the world, Foxwoods. She traces political maneuvering from the bureaucratic jungles of Washington to the state halls of power in Hartford, and then to the pocketbooks of a Malaysian investor who made a secret alliance that resulted in much of the gambling money won by the tribe leaving the country. Eisler appears to be telling an insider's story but does so with sympathy for the tribe and its casino venture. Another book from Jeff Benedict (see above) tells quite another story as he follows the same events.

Fine-Dare, Kathleen S. *Grave Injustice: The American Indian Repatriation Movement and NAGPRA.* Lincoln: University of Nebraska Press, 2002. 250 pp.

The author examines the rationale and process involved in passing the Native American Graves Protection and Repatriation Act of 1990. Fine-Dare looks at the Repatriation movement in a context of calling attention to major internal differences among Native peoples. She documents problems with military and scientific organizations seizing Native remains and follows these with many case studies. She focuses on implementation problems following passage of the Act.

Fixico, Donald Lee. *Termination and Relocation: Federal Indian Policy, 1945–1960.* Albuquerque: University of New Mexico Press, 1986. 268 pp.

Native American Donald Fixico holds a doctorate in history from the University of Oklahoma. He is now a professor at Western Michigan University. He is married to author Sharon Lynn O'Brien. This book is an outgrowth of his doctoral research. It presents a detailed account of the midcentury policies of assimilation: tribal termination, relocation of Natives to urban centers, and state takeover of criminal jurisdiction in Indian Country (Public Law 280).

Fleras, Augie, and Jean Leonard Elliott. *The "Nations Within": Aboriginal State Relations in Canada, the United States and New Zealand.* Toronto: Oxford University Press, 1992. 267 pp.

The authors examine Native peoples in a comparative framework. However, the main emphasis (nine chapters of twelve) is on relationships between the federal and provincial governments of Canada and the First Nations of that land.

Frantz, Klaus. *Indian Reservations in the United States.* Chicago and London: University of Chicago Press, 2001. 370 pp.

Reservations in the forty-eight contiguous states are described in terms of contemporary life. Economic resources are highlighted and are seen as major links in the crucial issue of sovereignty. Gambling is seen as a resource that is fleeting, one that must be exploited now as it may soon disappear. The book is full of facts, history, and photographs. It has been called the "most comprehensive and detailed cultural-geographic study ever conducted" about reservations.

Friar, Ralph E., and Natasha A. Friar. *The Only Good Indian . . . The Hollywood Gospel.* New York: Drama Book Specialists, 1972. 332 pp.

The Friars offer evidence of the bigotry in film images of Native Americans. An in-depth history of Hollywood is documented with many graphic illustrations. An appendix lists white actors who played Natives, as well as the titles of nearly a thousand films about Native Americans dating from 1894 through 1971.

Furniss, Elizabeth. *Victims of Benevolence.* Vancouver: Arsenal Pulp Press, 1995. 128 pp.

Furniss presents an accounting of the benefits and costs, emphasizing the latter, of Indian residential schools. Her focus is on a single school at Williams Lake, British Columbia. The school was operated by missionaries of a French Roman Catholic order. The value of the study lies in her depth of history, as she covers events and life in the school from 1891 to 1981, and even beyond.

She describes a 1994 report by the Assembly of First Nations on residential schools in Canada.

Getches, David, Charles Wilkinson, and Robert A. Williams Jr. *Cases and Materials on Federal Indian Law.* 3d ed. St. Paul, MN: West Publishing Co., 1986. 1055 pp.

The authors have prepared the leading law school textbook on Native American law. The thorough work presents cases, statutes, and commentary giving the reader insights into all aspects of pertinent law: states' rights and sovereignty; jurisdiction; taxation; religion; water, hunting, and fishing rights.

Giago, Tim. *The Aboriginal Sin.* San Francisco: Indian Historian Press, 1979. 86 pp.

The editor of *Indian Country Today* presents a first-hand account of his childhood experiences as a student at the Holy Rosary Mission School in Pine Ridge, South Dakota. With wry humor, he decries the frustrations of being confronted with teachers trying to deprive him of his cultural foundations.

Grobsmith, Elizabeth. *Indians in Prison: Incarcerated Native Americans in Nebraska.* Lincoln: University of Nebraska Press, 1994. 210 pp.

The prison experience presents many problems that are specific to Native American inmates. The author ventures into the Nebraska prison system as an observer-researcher. She examines mutual accommodations to prison life between Native inmates and prison authorities. Attention is given to discipline behind the "walls" as well as work experiences and educational programs. The author also discusses special programs for substance abuse for both inmates and former inmates. The book focuses on litigation involving religious freedoms—use of the sacred pipe, sweat lodges, and access to medicine men. Grobsmith finds that the prison experience heightens cultural awareness among the inmates.

Gross, Emma R. *Contemporary Federal Policy Toward American Indians.* Westport, CT: Greenwood Press, 1989. 144 pp.

In this volume, Richard Nixon emerges as a leading proponent of policies sympathetic with Native interests. The author directly interviewed many of the figures—Native and non-Native—

involved in the struggles for religious freedom, tribal restoration, land claim settlements, self-determination, and child welfare during the Nixon administration.

Guyette, Susan. *Planning for Balanced Development: A Guide for Native American and Rural Communities.* Santa Fe, NM: Clear Light Publishers, 1996. 312 pp.

Guyette has written a guide for business development in the context of preserving cultural values. She examines several fields of opportunity and gives her greatest emphasis to the promotion of a tourism that highlights and seeks to preserve traditional Native customs and values. Many illustrations are presented along with checklists and charts.

Hagan, William T. *American Indians.* Chicago: University of Chicago Press, 1961. 190 pp.

This is the story of white-Native relationships from the colonial era through the New Deal. It is a well-written, concise book that presents the issues in very direct fashion. In painting his word pictures, the author suggests that in many ways the white-Native encounters mirror contemporary efforts of American leadership to deal with underdeveloped countries.

Haycox, Stephen. *Alaska: An American Colony.* Seattle: University of Washington Press, 2002. 372 pp.

Haycox offers a comprehensive history of Alaska that builds on the theme of exploitation by outside groups. First the Russians came, then individual gold seekers, and in the modern era, Americans in a quest for oil. Native peoples of Alaska are seen as the victims of the exploitation.

Hunter, Robert, and Robert Calihoo. *Occupied Canada: A Young White Man Discovers His Unsuspected Past.* Toronto: McClelland and Stewart, 1991. 271 pp.

A young man was being raised by whites in Edmonton, Alberta, when a family death resulted in his being returned to a Native family he had not known. The first part of the book deals with his troubled years as a delinquent, and the second part focuses on the Native man seeking his roots by critically examining Canadian policy toward Natives in recent centuries.

Hurtado, Albert L., and Peter Iverson. *Major Problems in American Indian History: Documents and Essays.* Lexington, MA: D. C. Heath, 1994. 570 pp.

Two history professors at Arizona State University have drawn together seventy-seven important documents and first-person statements covering Native history from the period of Contact through the 1980s. These are presented in chapters devoted to each major period of development. The chapters also contain twenty-eight analytical essays that provide added insights for interpreting the documents.

Jackson, Helen Hunt. *A Century of Dishonor.* New York: Harper and Brothers, 1881. 342 pp.

This impassioned book attacked U.S. government policies toward Native America in order to arouse public demands for reform. Jackson provided the first concise documentation of the cruelty toward Natives across American history and across the American continent. Chapters focus on the abuses of Delaware, Cheyenne, Nez Perce, Sioux, Ponca, Winnebago, and Cherokee peoples.

Jackson, Helen Hunt. *Ramona.* Boston: Roberts Brothers, 1984. 490 pp.

This best-known work of Helen Hunt Jackson has seen over 300 printings. The novel traces the sad life of a poor Native woman in Southern California from a time of Spanish, then Mexican, and finally American domination of her peoples. The work was an appeal for justice, and it aroused great sympathy for the burdens carried by Native peoples. It was compared with *Uncle Tom's Cabin* as it was called "one of the two great novels of the 19th Century."

Jaimes, M. Annette, ed. *The State of Native America: Genocide, Colonization, and Resistance.* Boston: South End Press, 1992. 447 pp.

As the title may suggest, this is a series of critical essays attacking U.S. policies toward Native America. The essays include pleas for the release of Leonard Peltier, descriptions of the Sand Creek massacre, estimations of Native population at the time of Contact, and the usurpation of indigenous sovereignty, as well as Native hunting, fishing, and water rights.

Johnson, Troy, Joane Nagel, and Duane Champagne. *American Indian Activism: Alcatraz to the Longest Walk.* Urbana: University of Illinois Press, 1997. 297 pp.

The editors' collection of essays is based on the premise that the occupation of Alcatraz Island by Native Americans between November 20, 1969, and June 11, 1971, was "the" watershed event in modern activism for Native interests. Since that occupation, seventy-four other occupations of federal facilities have followed. A culminating event in the rise of activism was the 1978 "Longest Walk" from San Francisco to Washington, D.C. The focus is on Alcatraz, yet a book written as late as 1997 should have looked at other more critical sources of Native power—namely, the effects of gaming revenues.

Johnston, Basil H. *Indian School Days.* Norman: University of Oklahoma Press, 1989. 250 pp.

The author describes his youthful years in attendance at a residential school for Native Americans in Canada. It is a comic-tragic narrative told in anecdotal fashion. The schoolchildren maintain dignity by participating in sports and by fighting the authority of the Jesuit teachers.

Josephy, Alvin. *Five Hundred Nations: An Illustrated History of North American Indians.* New York: Alfred A. Knopf, 1984. 468 pp.

This epic book details life in generation after generation of Native peoples. Josephy records the events that resulted in a conquest but not elimination of 500 Native Nations. The book became the source for a major film script for Public Television.

Josephy, Alvin M. *The Native Heritage of America.* Boston: Houghton Mifflin, 1991. 416 pp.

Josephy's highly illustrated volume examines the development of Native American history by geographical region extending from Alaska south to the tip of the South American continent. The book is detailed but very readable. It contains an extensive bibliography.

Josephy, Alvin. *Now That the Buffalo's Gone: A Study of Today's American Indians.* New York: Alfred A. Knopf, 1982. 300 pp.

Yesterday was the inheritance, today is the struggle to survive, but tomorrow is a chance to "walk tall." Josephy points to the future by looking at contemporary Native attitudes toward individual life and society. Various chapters focus on the "will to endure," racial stereotypes, spirituality, and the connections to the land.

Josephy, Alvin. *Patriot Chiefs: A Chronicle of American Indian Resistance.* Rev. ed. New York: Viking Press, 1958; rev. ed. Penguin Books, 1993. 364 pp.

Josephy places nine Native leaders within a broad historical context in order to give a strong factual foundation for their efforts to preserve Native community. His selected patriots include Chief Joseph, Black Hawk and Keokuk, Osceola, Tecumseh, Pontiac, Popé, King Philip, and Hiawatha.

Josephy, Alvin, ed. *Red Power: The American Indians' Fight for Freedom.* New York: American Heritage Press, 1971. 259 pp.

The book offers a series of essays and documents from the 1960s era of emergent activism among Native American peoples. Included are statements from Vine Deloria, Clyde Warrior, George McGovern, and Richard Nixon, as well as reports from several conferences and meetings of Native leaders.

Kelly, Lawrence C. *The Assault on Assimilation: John Collier and the Origins of Indian Policy Reform.* Albuquerque: University of New Mexico Press, 1983. 445 pp.

Kelly has written the political biography of John Collier, commissioner of the Bureau of Indian Affairs in the New Deal Era. Collier engineered policies that effectively ended the national drive for assimilation through the process of allotment.

Kickingbird, Kirke, and Keren Ducheneaux. *One Million Acres.* New York: Macmillan Co., 1973. 240 pp.

The first chapter is entitled "Everything You Always Wanted to Know about Indian Lands, But Didn't Know Who to Ask." The book seeks to provide the substance of that title. The authors conclude that all Native lands must be given a new status, free from exploitation and under complete control of the Native peoples.

Krotz, Larry. *Indian Country: Inside Another Canada.* Toronto: McClelland and Stewart, 1990. 254 pp.

The author explores the condition of Native peoples on the reserves of Canada. Case studies are built around the author's visits to five reserves of the Cree, Mohawk, Kiwakiutl, Maliseet, and Ojibwa. He emphasizes the role of politics in Native life.

Lew, Alan A., and George A. Van Otten. *Tourism and Gaming on American Indian Lands.* Elmsford, NY: Cognizant Communications, 1998. 249 pp.

The authors examine gaming operations on many reservations and assess the impacts on both tribes and nearby non-Native peoples. They are skeptical about the ability of gambling to solve many community problems for Native peoples. They are also wary that the uneven distribution of gambling funds among tribes may result in federal policies that could hurt many tribes, as lawmakers will assume that all tribes are receiving excess funds from casinos.

Little Bear, Leroy, Menno Boldt, and J. Anthony Long, eds. *Pathways to Self-Determination: Canadian Indians and the Canadian State.* Toronto: University of Toronto Press, 1984. 197 pp.

The editors have brought together Native leaders and policy experts to examine the issues of sovereignty and self-determination in the context of Native societies today, their spiritual life, their economic standing, and their aspirations. The essays examine issues from the perspective of the Native peoples themselves.

Llewellyn, Karl N., and E. Adamson Hoebel. *The Cheyenne Way: Conflict and Case Law in Primitive Jurisprudence.* Norman: University of Oklahoma Press, 1941. 360 pp.

Native Americans have always had judicial systems. Some systems were complex and advanced. Here a lawyer and an anthropologist explore the operations of an advanced Native system using actual cases drawn from oral histories for points of reference.

Long, J. Anthony, and Menno Boldt, eds. *Governments in Conflict? Provinces and Indian Nations in Canada.* Toronto: University of Toronto Press, 1988. 296 pp.

This book includes seventeen essays on the relationships of Native Nations and the provincial governments of Canada. The essays explore issues such as sovereignty, self-government, questions of jurisdiction, land claims, and constitutional interpretation.

Lyden, Fremont J., and Lyman H. Legters, eds. *Native Americans and Public Policy.* Pittsburgh: University of Pittsburgh Press, 1992. 331 pp.

A series of academic articles deal with several subjects such as how national policy has failed to achieve goals of development. They also examine confusion over "blood quantum" and ineffective political methods to separate "true" Native societies from impostors.

Manuel, George, and Michael Posluns. *The Fourth World: An Indian Reality.* Don Mills, Ontario: Collier Macmillan Canada, 1974. 278 pp.

The Native authors present an overview of problems facing the First Nation peoples of Canada. They provide personal experiences and insights into Native–non Native American government relationships.

Mason, W. Dale. *Indian Gaming: Tribal Sovereignty and American Politics.* Norman: University of Oklahoma Press, 2000. 330 pp.

Mason reviews the general history of U.S. policy toward Native peoples before he explores policy on tribal gaming. He then looks at tribes as groups in the context of political interest group theory, followed by a focus on the development of gambling among Oklahoma and New Mexico tribes. He concludes that gambling has provided resources so that tribes can more fully play not only the roles of political interests but also the role of governments within the federalist fabric of American polities.

Matthiessen, Peter. *In the Spirit of Crazy Horse.* New York: Viking Press, 1983. 628 pp.

The author seeks to vindicate the actions of the American Indian

Movement in the 1970s. His specific goal is to establish the case of innocence for Leonard Peltier in the FBI shoot-out episode at the Pine Ridge Reservation in 1975. The book is detailed and intense. Its tone is pessimistic, however, and its conclusions seem to direct the flow of evidence presented. It is a disturbing work, but it is important for understanding all viewpoints of the Native American struggles today.

Mawhiney, Anne-Marie. *Towards Aboriginal Self-Government: Relations Between Status Indian Peoples and the Government of Canada 1969–1984.* New York and London: Garland Publishing, 1993. 143 pp.

In 1969, Prime Minister Trudeau issued his "White Paper," which essentially called for the termination of special recognition for Native peoples in Canada. The author's sociological analysis examines how Native peoples resisted this policy and moved Canadian leaders toward accepting self-determination as a goal for their First Nations.

McDonnell, Janet A. *The Dispossession of the American Indian, 1887–1934.* Bloomington: University of Indiana Press, 1991. 163 pp.

According to the author, the roots of Native American poverty today can be found in the Dawes Act of 1887. The reservation lands in 1887 were adequate for supporting Native populations. However, the Act not only broke up the lands into inefficient small parcels, but those implementing the allotment process consciously sought to apply the Act to the lands most desired by others, so that non-Natives could take over the lands.

McNickle, D'Arcy. *Native American Tribalism: Indian Survivals and Renewals.* New York: Oxford University Press, 1973. 182 pp.

This book, written in McNickle's later years, demonstrates the persistence of tribal life in America even while Native communities are embracing modern technology. The author walks the reader through the events of Termination and renewal in the mid-twentieth century.

Miller, J. R., ed. *Sweet Promises: A Reader on Indian/White Relations in Canada.* Toronto: University of Toronto Press, 1991. 468 pp.

Miller presents twenty-five essays, most of which were written by historians for other publications. The book is put together almost totally from a non-Native (Canadian) point of view. Only three essays are by Native authors.

Moore, John H., ed. *The Political Economy of North American Indians.* Norman: University of Oklahoma Press, 1993. 320 pp.

This collection of essays on the economics of Native life is presented in a framework of Marxian rhetoric—ruling classes, proletariat, and so on. Nonetheless, the message is clear that strategies are necessary for economic development and that the governmental bureaucracy has stifled opportunities for tribes to become self-sufficient and to enjoy self-determination.

Morrison, R. Bruce, and C. Roderick Wilson, eds. *Native Peoples: The Canadian Experience.* 3d ed. Oxford: Oxford University Press, 2004. 504 pp.

These Canadian essays are built upon the premise that Native (called Aboriginal) societies must be seen on "their own turf" before we examine broader relationships between the societies and other Canadian communities. This approach will reveal the nature of how they have been "encapsulated within a colonial state." The sociologist authors believe that our understanding of Aboriginal life requires an appreciation of many shared experiences. Therefore, the essays look at life in many different communities in several Canadian regions from the Eastern Woodlands through the Plains to the Northwest Coast and the Arctic.

Moses, L. G. *Wild West Shows and the Images of American Indians, 1883–1933.* Albuquerque: University of New Mexico Press, 1996. 364 pp.

Moses presents a positive image of William Cody's (Buffalo Bill's) "Wild West Shows." He counters criticism from those who view the shows as demeaning to Native Americans by casting them into false stereotypes. Instead, he claims that the shows gave economic opportunity to many Native people as they revealed participants and their culture in a positive way for audiences. He rejects the notion that Cody exploited the performers. Moses laments that the film industry did not follow Cody's lead, but rather chose to use white actors to portray Natives and accordingly deprived many of an economic opportunity, while opening the door to inappropriate stereotypes.

Moses, L. G., and Raymond Wilson, eds. *Indian Lives: Essays on Nineteenth and Twentieth Century Native American Leaders.* Albuquerque: University of New Mexico Press, 1985. 227 pp.

Eight essays record the role of leadership in the survival and adaptation of Native America to coexistence with non-Natives. Insightful biographies include lives of Maris Bryant Pierce, Nampeyo, Dr. Susan La Flesche Picotte, Henry Chee Dodge, Charles Curtis, Luther Standing Bear, Minnie Kellogg, and Peterson Zah.

Neihardt, John. *Black Elk Speaks: Being the Life Story of a Holy Man of the Ogallala Sioux.* Lincoln: University of Nebraska Press, 1979. 280 pp.

Author Neihardt met Black Elk in 1930 and engaged the Native elder in a series of conversations. Black Elk reminisced about the events surrounding Little Big Horn, the killing of his cousin Crazy Horse, and the massacre at Wounded Knee. He revealed details of his sacred visions and how they led him in his pursuits as a Holy Man. This is a classic of vital importance in understanding Native community.

Nichols, Roger, ed. *The American Indian: Past and Present.* New York: McGraw-Hill, 1986. 312 pp.

A leading historian has gathered twenty-five essays that interpret political and economic experiences in Native American life from the colonial years to the post-Termination era.

O'Brien, Sharon. *American Indian Tribal Governments.* Norman: University of Oklahoma Press, 1989. 349 pp.

O'Brien's work is the most comprehensive single-volume treatment of tribal governments, their organization and operations. Five tribes are selected for special case treatment: Senecas, Muscogee Creek of Oklahoma, Cheyenne River Sioux, Isleta Pueblo, and Yakima. Other chapters examine issues of sovereignty and relationships of Native governments and states and the federal government.

O'Connor, John E. *The Hollywood Indian: Stereotypes of Native Americans in Film.* Trenton: New Jersey State Museum, 1980. 80 pp.

This book reviews the history of stereotyping of Native Americans in films. The author examines the film industry's personnel as well as the political considerations behind the biases produced. The illustrated book presents ten essays on ten leading films: *America* (1924); *The Vanishing American* (1926); *Massacre* (1934); *Drums Along the Mohawk* (1939); *They Died with Their Boots On* (1941); *Devil's Doorway* (1949); *Broken Arrow* (1950); *Cheyenne Autumn* (1964); *Tell Them Willie Boy Is Here* (1969); and *Little Big Man* (1970).

Otis, D. S. *The Dawes Act and the Allotment of Indian Lands.* Norman: University of Oklahoma Press, 1973. 206 pp.

This is a study of how well-meaning reformers contributed toward a federal policy that tore apart Native cultures and destroyed opportunities for economic development. The manuscript first appeared as a report to Congress in 1934 in support of the repeal of the Dawes Act.

Philip, Kenneth R. *John Collier's Crusade for Indian Reform, 1920–1954.* Tucson: University of Arizona Press, 1977. 304 pp.

This book records the complexities and conflicts in the life of John Collier. While he wanted self-determination for Natives, he could not resist telling them what they wanted and then fixing his ideas into federal policy. He turned the federal government away from the dismal Dawes Act allotment practices, but his paternalism would not allow him to let Native America decide for itself.

Pritzker, Barry. *A Native American Encyclopedia: History, Culture, and Peoples.* Oxford: Oxford University Press, 2000. 591 pp. (Originally published by ABC-CLIO, 1998.)

This encyclopedia is arranged by geographical region, starting in the Southwest and moving toward the Arctic of the far north. The last two sections focus on Canadian indigenous peoples. Entries are presented for each tribal group, and they are subdivided into descriptions of location, population, language, history, customs, religion, and governmental arrangements. Each entry concludes with a contemporary picture of the tribe, its legal status, economy, and daily life. A glossary follows. The book features color illustrations of Native life.

Purich, Donald. *The Inuit and Their Land: The Story of Nunavat.* Toronto: Lorimer, 1992. 192 pp.

In 1992, the Inuit of Canada won a land claim and the right to have their own territorial government on lands comprising the eastern part of the Northwest Territories. This book examines economic and political conditions of the Inuit and their struggle for control of their lands.

Sayer, John William. *Ghost Dancing the Law: The Wounded Knee Trials.* Cambridge, MA: Harvard University Press, 1997. 310 pp.

In 1973, Russell Means and Dennis Banks, leaders of the American Indian Movement, participated in a "takeover" of the reservation at Wounded Knee, South Dakota. The action was prompted by a desire to gain attention for wrongs committed against Native peoples. The government responded by suppressing the "uprising" and putting Means and Banks on trial for criminal charges from obstruction of justice, possession of illegal arms, burglary, and assault. Attorneys for the two were successful in making the 1974 trials a political referendum on failed and abusive government policies. The essays in this book describe how the trial became a political forum and led to a verdict of not guilty.

Sayre, Robert F. *Thoreau and the American Indians.* Princeton, NJ: Princeton University Press, 1977. 239 pp.

Henry David Thoreau fascinates persons concerned with nature. In his early life he had very little contact with Native Americans. However, upon learning of their interrelationship with the natural world, he ventured to Maine to observe their lives. He wrote twelve notebooks of his observations. Sayre takes the reader into the mind of this great naturalist and his ideas about Native Americans.

Shaeffer, E. G. *Indian Casino.* Bloomington, IN: First Books (Author House), 2002. 130 pp.

Shaeffer dares to reveal the inside culture of a remote Native casino. She does not attempt to be politically correct. Instead she exposes organizational values that we would expect to find in some Third World dictatorship.

Non-Native Shaeffer was formally empowered to be the manager of the casino, but she was not given tribal support to do her job. She had to hire tribal members for casino jobs, and she felt she had to discipline and fire several who were related to tribal council members for offenses such as drug use, cheating customers, stealing, and failure to appear for work. The episodes involved confrontations in which she thought she might be the one fired. The council held on to her but treated her rudely. Her account tells of personal insults that were not at all subtle. Amazingly, she survived for two years and was able to escape with some sense of accomplishment. The book is an eye-opener and offers a perspective (not anti–Native American, but skeptical of tribal leadership) that deserves to be examined.

Shoemaker, Nancy, ed. *Negotiators of Change: Historical Perspectives on Native American Women.* New York: Routledge, 1995. 320 pp.

The editor has assembled essays on critical roles played by Native women after the time of Contact. The women are seen as active negotiators seeking to preserve traditional family life. Many found empowerment in new religions, as they resisted efforts to have them adapt to European notions of gender subservience. Their roles as economic participants are also highlighted. The book presents some insights into how women have participated in modern tribal governments, but most of the entries cover generations long in the past.

Skogen, Larry C. *Indian Depredation Claims, 1796–1920.* Norman: University of Oklahoma Press, 1996. 290 pp.

Skogen has revealed part of our "lost" history. He examined claims made mostly by non-Native peoples to the U.S. Court of Claims for recovery of damages inflicted upon them by Native peoples. In the period when such claims were heard, the Court awarded $5.5 million in damages, for the most part for destruction of property. While Congress awarded the sums in many cases, in many other cases, the money awarded was deducted from allotments authorized for tribes—ergo the full tribe was punished for individual wrongs. Skogen also notes that there was considerable fraud in the claims process. He finds that the program failed to realize the objective of the claims program—peaceful relations between Natives and non-Natives.

Spring, Joel. *The Cultural Transformation of a Native American Family and Its Tribe 1763–1995: A Basket of Apples.* Mahwah, NJ: Lawrence Erlbaum Associates, 1960. 210 pp.

Spring traces a mixed-blood Choctaw-Cherokee family's history from the eighteenth century to the end of the twentieth century and looks at governmental activity toward the family and tribe during each generation. He walks with the family through the era of civilization policies, to removal and reservation life, and then to the Dawes era and later eras of Termination. The book gives attention to the relationships of Native Americans and African Americans during and after the years of slavery. These flows of history are given flesh and blood with poignant accounts of "real" people seeking to survive with an identifiable heritage. He leaves the reader with a reverse image of the "apple" metaphor— today the family is "white on the outside and red on the inside."

Stewart, Omer C. *Peyote Religion: A History.* Norman: University of Oklahoma Press, 1987. 454 pp.

This is the comprehensive history of peyote use in Native cultures and the political controversies that its use has generated. Stewart suggests that peyote has been both a unifying force for intertribal coalitions and a divisive force in tribal life.

Stuart, Paul. *Nations Within a Nation: Historical Statistics of American Indians.* Westport, CT: Greenwood Press, 1987.

Stuart provides readers with 160 tables full of information gathered from almost as many sources. Much of the information is historical. It is organized into nine chapters, each of which has an introductory text: land base, climate, population, relocation, health, government activities, education, employment, and economic resources.

Surtees, Robert J. *Canadian Indian Policy: A Critical Bibliography.* Bloomington: Indiana University Press, 1982. 107 pp.

Surtees walks the reader through four centuries of Canadian history using a continuing flow of references to books and articles on the relationships of Native peoples with Canadian authorities.

Titley, E. Brian. *A Narrow Vision: Duncan Campbell Scott and the Administration of Indian Affairs in Canada.* Vancouver, BC: University of British Columbia Press, 1986. 245 pp.

Duncan Campbell Scott served as a bureaucrat in the Department of Indian Affairs for fifty-two years. He rose to the post of deputy superintendent and held this top policy-making position for almost twenty years. From 1913 to 1932, while he was in charge of policy, he steadfastly remained an assimilationist and showed no grasp of the feelings and attitudes of Native peoples. The book records the history of his era.

Utter, Jack. *American Indians: Answers to Today's Questions.* 2d ed. Norman: University of Oklahoma Press, 2001. 494 pp.

Utter presents a powerful body of information formatted as direct answers to several hundred questions (e.g., Who is an "Indian"?, How is tribal membership determined?, What is the present status of Indian-U.S. treaties?). Many statistics support the answers. Context is provided by the introduction and concluding sections on early history and recent self-determination efforts. Utter's last question is: "What is the greatest issue facing American Indians in the future?" His answer is "survival—environmental survival . . . [and] cultural survival."

Washburn, Wilcomb E. *Red Man's Land, White Man's Law: The Past and Present Status of the American Indian.* 2d ed. Norman: University of Oklahoma Press, 1995. 314 pp.

This book has three sections: historical survey, the land, and the people. Washburn provides a basic background and a social context for examining general questions of land title, land claims, and for specific treatment of Native lands in Alaska, Oklahoma, and New Mexico.

Weatherford, Jack. *Indian Givers: How the Indians of the Americas Transformed the World.* New York: Fawcett Columbine, 1988. 272 pp.

Weatherford provides a case that Native America has given wisdom to the world regarding democracy, medicine, foods, architecture, and ecology. He concludes that the real "America" has yet to be discovered by the newcomers to the land.

Weatherford, Jack. *Native Roots: How the Indians Enriched America.* New York: Fawcett Columbine, 1991. 310 pp.

Anthropologist Weatherford offers strong support for the thesis that newcomers of European heritage incorporated many values from Native America into the culture that they developed on the continent. From Natives they learned farming techniques, hunting and fishing methods, and the means to conduct warfare. The author builds the case that American civilization today is made up of the heritages of all its peoples.

Weaver, Sally. *Making Canadian Indian Policy: The Hidden Agenda, 1968–1970.* Toronto: University of Toronto Press, 1981. 236 pp.

The author provides a close examination of the way the White Paper of 1969 was formulated and the consequences of the policy initiative. The Canadian policy position taken by the Trudeau government favored the national government's termination of Native tribal recognition. Original interviews and documents develop the case that this policy was not well thought out and was doomed to fail from the outset.

Weibel-Orlando, Joan. *Indian Country, L. A.: Maintaining Ethnic Community in a Complex Society.* Rev. ed. Urbana: University of Illinois Press, 1999. 364 pp.

With 50,000 residents, the Native American community in Los Angeles is the largest urban indigenous community in the United States. The author provides ground-breaking research by providing a demographic profile of the residents and tracing 300 life histories within the community from 1973 to the time of publication. She seeks to give the reader a holistic understanding of a very complex social mosaic. Weibel-Orlando presents a definition of "community" that emphasizes collective rights and responsibilities, location, institutional integrity, cultural continuity, public ritual, communication networks, and collective participation. Specific attention is given to celebrations such as pow wows and 5th Sunday Sings, and to the institutional crisis engendered with the closing in 1986 of a critical community center operated by Indian Centers, Inc.

Welch, James, and Paul Stekler. *Killing Custer.* New York: W. W. Norton, 1994. 320 pp.

This is a deeply personal account of the Little Big Horn Battle of 1876 written from the perspective of Native Americans. The battle is defined as a major event in Native history. It was one of but a few events in which Native military forces actually overcame opposition from the U.S. Army. The era of General Custer was in reality an era of destruction for Native community and culture on the American Plains.

White, Robert. *Tribal Assets: The Rebirth of Native America.* New York: Henry Holt, 1990. 291 pp.

White examines the impediments that have stopped tribes from exploiting opportunities for economic success. He provides extensive case studies of the struggles of the Passamaquoddies, Mississippi Choctaw, Ak-Chin, and Warm Springs peoples to achieve economic growth and development.

Wilkins, David E. *American Indian Politics.* Lanham, MD: Rowman and Littlefield, 2002. 365 pp.

Wilkins looks at the history, political structures, and political functions of tribal governments in America. He examines politics within tribes, as well as the political influence of Native peoples in local, state, and federal politics away from the reservations. He offers portraits of leading figures in Indian politics today, along with a chronology, a listing of federally recognized tribes, and a glossary of terms.

Wilkinson, Charles F. *American Indians, Time and the Law: Native Societies in a Modern Constitutional Democracy.* New Haven, CT: Yale University Press, 1987. 225 pp.

The author examines the new era of Supreme Court cases on Native American law. Beginning with the *Williams v. Lee* decision in 1959, Wilkinson looks at eighty cases over a twenty-six-year period. The *Lee* case is notable because it ushered in an activist approach by a Court willing to consider major issues concerning tribal power. The analysis is augmented with a depth of commentary on the historical development of the law.

Zanjani, Sally S. *Sarah Winnemucca.* Lincoln: University of Nebraska Press, 2001. 368 pp.

Sally Zanjani, a professor at the University of Nevada in Reno, provides a comprehensive biography of Sarah Winnemucca, whose Native American name was Thocmetony, or "Shell Flower." The thoroughly documented work delves into controversies over Winnemucca's role as a negotiator and compromiser who used her personality, wit, and quest to be a performer to win support for her Paiute peoples. She helped restore reservation lands in northern Nevada, and she opened an Indian School that taught Native languages and culture. Zanjani makes the case that Winnemucca was the leading Native woman of the nineteenth century.

Journals and Periodicals

Akwesasne Notes
Kahiakehaka Nation
P.O. Box 366
via Roseveltown, NY
(518) 358-3326
$25 a year (quarterly)

Akwesasne Notes is a journal dedicated to issues of concern to Native peoples. It seeks to preserve and perpetuate the cultural values and attributes of Natives throughout the Americas.

American Indian Culture and Research Journal
American Indian Studies Center
University of California, Los Angeles
3220 Campbell Hall
405 Hilgard Avenue
Los Angeles, CA 90024-1548
(310) 206-7508
$25 a year
Edited by Duane Champagne

This quarterly journal offers scholarly, interdisciplinary articles that seek to advance knowledge about North American Native peoples—within both Canadian and U.S. boundaries. Of special value is an extensive book review section in each issue.

American Indian Law Review
College of Law
University of Oklahoma
300 Timberlake Road, Room 335
Norman, OK 73019
(405) 325-2840
$20.00 a year (biannual)

This standard law review is devoted to topics relevant to Native America, including processes of justice and dispute resolution within tribal court systems. Articles deal with historical as well as contemporary issues. Articles are contributed by professional scholars, and comments are written by members of the student editorial staff.

American Indian Quarterly
Department of Anthropology
University of Nebraska
233 N. 8th Street
Lincoln, NE 68588
(405) 325-3261
Edited by Devon Mihesuah
$30 a year (quarterly)

A quarterly journal with articles from many disciplines—history, anthropology, literature, and the arts. The articles are reviewed by referees before publication. The journal includes an extensive book review section.

American Indian Religions: An Interdisciplinary Journal
117 N. Church Street
Hillsborough, NC 27278
Edited by John Loftin
$30 a year

This quarterly publication examines sacred Native traditions of the past and present. The initial publication in winter 1994 included articles by Vine Deloria, Walter EchoHawk, and Tim Giago.

Canadian Journal of Native Studies
Department of Native Studies
Brandon University

Brandon, MB Canada R7A 6A9
(204) 727-9640
Edited by Samuel W. Corrigan
$30 a year (bi-annual)

This publication emphasizes the historical, political, sociological, and legal aspects of the life of First Nations peoples of Canada. However, it also gives attention to indigenous peoples everywhere. It is the official publication of the Canadian Indian/Native Studies Association.

Canadian Native Law Reporter
Native Law Centre
University of Saskatchewan
101 Diefenbaker Place
Saskatoon, SK Canada S7N 5B8
Edited by Zandra Wilson
$105 per year (quarterly plus special issues)

The *Canadian Law Reporter* presents a comprehensive list of all court cases and statutes with relevance to Native law in Canada. The publication includes a complete subject index as well as case listings and statute listings.

Indian Country Today
1920 Lombardy Drive
Rapid City, SD 57701
(605) 341-0011
Edited by Tim Giago
$48 a year (weekly)

The premier Native American newspaper is edited by Tim Giago. It is published in two editions, one for the Plains and the other for the Southwest. However, the scope in both editions is national. It is a balanced publication that may be considered a reliable source of information for research purposes. While editorially it is very supportive of Native peoples and the quest for full sovereignty, the editorials and the news pages will present items critical of Native Americans where the facts warrant criticism.

Indian Gaming Magazine
14205 SE 36th Street, Ste. 100
Bellevue, WA 98006

(425) 519-3710
Edited by Nicolle Burke
$85 per year (monthly)

This is the official publication of the National Indian Gaming Association. It presents profiles of Native American casinos as well as legal news, commentary, and statistical information on Native gaming operations.

Journal of American Indian Education
Center for Indian Education
Arizona State University
Tempe, AZ 85287
http://jaie.asu.edu
Edited by David Beaulieu
$45 a year (three times a year)

This is a scholarly journal that publishes papers pertaining to the education of all Native peoples. The emphasis is on articles with an applied focus. The *Journal of American Indian Education* has been in continuous circulation since 1961.

Native Peoples Magazine
5333 N. 7th Street, Ste. 224
Phoenix, AZ 85012
(602) 265-4855
Edited by Gary Avey
$19.95 per year (quarterly)

This magazine was created by the editor for the Heard Museum in Phoenix 1987. It seeks to portray Native life in America. Each issue has thirty-two pages of text and colorful illustrations.

Nonprint Resources: Native America in Film and Video and on the Internet

Films

Unlike print literature, which presents essentially the single view that Native America has been universally "wronged" by non-

Native societies and governments, films are criticized for presenting an almost totally opposite view. Indeed, Hollywood has been called a "co-conspirator" with the rest of America in "committing cultural genocide by subverting the Native American's various ethnic identities and retaining him as a racial scapegoat" (Friar and Friar 1972, p. 2).

This is a rather healthy indictment of a filmmaking industry that has produced literally thousands of feature films around Native American themes and characters. Of course, not all the films can be reviewed here, but any random collection of films from the past might indeed suggest that Hollywood films have not been made to glorify Native peoples. Nor do they seem to enhance general understandings of problems faced by Native peoples today.

On the other hand, some films are accurate and positive in their presentation. Also, several well-prepared documentaries do help in building understandings, and in that sense they can be considered as promoting community values.

Many films have become the object of attacks by Native American groups and many others. Objections are generally on two levels. One is that Native Americans have not been used in sufficient numbers in production of the films—indeed, that non-Natives play leading Native roles. The second objection is that the films offer negative (and patronizing) stereotyping of Native Americans.

In 1970, the American Indian Movement picketed a Minneapolis theater's premier of *A Man Called Horse*. Members passed out leaflets contending that movie-goers were "voting at the box office" for "bigotry." Later, in 1973, actor Marlon Brando instigated a boycott protest of the Academy Awards ceremony because of Hollywood's mistreatment of Native Americans. Actually, protests had been ongoing since the earliest days of filmmaking, and the protests continue today. More recently, the making of a film about Sioux leader Crazy Horse caused an outcry that the imaging of such a sacred leader was in and of itself a sacrilege (much as the imaging of Muhammad would be for fundamentalist Muslims). The made-for-television film, *Crazy Horse*, produced by Turner Network Television was released in 1996.

A documentary entitled *Images of Indians* appeared as a five-part series on television and reviewed the nature of the disappointments Native Americans have experienced with their portrayals on film. Four books have been explored dealing with

Native Americans and film. They are reviewed in earlier sections of this chapter: O'Connor, *The Hollywood Indian: Stereotypes of Native Americans in Films* (1980); Friar and Friar, *The Only Good Indian . . . The Hollywood Gospel* (1972); Hilger, *The American Indian in Film* (1986); and Weatherford and Seubert, *Native Americans on Film and Video* (1981).

No attempt is made to review all films or even all important films and videos with significant Native American themes. The following list is extremely selective, and it is arbitrarily confined to films and videos released since 1950. Materials presented in the four books just mentioned are used, as well as references in several film guides, including: L. Maltin, *2002 Movie and Video Guide* (New York: Plume, 2002); M. Martin and M. Porter, *Video Movie Guide* (New York: Ballantine, 2005); D. Ellery, *Variety Movie Guide* (New York: Perigee, 2000); and Videohound's *Golden Movie Retriever 2005* (Farmington Hills, MI: Gale, 2004).

Feature Films
Billy Jack (1971)
Warner Home Video
112 minutes
VHS

Prejudices against Native Americans are central to the story line about a "half-breed" Vietnam veteran and hero, Billy Jack, played by Tom Laughlin. Billy Jack defends a teacher and students at an "alternative" school on an Arizona reservation against the bigotry of nearby residents. Sequels include *Trial of Billy Jack* (1974) and *Billy Jack Goes to Washington* (1977)

Broken Arrow (1950)
CBS/Fox Video
93 minutes
VHS

A sympathetic film portrays peace efforts between true-life characters Tom Jeffords, a U.S. scout, and Chiricahua Apache Chief Cochise. The film has been faulted for its emphasis on a patronizing "noble savage" stereotyping of Native leaders.

Buffalo Bill and the Indians, A.K.A. Sitting Bull's History Lesson (1976)
DeLaurentis/Lion's Gate; CBS/Fox Video

135 minutes
VHS/DVD

This film is directed and produced by Robert Altman. Lead actors Paul Newman and Burt Lancaster take the viewer through a plot exposing Buffalo Bill as a fraud. The cast includes Native American actor Will Sampson.

Cheyenne Autumn (1964)
Warner Brothers/Warner Brothers Home Video
156 minutes
Video/VHS

Director John Ford seeks to atone for earlier films that denigrate Native Americans. Here he portrays with sympathy the flight of 286 Cheyennes from confinement of an Indian Territory (Oklahoma) reservation to their homelands 1,500 miles away in Wyoming. Native critics fault the film for costume and location inaccuracies, as well as the use of Navajo actors to portray Cheyenne people.

Chief Crazy Horse (1955)
Universal
86 Minutes
no video

Victor Mature is the proud, noble, stoic Crazy Horse in a caricature somewhat akin to that of the stereotypical "wooden Indian." The sympathetic account challenges realism with a constant flow of clichés.

The Company of Strangers (1990)
National Film Board of Canada
100 minutes
no video

Nonactors play themselves in a fictional setting. Seven elderly women are stranded in an abandoned country house. One is a Mohawk. In their quest for immediate survival, all make contributions. The Mohawk woman teaches the others how to fish without modern gear.

Crazy Horse (1996)
Warner Home Video

93 minutes
VHS

This protested film offers the story of Crazy Horse, the Ogallala Sioux who stood against the U.S. military, and General George Armstrong Custer, in defense of Native lands.

Dances with Wolves (1990)
Tig/Majestic; Orion Home Video/Image Entertainment
181 Minutes
VHS/DVD

Lead actor Kevin Costner—also the director and producer—discovers Native cultures among the Sioux Nation in the 1860s. The Army lieutenant is assigned to a western outpost where he gradually enters into a Native lifestyle. Much of the film dialogue is in the Lakota language. The Academy Award–winning film captures the dramatic landscapes of the Dakotas. Protests against this film emphasized the Sioux' desire to have the lands used in the film returned to their control.

Devil's Doorway (1950)
MGM
84 minutes
No video

The leading character, Broken Lance, played by Robert Taylor, is a Shoshone who has served with the Union Army in the Civil War. He comes home bearing the Congressional Medal of Honor only to find that his Native family has lost its homelands due to a corrupt land agent who has sold the lands to settlers. Broken Lance dies fighting to regain the lands. The film represents a shift toward a sympathetic treatment of Native Americans in the context of a plea for racial justice in America. At the time the film was being made, blacks, Jews, as well as Native Americans were returning from military service and facing a world of segregation in their homeland.

Distant Drums (1951)
United States/Warner; Republic Pictures Home Video
101 minutes
VHS

Gary Cooper appears as an army captain in the Florida Everglades. His mission is to break a supply line that is bringing guns to the Seminoles in the 1840s.

Drum Beat (1954)
Warner/Jaguar
111 minutes
VHS

The film focuses on Captain Jack's leadership of the Modoc Nation in their 1869 uprising against the U.S. Army on the California-Oregon border. Alan Ladd is the frontier agent who negotiates a peace.

The Education of Little Tree (1997)
Paramount
112 minutes
VHS/DVD

A Depression-era Cherokee boy, Little Tree, loses his parents, and as a result he goes to live with his Native American grandparents. In their community he learns about Native culture and the Cherokee way of life.

Flaming Star (1960)
20th Century Fox; CBS Fox video
101 minutes
VHS

Elvis Presley stars as a "half-breed" son of a Kiowa mother and a white father. He is a victim of prejudice from two sides during wars between Texas settlers and Native Americans. The Kiowas kill his father, the whites kill his mother. In the pathos of the saga, Elvis fails to pull off a realistic portrayal of his role.

Geronimo: An American Legend (1993)
115 minutes
Columbia Tri-star Home Video
VHS

This film focuses on the years 1885 and 1886 when 5,000 U.S. Army troops sought to pursue and capture the Apache chief, who refused to accept the confinement of a reservation. Directed and produced by Walter Hill.

Incident at Ogallala (1992)
Facets Multimedia, Inc.; Live Home Video
90 minutes
VHS/DVD

This docudrama sets forth the case for a new trial for Leonard Peltier. Peltier was convicted of murder as a consequence of a shoot-out between the FBI and Native Americans on Sioux lands in South Dakota. He remains in prison.

Jim Thorpe, All American (1951)
Warner Brothers; Warner Home Video
105 minutes
VHS

The story line focuses on the life of Jim Thorpe, the great Sauk and Fox athlete. Thorpe is played by Burt Lancaster. His triumphs on the playing fields end as he ages, after which Thorpe recedes into a moody depression and despair exacerbated by divorce and the death of a child. Lancaster presents a sympathetic portrait of a fragile Native American, all-American hero.

The Last of His Tribe (1992)
Warner Home Video
90 minutes
VHS/DVD

The last survivor of the Yahi tribe is discovered by an anthropologist who communicates with him. Ishi reflects upon his early life and how his peoples were destroyed by greedy gold-seekers. The film is a realistic portrayal of a true situation. Ishi died in 1917.

The Last of the Mohicans (1992)
20th Century Fox
114 minutes
VHS/DVD

Native activists Russell Means and Dennis Banks play leading roles in James Fenimore Cooper's classic novel about the French and Indian War.

Little Big Man (1970)
National General; CBS Fox Video

135 minutes
VHS/DVD

Actor Dustin Hoffman plays a 121-year-old white man who reminisces about being raised by the Cheyennes after his family was killed on the frontier. He presents a very human view of Native peoples during an era when they were being overwhelmed by massive numbers of intruders upon their lands. Subthemes imply relationships between the futility of struggles in the West with the futility of American involvement in Vietnam. Squamish Nation Chief Dan George also appears in the film.

The Lost Child (2000)
Hallmark Home Entertainment
99 minutes
VHS/DVD

Rebecca was adopted by non-Natives. Years later, after her mother dies and her father remarries, she seeks to find her tribal roots and her natural parents. In her search, a Navajo woman who is seeking her sister who was stolen from their home emerges. The women discover that they are sisters. Rebecca is welcomed as she visits her tribal homelands, and she seeks to become part of her original family's culture. But her husband, Jack, does not fit well into the new scenario as differences between the two cultures surface. Rebecca seeks to integrate the old and the new so that her whole family can come together in peace.

A Man Called Horse (1970)
National General; CBS Fox Video
114 minutes
VHS/DVD

The film features actor Richard Harris as an English gentleman captured by Lakota Sioux warriors. He is called "Horse" and is abused, but soon he adapts to Native life and he plays an important leadership role in Sioux battles with hostile Shoshones. The film depicts the Sun Dance ceremony. The film has been attacked by Native activists for its dialogue, for its implication that the white man is superior in all activities illustrated, and for historical inaccuracies, notably that the Lakota did not follow the Sun Dance procedures portrayed. Two sequels were released: *Return of a Man Called Horse* (1976) and *Triumphs of a Man Called Horse* (1984).

Massacre at Sand Creek (1956)
Columbia Pictures
80 minutes
no video

This film depicts the U.S. Army's raid on a defenseless Cheyenne camp in Colorado Territory in 1864. General Chivington is characterized as a lunatic as if to get the white government "off the hook." In reality, Chivington's role was probably quite calculated as a means to carry out the wishes of white settlements in the Territory.

Naturally Native (1998)
Red Horse Native Productions
110 minutes
VHS

This sympathetic film looks at three Native sisters, all of whom have been adopted by non-Native parents as they seek to start a business. They have to overcome obstacles of the business world as well as barriers imposed by their parents. Insights are presented regarding tribal organizations and the gaming enterprise. The film stars Native women, and it was also written and directed by Native women.

The Outsider (1961)
Universal
108 minutes
no video

The film, staring Tony Curtis in the lead role, portrays the life and tragic death of Ira Hayes. Hayes, a Pima, was one of the United States Marines who raised the flag at Iwo Jima in World War II. Hayes returned to his people a "hero" only to be unable to cope with the impoverished conditions of life he found on the reservation. He is uncomfortable with his status as he drifts into a life controlled by alcoholism. He dies at age thirty-two. While there is a strong message in his story, the film is not the best vehicle for telling it. Friar and Friar (p. 217) criticize the film as a "tasteless distortion of his life as well as his tragic death."

Pocahontas (1995)
Walt Disney Pictures

87 minutes
VHS/DVD

This animated Disney feature has a musical script that deviates considerably from the historical reality of the European settlement of Virginia and the relationships of John Smith's colony with Chief Powhatan and his daughter Pocahontas. In a frenzy of "political correctness" Native Americans appear as one with nature, living a bountiful idyllic life. With the exception of Smith, the English are painted with a single brush as total brutes killing the land and its people in their search for mineral wealth. It is a fun movie for children, and it provides a sympathetic understanding of Native peoples being confronted by an invading culture.

Pow Wow Highway (1988)
Warner Home Video
105 minutes
VHS/DVD

This comedy is built around serious issues of Native American rights, welfare, and control of tribal resources. The hero is on the tribal board and wishes to have a contract with an energy extracting company revised. Tribal opponents and the company contrive a situation that takes him off the reservation so that he cannot vote against the contract they desire. He travels to New Mexico to help his sister deal with trumped-up legal problems. He makes the journey with a friend, who introduces him to the traditional customs of his culture.

Running Brave (1983)
Walt Disney Home Video
90 minutes
VHS

The film presents the true story of Native American Billy Mills and his struggles to beat the odds. Mills trains and achieves his goal—a gold medal at the 1964 Olympic games for his victory in the 10,000-meter race.

Skinwalkers (2002)
Warner Home Video
100 minutes
VHS/DVD

Skinwalkers is a bad medicine man who appears to be the culprit as Navajo tribal police are confronted with the murder of three medicine men. Cultural restraints complicate the work of detectives seeking to find justice.

Smoke Signals (1998)
Miramax Home Entertainment
89 minutes
VHS/DVD

Two friends leave their Idaho reservation to go to Phoenix to recover the remains of the father of one of them. The son recalls his father as an alcoholic, while the friend reveres him as a hero who saved him from a fire when he was a very small child. Reality comes to both in a moving climax that gives both a better sense of the heritage of their people.

Soldier Blue (1970)
Avco Embassy/Columbia Tri-star Home Video
109 minutes
VHS

While this film has been called a "cutesy romance," it is anything but that. A soldier who has survived a massacre meets a young woman who had been raised among Native peoples. Their young romance is punctuated by arguments over the "American" and the "Native" causes. The arguments come to a tragic conclusion as the film's plot leads them to the Native village at Sand Creek, Colorado, where the U.S. Cavalry has slaughtered innocent Native women and children. The mass killing at Sand Creek is portrayed as analogous to army atrocities in Vietnam.

Song of Hiawatha (1997)
Hallmark Home Entertainment
114 minutes
VHS

The film presents Native history and cultural and religious life in a respectful, reverential context. The story line is based on Henry Wadsworth Longfellow's epic poem, *Song of Hiawatha.*

Tell Them Willie Boy Is Here (1969)
Universal; MCA/Universal Home Video

98 minutes
VHS

The film records a semi-true story about a young Paiute's heroic run from the law alongside his non-Native girlfriend. Willie Boy seeks to escape from hostile prejudiced townspeople who believe he murdered the girl's father—in fact, his death was accidental. His run is futile as the girl and then Willie Boy are gunned down. The film features Robert Blake as Willie Boy, Katherine Ross as the girl, and Robert Redford as a sympathetic police chief compelled by public opinion to pursue Willie Boy. The symbolism relates to youth conflict and attempts to avoid military service in the Vietnam era.

Thunderheart (1992)
Tribeca-Waterhorse; Columbia Home Video
118 minutes
VHS/DVD

The story revolves around a murder investigation on a Sioux reservation. A part-Native FBI agent is assigned to the case. He gains a sense of his heritage as he is exposed to Sioux spirituality and ways as he makes his investigation. The actors include Fred Thompson and Dennis Banks. Produced by Robert DeNiro.

Two Rode Together (1961)
Columbia Home Video
109 minutes
VHS

James Stewart stars as a marshall hired to rescue settlers who were captured by Commanches many years before. After the rescue, Stewart finds that the captives now have their feet in two cultures and are reluctant to be "saved." Directed by John Ford.

War Party (1988)
Hemdale; HBO Home Video
99 minutes
VHS

The non-Native mayor of a Montana town invites local residents and Native Americans to recreate a massacre that had occurred a hundred years before. In preparation for the celebration, a "drunken white man" kills a Native in a fight. Racial tensions of generations are rekindled, engulfing the entire town. The violence escalates, and soon the state police and the National Guard are tracking down Natives. There is no happy ending in this chase either.

Windtalkers (2002)
John Woo/MGM
134 minutes
VHS/DVD

This is a story about a young Navajo soldier trained to be a code talker—a person who communicated behind enemy lines using the Navajo language code. The code talkers were assigned Marine guards as they went into action. However, because of their secret work, the code talkers were to be killed if it appeared they would be captured. Here the essence of the film comes to the viewer. What should the code talker's Marine guard who has befriended him do as the enemy surrounds them?

Documentaries
Acts of Defiance (1992)
First Run/Icarus Films
104 minutes

This excellent production, voted best documentary at the 1992 American Indian Film Festival, is a detailed account of the Mohawk people's struggle against the aggressive land annexation policies of the Canadian government that led to the 78-day blockade of a major bridge leading into Montreal in 1990.

Black Coal, Red Power (1972)
IU/UCEMC/UAZ
41 minutes

This documentary addresses the environmental damage caused by energy companies that have conducted strip mining operations on Hopi and Navajo lands.

Broken Treaties (1989)
Coronet/MTI Film and Video
33 minutes

This dramatic video provides an account of the history of the government's repudiation of its own treaties with Native Americans. The presentation is made in the form of a courtroom trial. The United States is found "guilty as charged."

Broken Treaty at Battle Mountain (1974)
Cinnamon Productions
UNI/UNV/MICH
60 minutes

This is a documentary about the struggles of the Western Shoshone to regain their Native lands in Nevada—twenty-four million acres of them. The film also shows their struggle to hold onto traditional cultures in the face of disputes with assimilated tribal members. It is narrated by Robert Redford.

By No Means Conquered (1979)
Lund
26 minutes

The video documents the coast-to-coast "Longest Walk" of 1978. The walk was a demonstration of Native concerns about treaty rights and other social issues. Included in the film are speeches by Clyde Bellecourte and black activist Dick Gregory.

Civilized Tribes (1976)
Document Associates and BBC Dist. DA/IU
26 minutes

The television documentary examines contemporary life among peoples of the five Southeastern "civilized tribes": Seminoles, Choctaw, Creek, Chickasaw, and Cherokee. Attention is given to the need for economic development activities.

Concerns of American Indian Women (1977)
WNET Dist./PBS
30 minutes

This is part of a series on women's concerns. It features interviews with Marie Sanchez, a Northern Cheyenne judge, and Dr. Connie Uri, a Choctaw-Cherokee physician and law student. The talk is directed at health problems, children's needs, and environmental concerns.

Dineh: The People (1975)
Dist.: NAPBC
77 minutes

The film portrays contemporary problems and lifestyles on the Navajo reservation, the largest within the United States. The film involves extensive discussions with Peterson Zah, the head of a tribal legal aid program. Zah later becomes the president of the tribal government.

Dream Catchers (1994)
Legal Base Team
40 minutes

The is the first of a six-part video series on Native American cultures. The dream catcher is a crafted artifact that possesses magical powers. It is hung in Native homes and beside the cribs of babies to assure that good fortune will be present.

Federal Indian Law (1980)
Institute for the Development of Indian Law
19 minutes

Two series of films are included in this collection. Titles in these series include *Federal Indian Law, Indian Tribal Government, A Question of Sovereignty, Indian Treaties, Indians and the U.S. Government, Indian Jurisdiction,* and the *Federal-Indian Relationship.*

Forty-Seven Cents (1973)
UNI/UCEMC
25 minutes

The federal government took over 3.5 million acres of land belonging to the Pit River tribe of California. This film examines the process of "winning" a claim under provisions of the Indian Claims Act of 1946. The Pit River tribe was offered a "settlement" amounting to $0.47 per acre of land taken.

Geronimo (1993)
A and E Productions
100 minutes

Geronimo is the story of the legendary leader who led a band of his Apache tribe to act as guerrilla fighters against invaders on his land. This is also the tragic tale of a broken man who spent the last twenty-three years of his life in virtual confinement away from his Native lands.

I Will Fight No More Forever (1976)
MAC
106 minutes

The film tells the story of Chief Joseph's struggle to lead Nez Perce peoples across the Canadian border and to safety from their American pursuers. The film explores the chief's motivations as well as those of the leaders of the U.S. Army in this tragic chapter of the American West.

Images of Indians (1980)
KCTS/9/Seattle
Produced for National Public Television

This is a series of five films, each running 30 minutes. The series offers an in-depth examination of how filmmaking has stereotyped the Native American. Titles are: *The Great Movie Massacre, Heathen Injuns and the Hollywood Gospel, How Hollywood Wins the West, The Movie Reel Indians,* and *War Paint and Wigs.*

The Indian Experience: Urban and Rural (1979)
NAPBC Video
28 minutes

This film explores the life of Natives who have been relocated from reservations to urban centers. It contrasts the new life experiences with traditional cultures of the reservations.

Indian Rights, Indian Law (1978)
Dist.: Associate Films
Ford Foundation
60 minutes

This film focuses on cases handled by the Native American Rights Fund from its founding in 1971 to 1978. Cases include disputes about fishing and hunting rights, religious rights of prisoners, and land claims.

In the Land of the War Canoes (2000)
Image Entertainment
59 minutes

A docudramatization of a folk legend about the Kwakiutl of Vancouver. The film makes a strong presentation of the Kwakiutl culture, including their heritage of fabric arts, wood carving, costuming, and dance. The animal-spirit costumes stand out as do huge canoes and lodges. It was filmed over a three-year period by folklorist Edward S. Curtis.

The Long Walk (1970)
UCEMC Producer: KQED-TV San Francisco
60 minutes

The film portrays life on the Navajo reservation today, along with discussions of social problems, relocation programs, and the control of Native American schools. An elder reflects back on stories of the Long Walk of 1863 as told to her by her elders.

Menominee (1977)
NAPBC
Produced: WTNE-TV
60 minutes

The film depicts the contemporary history of the Termination policy and its effects on one Nation. It portrays how the Menominees were able to build a political campaign in the 1970s to restore their status as a Nation through legislation.

Myths and Mound Builders (1981)
Dist.: DER
59 minutes

An exploration of the Hopewellian and Mississippian cultures of a thousand years ago. These cultures left their imprint on the middle of the North American continent with a series of massive mounds. The film explores the origins and purposes of the mound-building activity as well as the fate of the mound builders.

Potlatch: A Strict Law Bids Us Dance (1975)
Dist.: Pacific Cinemateque
55 minutes

Two years of research reveal specifics of a 1922 trial of Kwakiutl Natives of the Pacific Northwest for participating in a Potlatch ceremony. The Potlatch is a traditional event in which people give away their property. This giving of gifts was actually outlawed by the Canadian government and was actively discouraged by actions of the U.S. Army in the West. The film shows a Potlatch ceremony.

Powerless Politics (1975)
KNBC-TV
Dist.: BYU-NAS
28 minutes

This film is from a series written by Native Americans. It focuses on the relationship of tribes to officials of the Bureau of Indian Affairs.

Primal Mind (1984)
Corporation for Public Broadcasting
60 minutes

This documentary is drawn from a book of the same title by Jamake Highwater of the Blackfoot Nation. Highwater narrates the film. The *Primal Mind* celebrates the cultural differences that separate Euro-Americans from Native peoples. These include the way people look at God, nature, building structures, concepts of time, place, and space, change, and property.

The Right to Be Mohawk (1989)
New Day Films
15 minutes

The Mohawk Tribe has been left with a reservation that straddles the international border of upstate New York. This video explores tribal attempts to maintain traditional values in the modern society.

Six Nations (1976)
Document Associates and the BBC
26 minutes

The film presents a survey of current problems and concerns facing the Nations of the Iroquois Confederacy. Particular attention is given to relationships between Senecas and white residents in the town of Salamanca, New York. The town land is owned by the Seneca Nation.

Wilma Mankiller (1992)
Woman Makes Movie
29 minutes

This video examines how Wilma Mankiller rose from humble origins to the leadership of the Cherokee Nation. Her story is told with interviews of fourteen Native Americans who witnessed her rise and her success as a Native American leader.

500 Nations Vols. 1–8 (1995)
Warner Studios

This is an eight-part documentary on Native peoples. It begins from Pre-Columbian history and covers the arrival of Europeans through events of modern times. Rich civilizations proliferated in ancient times, but they could not all survive. Attention is given to the current efforts of Native Americans to regain their cultural life. *500 Nations* uses a variety of sources, including documents, photographs, and eyewitness accounts.

Internet Sources on Native America

Administration for Native Americans
http://www.acf.hhs.gov/programs/ana

Website offers information about the Administration for Native Americans (ANA), many grant programs, training and technical assistance, peer panel reviewers, publications, resources, and employment opportunities with ANA.

James Madison University Native Americans—Internet Resources
http://falcon.jmu.edu/~ramseyil/native.htm

On this website, one will find bibliographies, directories of individual tribes, history and historical documents, periodicals, and general links. This site is for teachers, librarians, students, and anyone else with an academic or personal interest in Native Americans.

Native American Resources at the Smithsonian
http://www.si.edu/opa/amind

The website has information on the National Museum of American Indians, American History, and American Art. This site gives contact information along with a preview of what one may expect to find when he or she visits one of these museums.

Native American Websites
http://www.jammed.com/~mlb/nawbt.html

This index gives information on Native Americans such as language, environment, genealogy, anthropology, art, film, museums, literature, music, online books, history, travel and tourism, science and technology, health and social issues, education, law, politics, miscellaneous, news, and comment.

Pride
http://www.pride-net.com/native_indians

This is a link to information on Native Americans, their past and their present.

The Topic: American Indians
http://www.42explore2.com/native.htm

This index includes resources on American Indians and offers links to other American Indian websites.

The Wild West Organization
http://www.thewildwest.org/native_american

This Web site has links to information on Native American society, wisdom, places, art, religion, legends, and faces.

Other Sources of Information
Native Web
http://www.nativeweb.org

This site is sponsored by the Maxwell School of Syracuse Univerity. It contains resources for indigenous cultures around the world.

Glossary

Aboriginal A general term referring to the original indigenous inhabitants of a region. It has sometimes been appropriately used as a specific reference to Native peoples of a single region (Australia); in many other places the term has been considered a derogatory one, especially if spoken in an "abbreviated" form.

Allotment The government procedure established in the Dawes Act of 1887 whereby common tribal lands were broken up into smaller parts for distribution to individual members in hopes of turning the Native Americans into individualists—like the non-Natives of European heritage. The procedure was part of the assimilation policy.

American Indian A commonly used reference for all Native Americans. As with the terms *Amerind* and *Amerindian*—used mainly by scholars—the term helps distinguish "Indians" of North America from the inhabitants of the nation of India. A 2004 poll of Native Americans demonstrated majority support for this term of identification.

Amerindian A term used by scholars to refer to Native Americans. Its use is more prevalent in Canada than in the United States.

Annuity An annual (or periodical) payment of money or other goods (food, clothing, tools) given to tribes and their members in exchange for their forfeiture of their lands and/or resources. In recent years, the term has been used to refer to payments given to tribal members as a result of profits from gambling establishments (also called per capita payments).

Assimilation The policy of absorbing Native Americans into the dominant non-Native American economy, culture, and society. The policy idea, which gained credence as early as the Jefferson administration, formed the basis for the Dawes Act of 1887 and other decisions fostering the breakup and termination of tribal landholdings.

Band A part or subunit of a tribe. The term is widely used in Canada, as bands are the basic political and landholding units. There are approximately 614 bands, though the Parliament of Canada may recognize more bands or change the status of existing bands.

Boarding School   A term referring to schools often run by the Bureau of Indian Affairs or by religious groups. Native students were sometimes removed from their reservation homes against their will and placed into the schools. There attempts were made to deprive them of their cultural heritage by changing their names and making them dress in non-Native clothing in furtherance of assimilation policies.

Chief   Top-ranking leader or advisers of some tribes. Tribes often had several chiefs as the term applied to military, political, or spiritual leaders. Some chiefs were elected, others gained the position through inheritance or performance. Other terms also used for leaders included: *sachem, nantan, miko,* and *sagamore,* and in later years *president.*

Clan   A group of several generations of people who hold a blood relationship with one another, usually through a common ancestor.

Community   A population of people possessing geographical areas, having common ties with a sense of identification, and engaging in social interaction as groups. Communities are very important to human survival. A strong community provides individuals with an "internalized rationale for altruistic, humane, and moral behavior." A powerful community binds people with feelings of mutual security.

Contact   The time when Europeans first came to settle and permanently engage in economic activities on the North American continent. Sometimes the specific date of Columbus's landing—1492—is used as a time of Contact.

Creation Story (Creation Myth)   Tribal legends that describe how the earth and all people began, but usually specifically how their tribal people began, and how they came to occupy their lands. The stories often refer to the intervention of a Great Spirit of life giving. The stories establish a religious justification for tribal members to occupy specific lands of the earth, as the lands have been given to "their" people alone.

Domestic Dependent Nation   A term used by the U.S. Supreme Court to describe the limited sovereign condition of Native peoples within the structure of the new nation of the United States.

Eskimo   A general term used to refer to groups of Native Americans who live in Arctic and far north regions of the United States (Alaska) and Canada. It is also used to describe peoples who reside in Siberia and Greenland. The term is considered a derogatory one (it is related to words that mean "one who cooks meat") in Canada where the term *Inuit* is the acceptable reference to the peoples.

Fee Lands (Fee Simple Ownership)   Private ownership of land, including the right to use the land and to sell the land. An objective of assimilation policies was to split tribally controlled (community) lands into fee lands to be held by individual tribal members.

Ghost Dance   A ritual used in Native religious ceremonies after 1870. The ceremony was developed and spread by Paiute Holy Man Wovoka. By participating in the dance, Native Americans in the West were to be returned to their traditional ways, the non-Natives would leave their lands, and the buffalo and other resources would return. Although it was a peaceful religious practice, the U.S. Army considered the dance to be hostile and therefore sought to repress it. The Army's suppression of the ritual led to events culminating in the Wounded Knee massacre of 1891.

Great Spirit (Wakanda, Wakan Tanka, Manitou, Orenda, All Father) A term referring to an all-powerful divine force that is revealed through nature, the earth and sky, and all life forms. Many traditional Native religions directed worship toward objects in nature rather than toward the unseen intangible "god" of Western religions.

Half-Breed   A term, usually considered derogatory, that refers to persons whose parents belong to different races. In Canada the term *Metis* was generally used for these people, but later it became a specific reference to communities of people with French and Native heritage. In Mexico and South America the term *Mestizo* was used for people of mixed heritage.

Indian   A term used by Christopher Columbus to refer to the Native inhabitants of the American continent. He so named them because he thought he had reached India rather than the New World. Many Native Americans resent the term; all the same, it continues to be commonly used.

Indian Country (Indian Lands)   A term(s) that has had a confusing mix of meanings over history. Currently, it is accepted as a reference to all lands within the outer boundaries of a Native American reservation. Within "Indian Country" there are tribally held (common) lands, lands allotted to individual Native Americans (some of which are fee lands), and fee (private) lands held by non-Native owners.

Indian Territory   Parts of the western United States that at one time were reserved as a permanent homeland for Native Americans of many different tribes. The territory encompassed most of present-day eastern Oklahoma as well as parts of Kansas. Policies of assimilation led the United States to break up the territory and incorporate most of it into the American-controlled state of Oklahoma.

Inuit   Native peoples of northern Canada; a term used in place of the unacceptable term *Eskimo*. The Inuit are also known as Nunavut peoples. The Inuit Nation has been officially recognized as the controlling entity over a new territory called Nunavut, which began political operations in 1999.

Kachina   A doll or mask that represents the personification of a god for certain Native peoples mostly in the Southwest region of the United

States. The Kachina is used in religious ceremonies and also as an object for good fortune.

Manifest Destiny A notion popularized in the nineteenth century that non-Native Americans had a mission, divinely inspired, to dominate the entire North American continent—even if the mission required the taking of Native lands and submission of Native peoples to the ultimate political control of non-Natives.

Medicine Bundle A sacred collection of objects placed in a small pouch and used by holy persons for healing ceremonies or by others desiring good fortune. Such bundles became the focus for legal controversies as Native holy persons gathered materials for bundles in Canada and then refused to open the bundles for border inspectors when they reentered the United States. An opening of the bundles destroyed their religious values.

Metis Individuals of mixed heritage usually French (but sometimes other European) and Native. Communities of Metis in Canada are considered to be a separate cultural group with some group rights and legal standing within provincial laws but not national law.

Mounds Sacred ceremonial and burial sites constructed by Native peoples mostly in the pre-Contact era. The Mounds areas are protected by federal legislation from desecration. The most prominent mounds in the United States are located in Ohio, Illinois, Mississippi, and Louisiana.

Nation A permanent or semipermanent community of people having common cultural bonds—history, language, religion—common political structures, and a fixed territory. The term *nation* has sometimes been used as a synonym for tribe, although some argue that tribes did not necessarily possess all the attributes of the modern nation-state.

Native American A term referring generally to all of the peoples whose ancestors were the indigenous people of the American continents; that is, their heritage dates back to persons on the continents many thousands of years ago. The term is synonymous with Indian, American Indian, Amerind, and Amerindian but is more acceptable in use by many Natives, but certainly not all, today. Some Native peoples do not like the reference term *American* as it is derived from the name of an Italian map maker, Americus Vespucci. The term has been used in federal legislation since 1991.

Nonstatus Indians Canadian Natives who do not have a special status as Natives. They are not enrolled with bands, and they usually do not live on reserves. They may have given up their status voluntarily or through marriage with non-Natives, although intermarriage is not always a bar from status as a recognized Native person.

Nunavut   A territory of Canada created in 1999 to be governed by the indigenous Inuit peoples. The territory was split off from the Northwest Territories, and it occupies 1.9 million square kilometers, an area that is one-fifth of all of Canada. Nunavut means "our land."

Per Capita Payments   Payments distributed by some tribes with casino establishments to their members as a result of gambling profits.

Peyote   An indigenous cactus plant that produces a shoot (or button) that is eaten or imbibed in tea form. The peyote is used as part of some Native religious ceremonies. The plant contains mescaline, a chemical that as a hallucinogen aids peoples in achieving visions. The use of peyote is an important part of ceremonies of the Native American Church, and it has received some exemptions from the laws against drugs when used in this way.

Plenary Powers   The doctrine that the United States Congress has complete political control over Native American reservation lands if they choose to exercise it. The doctrine has been well established in U.S. Supreme Court cases, but is still challenged philosophically by those who espouse the notion that tribal governments are (or should be) fully sovereign political units.

Potlatch   A tribal ceremony common among many Nations of the Pacific Northwest. Wealthy tribal members exhibit their prestige by giving away expensive gifts. The potlatch was considered by Canadians and Americans as evidence of a primitive anticapitalist spirit in Native communities. In Canada the practice was outlawed for several years. Native Americans skirted prohibitions by calling the ceremonies "Christmas" and "birthday" parties. The laws are no longer enforced.

Pow Wow   A tribal festival during which members socialize, participate in dancing, games, and trade goods. The pow wow is a community-building event.

Red Power   A political movement of Native peoples from many tribes. Peoples demanded a greater recognition of tribal sovereignty and Native human rights. The leading group identified with Red Power was the American Indian Movement.

Relocation, Removal   The practice of moving peoples off of certain lands onto new places of residence. Relocation and removal was a major policy in the nineteenth century as Natives were deprived of lands during the movement called Manifest Destiny by non-Natives. In the Termination era of the post–World War II period, efforts were made to relocate large numbers of Native peoples into large American cities where they would be able to have greater job possibilities. In this way they could be assimilated. The efforts were not considered a success. Removal of persons from their homes, whether by force or more often by misguided incentives, is considered one of the most cruel actions of a government, and under American legal standards it is not done except for definite public needs and with full compensation. The Fifth Amendment offers a blanket protection for one's property. Nonetheless, in practice, the principle of having a home was not legally recognized for Natives during much of the early history of the United States.

Reservation, Reserve   Lands retained by or set aside for tribes and bands for their exclusive use. The lands were set aside as a result of treaties, laws, or executive actions of the federal governments of the United States and Canada. The term *reserve* is used in Canada. Other terms apply to some U.S. reservations: *rancheria* (in California), *colony, settlement,* and *pueblo.* Reservation lands are held in trust by the federal government. State governments also recognize reservations, but these do not enjoy the benefit of rights and programs provided for federally recognized Native lands.

Reserved Right Doctrine   The doctrine that tribes hold inherent rights to control their lands and resources, unless the rights are specifically given up in treaties or by law. The doctrine was put forth by the U.S. Supreme Court in the *Winters* case in order to establish that reservations had water rights in the West.

Self-determination   The notion that Native peoples should control their own political and economic affairs to the end that they do not depend upon outside help to sustain the life of their communities. The idea of self-determination was behind the passage of much federal legislation in the last decades of the twentieth century.

Smoke Shop   A tribal business that sells cigarettes and other products to the public. The smoke shop offers prices lower than those of non-Native competitors as the goods are not subject to sales taxes as a practical matter. There is some legal controversy over the imposition of taxation over sales to non-Natives.

Sovereignty   The supreme power to control political affairs within a territory. In general, Native American tribes had a sovereign condition in the pre-Contact era. Some assert that the power remains today. In practice, sovereign powers are always shared in "Indian Country," as some powers are exercised by tribal governments, others by the federal government, and, under some circumstances, powers are exercised by state governments. Political power, even in the hands of the federal government, can never be unlimited. There are always checks and balances, as well as constitutional limits to political power. Therefore, sovereignty is a concept of philosophical or theoretical significance.

Status Indian   A term used in Canada to refer to Native peoples who are registered as members of one of the 542 recognized bands. Most Status Indians live on reserves. They are given special rights and programs.

Sun Dance A traditional religious ceremony that was practiced among some Plains tribes. A young man would sacrifice his flesh and undergo self-torture in order to bring good fortune to his peoples. The man's skin would be broken by skewers to which ropes would be fastened. He would then be placed on a vertical stick and pulled while the sun beat down on his face. During this time the man might experience visions. Other tribal members would dance and sing during the ceremony.

Sweat Lodge A place for purification ceremonies. Tribal members go into small enclosures that are built into the ground. The participating people first drink a tea and then fast. They go into the lodge where heated stones are sprinkled with water causing steam to rise among the people. While in a state of intense perspiration, the people pray and seek to communicate with the Great Spirit through visions.

Termination and Restoration An assimilation policy most prominently implemented in the post–World War II era by the Truman and Eisenhower administrations. The federal government of the United States withdrew recognition of some reservation lands in exchange for grants of money. This was done in the hopes that the Native peoples would thereby assimilate and conduct their affairs without the need of future federal moneys. The movement was recognized as a clear failure, and terminated tribes—the two largest ones being the Menominees and Klamaths—regained status through new legislation. A Canadian effort to establish a termination program in 1969 was rejected before it could be implemented.

Totem A symbol of a family or clan honoring ancestors or great events of the past. The totem may take many forms. In the Northwest, tribes have totem poles that are placed into the ground near the homes of chiefs.

Treaty A formal agreement between autonomous political units. The treaty process was used in relationships between Native Americans and federal governments (the United States until 1871 and the Canadian government) for transfer of lands. The Twenty Points presented to President Nixon in 1972 demanded a restoration of the treaty relationships between tribes and the national government.

Tribe A group of Native clans who share a common history, culture, traditions, language, and territory. Tribes are communities. The term is analogous in some ways to the American concept of "nation," although it can be argued that the terms are not exactly the same.

Twenty Points A position statement made by Native leaders who brought a caravan of protesters over what they called the Trail of Broken Treaties to Washington, D.C., in 1972. The protest led to the occupation of the BIA building. Many of the "Points" concerned demands to restore treaty relationships with Natives.

Vision Quest A young man's personal religious rite of passage. The youth purify themselves in sweat lodges or by other means. Then they venture off to a lonely place, often a religious place. There they seek communion with the Great Spirit. The exercise may be repeated over and over until a vision is experienced, and then adulthood begins.

Wampum Belts Belts that have patterns of beads woven into them. The patterns were messages or records of history. The belts were considered very valuable property, and they were exchanged as expressions of peaceful relationships or in settlement of disputes.

Index

About the Author

William N. Thompson is a professor of public administration at the University of Nevada, Las Vegas. He received his doctorate in political science from the University of Missouri, Columbia. Thompson is a noted authority on gambling, has researched and written extensively on the topic, and has served as a consultant on gambling for Native Americans as well as national and international businesses and organizations.